ASTRIDE THE WHEEL

ASTRIDE THE WHEEL
YANTRARUDHA

Chandrasekhar Rath

Translated from Oriya by

Jatindra Kumar Nayak

OXFORD
UNIVERSITY PRESS

OXFORD

UNIVERSITY PRESS

YMCA Library Building, Jai Singh Road, New Delhi 110 001

Oxford University Press is a department of the University of Oxford. It furthers the
University's objective of excellence in research, scholarship, and education
by publishing worldwide in

Oxford   New York

Auckland   Bangkok   Buenos Aires   Cape Town   Chennai
Dar es Salaam   Delhi   Hong Kong   Istanbul   Karachi   Kolkata
Kuala Lumpur   Madrid   Melbourne   Mexico City   Mumbai   Nairobi
São Paulo   Shanghai   Taipei   Tokyo   Toronto

Oxford is a registered trademark of Oxford University Press
in the UK and in certain other countries

Published in India
By Oxford University Press, New Delhi

© Oxford University Press 2003

The moral rights of the author have been asserted
Database right Oxford University Press (maker)

First published 2003

MR. Omayal Achi MR. Arunachalam Trust was set up in 1976 to further education
and health care particularly in rural areas. The MR. AR. Educational Society was
later established by the Trust. One of the Society's activities is to sponsor Indian
literature. This translation is entirely funded by the MR. AR. Educational Society
as part of its aims.

ISBN 019 566477 9

Typeset in Wilke Roman
by Eleven Arts, Keshav Puram, Delhi 110 035
Printed in India by Roopak Printers, New Delhi 110 032
Published by Manzar Khan, Oxford University Press
YMCA Library Building, Jai Singh Road, New Delhi 110 001

Contents

Acknowledgements

Author's Note

Yantrarudha is my basic identity. Other books written by me are attributes added to it. It came to me as a bird comes in late summer for nesting. On a quiet afternoon in 1963, Sanatan Dase walked into my field of vision to possess me and the small apartment I occupied at Baripada. I was then teaching English in the local undergraduate college which was closed for the summer months. Sanatan was not imaginary; not a recollection either. He was more tangible and real than anybody living around me in flesh and blood. Curiously I kept watching him. He moved about freely in that apartment and did not seem to notice me or my family. Interesting. Not only my residence but the entire locality, the roads and the dwarfish temple, a hundred yards to the left, were magically transformed into a silent and invisible witness to the panorama opening up before my eyes.

That afternoon I scribbled the first chapter on loose sheets of paper having absolutely no idea of what would follow next. *Yantrarudha* poured into me like a river in full spate. As I lay on a mat spread on the ground with a pillow to support my elbows, I reeled off a chapter a day in the quiet and hot afternoons. Getting up I went out for tennis and later to play billards at the only club in town. I never felt like reading the chapters as I thought I had lived them, saturated with the details of Sanatan's life and happenings. I was like a man possessed from the very beginning. That was why I chose the title *Yantrarudha* for the first chapter as well as for the book.

The eighth child of my parents, I remember my father in his fifties. Sanatan remotely resembles my father. I respect him. *Yantrarudha* is my first-born baby. I love it. The translation rendered painstakingly by Jatindra Kumar Nayak, edited most scrupulously, (over several years and numerous consultations with me) by Mini Krishnan and published by Oxford University Press is like sending my first child abroad.

CHANDRASEKHAR RATH

Translator's Note

In *Yantrarudha* (Astride the Wheel), the scope of the Oriya novel of social realism, which largely confined itself to exploring social processes as they shaped lives of individuals, widens to accomodate a profoundly mystical apprehension of life. Closely observed details of life in a traditional Oriya village as it undergoes change in the turbulent sixties, provides a passage to the rich inner life of the central character. Everyday speech of ordinary people living out their workaday lives alternates effortlessly with language saturated with allusions to scriptures and animated with a deep yearning for the infinite. This highly supple idiom, while effectively capturing the rhythm of a way of life rooted in caste, rituals and custom, enables the reader to accompany the protagonist in a unique spritual journey. Translating a densely textured novel like *Yantrarudha*, therefore, renders the task of the translator particularly challenging and difficult.

In translating *Yantrarudha*, I have benefited immensely from the advice and suggestions of its author, Professor Chandrasekhar Rath. I take this opportunity to express my deep gratitude to him. I feel a particular obligation to Ms Mini Krishnan, Editor, Translations, Oxford University Press, India. Her editorial comments and expert advice were extremely helpful at every stage of the preparation of the translation. I express my sincere thanks to my friend Mr Kamala Kant Mohapatra, for the encouragement I have always received from him. I am deeply grateful to my wife, Elly for her support and her patience.

JATINDRA KUMAR NAYAK

Introduction

The saga of Sanatan, epitomizes the widely-held Hindu belief in a pre-ordained life, finally released into a state of liberation. The psychosocial milieu of this novel is Orissa, India, and the characters and locale are set against this backdrop. To ease the non-native reader's response to the space-time dimensions in the novel, this introduction is in two parts. The first presents a brief outline of the region, history, people and seminal movements of Oriyan literature in a certain perspective. The second presents a profile of the author and a critical insight into the novel.

The Land Divine

Hemmed in by the Bay of Bengal on the east, guarded by mountainous ranges in the southwest and opening up to the northern plains, Orissa lies between an enchanted past and an inviting future.

In the fabled past, poised midway between dream and reality, the land washed her hair in the Ganga and rinsed her feet in the Godavari. In the Mahabharata she has been identified as *Udra Desha*. In the *Natural History* of the Roman historian, Pliny, she is *Oretes*. The Chinese traveller Hiuen Tsang has described this land as *wu-cha* (AD c. 639). Alberuni, in the 11th century AD, called her *Udra Visau*. 'Udissa' was used primarily by medieval Buddhist and Islamic writers. The ancient names of 'Odra', 'Kalinga' and 'Utkala' still weave magic in the historical memory of the people of this land.

Modern Orissa gained her present geographical map on 1 April 1936, after a long struggle with her British masters who had almost dismembered her for their own administrative convenience: the northern part was with Bihar and Bengal, the western part was tagged on to Madhya Pradesh, and the southern tip was telescoped into the Madras Presidency.

Orissa has five natural regions rising up from the coastal plains to the mountains like an upcurving and levelled theatre with the mountains as a backdrop. The plains, rivers, valleys or flood zones, the uplands, the hilly plains with elevations varying from 200 to 600 metres, and the green-robed mountains make this ancient land a veritable theatre of bio-diversity. To the delight of geologists, rocks of the pre-Cambrian and Gondwana varieties are found in the mountains. The Chilika Lake, naturally formed near Khallikote in the district of Ganjam bordering Puri, is the biggest in India. Chilika has given rise to various socio-literary myths. Poets like Radhanath Roy and Godavarish Mishra have deified her, seeing her as a protective spiritual presence, which man defies at his peril. Godavarish's ballad *Kalijai* and Radhanath's meditative epic *Chilika* have created living myths about her moral spirit and spiritual powers.

The rivers of Orissa are her nerves, both literally and figuratively. The economy of the state, which is primarily agrarian, is totally dependent on the river system. If the rivers have sustained the steady growth of folk culture in Orissa, then the sea has drawn the people of the coastal areas into adventure and roving commerce. Even today, on Karthik Purnima (full moon in October–November) day, a symbolic replica of paper, banana bark or cork boats is released ceremonially into the sea or river as a tribute to the sacred memory of great ancestors. Myths and folk tales, half-history and half-imagination, have grown around the sea adventures.

On the mountains of Orissa live the Adivasis and tribal people. The Adivasis are the autochthonous people of this land, perhaps driven up to the mountains by invading waves of plains people.

The primitives and the Adivasis were the original inhabitants of this coastal corridor. Worshipping stones and trees they survived for many centuries till they were absorbed by the invading Dravidians from the south and Aryans from the north. The autochthonous people were slowly Aryanized around Lord Jagannath whose reality and symbolism changed according to the new rulers' religion and politics. The Buddhas, Jains, Saibas and hosts of people of other faiths also came in successive waves refining, modifying and sharpening attitudes to a palpable synthesis.

The Oriyas have a double sense of history: one of myths, mysteries and innocence and the other of a visible chronology, morphologically divined. Filtered through the maze of time and its formal orchestration of values, the Oriya is both heroic and non-heroic, more often a victim of his own tentative encounters with reality. The recorded history of Orissa begins, it is safe to conclude, on the slender evidence of inscriptions, coins and oral traditions, from the Nandas of Magadha, particularly Mahapadma Nanda. Then came Asoka to conquer Kalinga in 261 BC. The horrors of war brought about a spiritual transformation in Asoka and he turned to Buddhism. But in the 1st century BC, Kalinga declared her independence under Kharavela of the Chedi dynasty. In the 2nd century AD this land again lost her independence and came under Satakarni of the Satavahana dynasty. The Nalas and the Gangas marched into the political vacuum created after the fall of the Satavahanas. Due to family feuds regarding the sharing of power they divided Kalinga into South, Middle and North Kalinga and ruled at their pleasure till the Sailodbhavas drove them out in the 6th century AD. The Sailodbhava rule made Orissa comparatively prosperous by expanding its trade overseas. The Bhaumakaras defeated the Sailodbhavas in AD 736 and ruled with a semblance of administrative skill. Their contribution to architecture is testified by the sixty-four Yogini temples at Haripur (now in ruins).

The golden age of Orissa, in her chequered history, was between the 7th and the 14th centuries when the Somavansi Kings—Janmejaya, Yayati I, Yayati II and Janmejaya II ruled, followed by the Gangas again in AD 1038. Under the powerful Chodaganga Deva, Orissa expanded territorially, spanning an area that had the river Ganga in the north as its border and the river Godhavari in the south. The modern temple complex of Lord Jagannath was built by Chodaganga and Orissa became an attractive intellectual and spiritual seat for visiting scholars like Sankara, Ramanuja and others. Anangabhima Deva completed the Jagannath temple and consolidated the empire by his military prowess. He established the city of Cuttack and his illustrious son Narasingha Deva I built the famous Konark temple. During the reign of the Gangas, Orissa enjoyed economic and cultural prosperity. The last Ganga ruler Bhanudeva IV was duped by his own general Kapileswar Routray who staged a coup, usurped the throne and renamed himself Kapilendra Dev. He was the greatest Gajapati king of Orissa, a scholar and a poet.

The Gajapatis ruled Orissa till the death of Prataprudra in 1540. The reign of Kapilendra—Purushottam—Prataprudra—is considered to be the most prosperous period in the history of Orissa. They ruled in the name of Lord Jagannath patronizing art, culture and literature.

The decline and fall of the Gajapati empire paved the way for an inevitable descent into gloom, apathy, lethargy and pessimism. A mighty people embraced indifference and indulged in the mysteries of otherworldly cults. Then came the Marathas and finally the British in 1803. A heroic people accepted their destiny of unresisted oppression and almost faced extinction in the worst man-made famine of 1866. But, strangely, after this soul-chilling famine a new surge of nationalism and Oriya pride awakened and united the first-generation recipients of modern education, (initiated by the British missionaries) to fight for Oriya identity. A quest for historical pride and language identity began under the leadership of patriots and litterateurs like Madhusudhan Das, Fakir Mohan Senapathi and others. In 1936, Orissa was carved out of Bihar–Bengal–Madhya Pradesh–Madras dominions as a separate state. The national freedom of 1947 gave her the status of a distinct cultural territory integral to the great civilization of India.

The People: The face of innocence

With a population of 35 million, Orissa has three progressive layers of civilization. The ancient Adivasis with their culture, almost untouched despite the ravages of other influences; the farmland workers in villages and the neo-urbanites in the growing cities—a typical pan-Indian feature: the Scheduled Tribes, comprising 62 tribes form 23 per cent of the population while the Scheduled Castes comprising 93 castes, form 17 per cent of the population of Orissa. The interface of the three layers of people leading up to an intermix of civilizational values is now increasing, thanks to the socio-economic measures of the state government. But the cultural identities of the primordial classes have not been totally defaced by modernity.

The average Oriya is reserved, god-fearing and emotional. His cultural hero and life source is Lord Jagannath and like the deity the Oriya believes in good food, dance, drama and music. The body and materiality, as well as the spirit and its essences are acknowledged. Yet a fatalistic otherworldliness runs along his oversensitive nerves as an inhibitive second nature. He loves gatherings, group functions, *mela*, *hat* and totemic festivals. He is essentially non-interfering and tolerant but his spirit unfailingly rises to vengeful heights when his pride is undermined by arrogance. He is flexible but not pliable. Literature and social rituals are his compulsive passions.

The Literary Efflorescence

The non-Aryanized autochthonous people of this land in their primary survival struggles connected themselves orally with the objects of nature—stones, trees and brooks with the luminous sky above. Their hunting, shelter-making, community-living, necessitated the oral consolation of songs and prayers to keep their survival on an even keel. They had no script and their oral rhythms sprang out of a defiance of the restraining order around. When the Dravidian and Aryan invasions threatened their existence further, they created martial rhythms to spur their resolve to survive. Gradually there was an inter-assimilation of certainties and ideas of form and perception of truth generated, the structures of a worldview. The Adivasis' oral tradition has three basic orientations: Dravidian, Austric Munda and Indo-Aryan. This is mainly folk literature and their written forms which came much later in Santal, Saora, Ho and Kui languages make very interesting reading.

Mainstream Oriya literature dates back to the 6th century AD. This is confirmed by the discovery in the Nepal Royal Palace in 1905 of the *Charyapadika* (Verses of Spiritual Exercise), by Haraprasad Shastri. Dr Karunakar Kar has shown that the language of these *Charyapadas* is Oriya by virtue of the singularities of the Oriya grammar. But Maithili, Assamese and Bengali linguists also stake their claim on it. The charya songs are mysterious and philosophical, reflecting the mode of the Buddhist mahayana lore. However the real beginnings of Oriya literature are to be seen in *Sisu Beda* (Splendour of the Inner Universe) (10th–14th centuries), *Amarkosa* (The Cell of Eternal Wisdom) (14th century), and *Kalasa Chautisa* (The Kalasa Verses) of Baccha Das (15th century). The influence of Vedic literature and philosophy is unmistakable in these works. All the bhasa literatures of India in the early centuries of the middle ages were impacted by Vedic literature; Oriya was no exception. But during the reign of Kapilendra Deva, epic or kavya literature was very popular. The most talented and unfading among them was Sarala Das, whose Oriya Mahabharata in eighteen long cantos, is the most widely and deeply read work in Oriya literature. This work modelled on the original Mahabharata of Vyasa excels in terms of its insight into human nature and its perception of the meaning and significance of life. Its worldview mitigates the tragic dénouement by ennobling the Pandavas' post-war deeds on earth and makes them natural worthies for heaven. Its canvas is vast, battles violent, descriptions often bordering on gory dehumanization and nihilistic frenzy. Written in the *dandi* style, its lines vary in length from 14 to 26 letters by combining the sanskritized lexicon of the palace with the speech rhythm and the vocabulary of remote villages. This late 15th century epic gives the Oriya language and literature its identity, strength and the intensity of a visionary gleam. Its range and sweep of vocabulary encloses reality with its beauty, grace, vitality, sublimity as well as profanity, and encounters the surreal and the mystical with plastic energy.

But the poet who made Oriya literature a household affair was Jagannath Das of the early 16th century. He wrote the Krishna *lila* in his *Bhagavatha* in the language of the common people. He took his material from the *Bhagavatham* and other Sanskrit sources but used the language of common speech of the villagers to reach the homes of ordinary people. It may not be an exaggeration to suggest that the *Bhagavatha* of Jagannath Das has familiarized the lettered and the unlettered Oriya alike, with the Vedic philosophy and worldview. At the same time it fashioned their literary tastes along moral lines. Written in the *Nabaksari Chhanda* (couplets of nine-lettered lines) the rise and fall of wave-like rhythms reconcile the Oriyan sensibility to the universal binaries of pleasure-pain, joy-sorrow, which are the composites of experience. The philosophical perspectives and mystic-tantric-yogic poetry of *Pancha Sakhas* (Five Friends) enriched Oriya literature with epic and Puranic themes and insights. The poet combines the mystic and the magical in kavya styles and recreates the vast universe of messianic characters operating in the world of classical values. The ways of man, abstracted from the coils of mortality, and attaining identity with the Brahman have been charted out by these sage poets without ostentation or sophistry.

The contrastive secular poetry in ornate style using sanskritized diction and aristocratic affairs for the creation of *rasa*, especially the primary passion of romantic love, came from the royal families of Ghumusar Ganjam and other areas. Although it was imitative of the *riti kavya* style of Sanskrit romances, the focus on love as the only liberation in this world of pain stands out as a 'secular' and more enjoyable path to bliss. Upendra Bhanja, venerated as *kavisamrat*, (the emperor of poets) removed the Oriya language from village homes and gave it a courtly character. His diction and rhythms had a scholarly orientation not meant for the common man. But he introduced a new dimension of Oriya poetry in respect of aesthetic joy and poetic purpose. His focus is on form and style. Love dominates worldly matters and releases all tensions that life presents. Love is the ultimate liberation of the spirit. Upendra Bhanja offers an alternative worldview where the mystical and the metaphysical merge in the physical, which is nature fulfilling its destiny of love. His depiction of love and union, separation and agony amongst royalty must be read as man's love transformed, where social and economic status are irrelevant. Bhanja's masterpieces are *Lavanyabati* (The Glowing Beauty), *Kotibrahmandasundari* (The Beauty of a Million Universes) and *Premasudhanidhi* (The Essence of Ambrosial Love). Dinakrushna Das and Abhimanyu Samanta Singhar are also important poets in the *riti* genre.

After the *riti* poets of the 17th and 18th centuries, poets wallowed in the themes and characters of the Ramayana or the Mahabharata or classical myths and episodes. The *kavya* gave way to shorter poems and lyrics. In this genre two prominent names may be remembered: Kavisurya Baladev Rath and Gopal Krushna Patnaik, both from south Orissa, like the *kavisamrat* before them. The religio-metaphysical and the secular kavya traditions dissipated as the new pressures of time manifested themselves in the 19th century. A lyrical impulse and growing humanist zeal surrounded the individual, however diminutive and small in comparison with the cult figures, epic heroes, gods and sages, and inspired the poets to a new realization of life. The poet's 'I' became more and more grounded in his practical viabilities. A moral strength and psychic power was discovered in man to confront his burdensome reality. Bhima Bhoi (whose congenital blindness is in dispute) in the 19th century asserted the Christ-like potential in man, capable of taking upon himself the burden of mankind. His immortal lines: 'let my life rot in hell, may the world be saved' sculpted a new image of man. Bhima Bhoi envisioned man as God. The void and the fullness are interchangeable and mutually fulfilling. In his *bhajans* and visions he saw a luminous form, a pantheistic presence and longed for a reunion and indistinguishable identification with it. The mystical and the divine for him are human too and the physical, non-physical. Bhima Bhoi searches for the primeval in the ephemeral and formal in the formless. But he gives man a measure of dignity amidst the wordly realities of pain. His *Stutichintamani* (The Thought-Jewel of Prayer) is an adored masterpiece.

Alongside these basic realizations of a derivative classical temper, the impact of modern education and English literature in the late 19th century stirred up a romantic quest for identity: identity of the self with time and place, history and spatial glory as its natural halo. The new generation of poets: Radhanath Ray, Gangadhar Mehar, Nandakishore Bal, Madhusudan Rao with Fakir Mohan Senapati, Madhusudan Das and others to follow, tried to create a sense of Orissa. Radhanath made the rivers, mountains, myths and mysteries of Orissa a visible presence in his *Chilika*, *Chandrabhaga* and *Nandikeswari* and also reinterpreted themes of love and incest in his *Kedar Gouri* and *Parbati*. Gangadhar Meher brought down to familiar human levels the hallowed heroes and heroines of classical antiquity and treated the themes of love, valour and sacrifice with 'sweet reasonableness.' Madhusudan and others struck a compromise with man's surrender and assertiveness in his relationship with the divine.

New forms—the sonnet, the lyric and essay emerged, and vistas of patriotism and paradigms of an identifiable Oriya culture appeared in explorative styles. Madhusudan Das and Gopabandhu Das later added the metaphysical-political dimensions of freedom to this edifice of cultural identity. The political movement for a separate Oriya state and the national movement for independence used literature as a catalyst to effect a perspectival metamorphosis in the people, midway between an uncharted past and a translucent present.

The Novel

And then came the novel. Although *Padmamali* of Umesh Chandra Sarkar, written in 1885, is honoured as the first Oriya novel, the form-perfect and genre-specific work of genius was *Chha Mana Atho Guntha* (Six Acres and Eight Gunthas) written by Fakir Mohan Senapati in 1898. The first short story *Rebati* by the same author also appeared in the same year. The other novels of Senapati are *Mamu* (Uncle), *Prayaschitta* (Atonement) and *Lacchama*, a historical novel. Fakir Mohan Senapati, for the first time in Oriya literature, demythologizes the classical verity associated with nature, God and man. In *Chha Mana Atho Guntha* nature's fertility is suspended. The village pond is filthy, polluted and is host to all sorts of manipulation and conspiracy. The village deity Budhimangala is a menacing force. The village *chowkidar* is an agent of evil. The landlord Rama Chandra Mangaraj is an outsider without viable roots who usurps 'Fatepur Sarasandha' by duping Dilbar Mian with a castrated he-goat, some ghee and a bag of coins for his revelry. The illegitimate gains legitimacy and authority by deceit and villainy.

He imposes the illegitimate relationship with Champa, his consort in evil, on his legitimate family which dissipates under the weight of its mute virtue. He then desires the only 'area of fertility', the *'Chha Mana Atho Guntha'* of Bhagia and Saria, to illegitimize the entire earthly space available in the novel. This plot of land of Bhagia and Saria is the fertility substitute of the childless couple, which they are prepared to mortgage to gain fertility through propitiation of the village deity, prompted by the ingenuous villainy of Champa. The victims of the Mangaraj-Champa machinations are absorbed by this earth as are Govinda and Champa in the end when they try to run away with Mangaraj's wealth after he is charged with Saria's murder. The lawyer Ram Ram Lala ultimately grabs the 'territory', the land of Mangaraj, perhaps to lose it to another, future usurper. Mangaraj dies, his penitence unarticulated. In Senapati's fictional world his death becomes him more than his life. The novelist posits in his omniscient narrative, an earth changing hands in time's fickle march while human beings chase manipulated goals of power and domination, trampling law, justice, God and morality under their heels. The good, the innocent and the honest as well as the bad, the evil and the foolish (like the Baghsingha family in the novel) perish. The earth, like man's plaything, responds to the person who holds the reins, however temporary.

This novel of Fakir Mohan presents a dark vision of man's cosmic totality. But it stands apart as the insight of a genius into the nature of things. It is a tragic perception of life in line with the vision in the Indian epics and the Pancha Sakhas' view of reality. And it stands out as a universal monad from which springs the multiple matrix of time's manifestations.

The major novelists that followed Fakir Mohan were fated to see both the separate state of Orissa and experience the freedom of India. In the wake of the new realities that emerged, new paradigms of man-society-nature-God symbioses were constructed by the novelists. Kalindi Charan Panigrahi showed the collapse of the joint family in his *Matira Manisha*. Gopinath Mohanty focused on the Adivasis in his *Paraja* and explored primordial man's existential relationship with the earth, the fertile land which feeds him and all creatures. In the three important Oriya novels—*Chha Mana Atho Guntha*, *Matira Manisha* (Man of the Earth) and *Paraja*—the earth-cult of man is the probing focus. In Nityananda Mohanpatra's *Hida Mati* (The Bund Earth) and Gopinath Mohanty's *Mati Matala* (The Loamy Soil) the same cult is looked at again in the changed contexts of society and man.

In Surendra Mohanty's *Andha Diganta* (Blind Horizon) the Oriya novel lifts itself from the man-earth bond to a value orientation of the spirit of man. The human spirit is always in quest of freedom, but political freedom and emancipation from foreign rule lift man up from the physicality of existence. *Andha Diganta* probes the spirit of human freedom and the quest for its attainment in the new context of Gandhian values. A new kind of betrayal and manipulative aggression for power opens up another void of nihilistic human wishes, in Surendra Mohanty's novel.

In the major novels of post-Independence Oriya literature like *Nara Kinnar* (Man and Phantoms) of Santanu Kumar Acharya, *Laya Bilaya* (Creation and Chaos) of Gopinath Mohanty and *Yajnaseni* (Draupadi) and *Maha Moha* (The Grand Desire) of Prativa Ray, the earth, freedom and existence are sublimated into a psychic thrust on reality, demanding a larger chunk of power for the individual. Acharya's individuals are mostly social outcasts who struggle with the burden of society. Prativa's women, mostly from the epics or myths (Draupadi and Ahalya) search for their cosmic souls, independent of men. The influence of the psychic enclosures of post-modernism goad these writers to psychoanalyse their characters within the frame of their operational spaces. The forms and styles of the post-Independence writers vary from writer to writer but the search for psychic certainty and existential attitudes often diverts them from the well-made or the stream of consciousness or psychological modes into the uncanny parameters of metafiction. Manoj Das, in his novel, *Amrita Phala* (The Ambrosial Fruit, 1996) has given us a well-made novel of the contemporary psyche and its turbulent contours. Myth and reality finally coalesce in his novel into a time continuum of human constants.

—

Against this backdrop of the Oriya novel, spanning about a hundred years, Chandrasekhar Rath's *Yantrarudha* maps a psychic transcendence of the earth and the mystique of life and death, in terms of experiences that are both real and surreal.

The Author

Born in 1929, Chandrasekhar Rath stands out among his contemporary writers in Oriya literature for his remarkable background and contributions to diverse literary genres like belles-lettres, fiction and poetry. His roots are in the legacy of a traditional brahmin family providing him with an early exposure to scriptural Sanskrit which is the fount of his pan-Indian thought and philosophy. Degrees in mathematics and English gave him both precision of expression and a rich sensibility for literatures available through English. His early exposure to Bengali and Hindi literatures, in the original, widened his acquaintance with life and society in the regions adjacent to Orissa. He had, therefore, a fairly well-cultivated mind and a sensibility enriched by the masterminds of the East and the West when he began to write seriously having already taught English literature for ten years. Painting and sculpting provided him with extra outlets for self-expression giving his images a distinct visual and tactile character both in prose and poetry. This kind of mental and psycho-spiritual preparation made a rare difference and earned for him, distinction in all those areas of literature where he chose to express himself.

He made his debut on the pages of a literary magazine called the *Jhankar* in a deeply reflective article written in a distinctive poetic-prose style. The title was 'Srastar Sweekar' or the 'Creator's Confession.' This was classified under 'essays' though Chandrasekhar was inclined to call it an 'open form' after Alfred Kazin, where poetry commingled with prose, philosophy, fiction and reflections on life with a sprinkling of dramatic dialogue. The first year (1963) of his literary career brought the first literary award and he moved ahead to author nine volumes of such reflective personal essays in an 'open form' of poetic prose. They are acknowledged as being in a class by themselves and a unique contribution to Oriya prose.

Fiction crept in almost around the same time. In fact his creative centre was a seedbed for stories, novels and poetry besides the kind of prose he was producing at that time. Fiction took the form of a novel which bears the title of the first chapter of *Yantrarudha*. It was published in 1967 though written four years earlier. Fakir Mohan titled every chapter of his novels separately not so much because Bankim did it in Bengali but because he was serializing it in a magazine. It did not serve as a model for the later novelists until Chandrasekhar deliberately named the chapters to give his novel a composition of apparently exclusive units strung together by the single thread of a central character. The protagonist of *Yantrarudha* passes through experiences on two different planes, one horizontal and the other vertical, separated by a critical point—the loss of his wife. On the horizontal plane lies the society around him and its typical religio-cultural and socio-political institutions ranging from cremation rituals to wedding ceremonies, recitals of holy texts to electioneering. At the turning point he takes off in a vertical lift to another plane of consciousness where the experiences are of yogic and spiritual richness and depth, culminating in a final burst far above the mundane level. Structurally, therefore, *Yantrarudha* is bipedal. But on both planes, the exterior comprising events and consequences has the interiorized flow of revelations, realizations and rationalizations of the experiencer. Psychological treatment was introduced by Gopinath Mohanty into Oriya novels but spiritual progress monitored by an unseen propellant (for which Chandrasekhar names his novel) was an untrodden path until the publication of *Yantrarudha*.

The Novel

The novel is set against two time scales, one the chronological calendar time, framing events and episodes in memory, and the other against the cosmic scale of which the consciousness gets glimpses in lucid or charged moments. The time scales have been contextually conceived by the novelist to synthesize his own comprehension of man's place and purpose in time's flux with the still and unmoving centre beyond the intractable process.

This is the world of Sanatan Dase. The only 'outsider' here is Satpathy, the scholar-professor-philosopher-guru who enters at a late stage as a uninvolved protagonist to lead the hero through a spiritual odyssey. In Satpathy one becomes conscious of the authorial presence but does not feel his power turning the wheel. He fades out as he appears with acontextual casualness. This novel is the story of Sanatan Dase, his reality, his village, his family, his psychosocial totality moving towards a personal release.

Sanatan Dase is touching fifty when the novel begins. The locale is rural, a village in post-Independence Orissa experiencing the first simmerings of western education, postal facilities, elections, politics and mobility. He is the third generation servitor of the Lakshminarayan temple, an inheritance gratefully accepted as the only choice available to him to eke out a living. His education is limited to the family expertise of the rituals of worship and spiritual texts. But his speciality is the recitation of Puranas and epics. He gets invititations to read the Puranas, the Mahabharata and other texts by merit-seekers and supplicants, wishing for relief. He recites the several texts in a mellifluous voice modulating the dramatic pitches with ease. This adds to his meagre income. Sanatan's reality comprises the self, the family, the temple and his functional society, the self being the epicentre of his indulgences, internal conflicts, worries and his relational totality of conscious existence. The physicality of the self, the body machine, moves within the perimeters of four existential obsessions: fear, lust, incomprehension of systems and uncertainty. These universal generalities of existence, in the case of Sanatan, could be summed up as the common mortal fears. Sanatan's family, work place (the temple), social relations and urge to move forward are all extensions of his self. In other words, the fictional world of his novel is the self of its hero. He determines within the operational parameters of his reality what to do, how to live and what relationships to nourish. His desires, aspirations and social manoeuvrability, however, stem from one certainty: his temple-priesthood. He locks and unlocks Lakshminarayan, serves the iconic Vishnu and his consort Lakshmi, for the survival and sustenance of his self (extended to his total psychosocial time space) with some self-assured certainty, which however, is under constant threat of being tentative.

He fears darkness, the canine instinct in animals and man: 'Bastards; They are the same: human beings, cows and dogs'. He fears the temper of his wife, fears his own inability to give her the minimum comforts of life while trying his best to feed and sustain his eight-member family. He spends his scanty leisure time in writing the Puranas on palm leaves which are then sold. Yet his ends never meet. He stifles his wife's desire to visit Puri, scolds his son for having contributed half a rupee to the war efforts of the country. Fear and poverty make his day of moodshifts ponder on fate, God, manhood, the soul and the world.

> But what a funny thing, this karma is. Hasn't the Lord himself said: 'I am the one who gets everything done. None can ever escape me'. It is he who resides in us and directs all our actions. Where does this thing known as karma come from and why should we suffer the consequences of our karma? Thus it is He who acts, and He who suffers. Where do we fit in?'

He suffers from incomprehension of life, man, the purpose of existence and the prevading divinity of the scheme of things. His daily worship of the deities, articulation of scriptures and sacred texts fail him in his apprehension of reality. Poverty and its humiliating faces in his home confront him with his own ineffective manhood. He doubts the metaphysics of spirituality. His loneliness, alienation and agony in the face of an eight-member family, and a world of views, conflicting voices and variety turn him inwards for sombre cogitation on finalities. But Sanatan Dase has the gift of rationalization. He consoles himself, nurses his agony and moves forward. His mercurical surges of thought pause on the practical. He also chooses to move forward, not towards a goal or destination but just forward in time to meet his responsibilities as a father, husband and priest. He has no vile gimmicks to wrench ease from society, nor does he have the bitter lowliness of spirit to tolerate indignities. He fantasizes in a half stupor about going to Puri, the crowded train compartment, the visit to the Garuda tower, the sea-bath, the final encounter with the rotund eyes of Lord Jagannath, the clamorous surrender, the fantasmagorial compensation for defeat, the untethered run to the heart of light, away from the enveloping gloom. Dase suffers alone, never inflicting his sorrows on anyone else. When his son sends money every month, he swells with satisfaction, even pride. When his daughter-in-law's feet get heavy his heart lightens. When the invitation to perform pujas for the Madanpur Marwari seth arrives, he relaxes in joyous anticipation of good money. A month away from home, children, wife and particularly the impending motherhood of his daughter-in-law disturb him but the expectation of money, 150 rupees plus gifts, goads him on. His dream of buying things for the family—an anticipatory joy—makes his difficulties, loneliness and suffering seem bearable. He faces every moment with fortitude.

During this tour to Dhabaleswar he chances upon a sober and staid intellectual, Satpathy, a mysterious character without a history. Only his physical appearance and cryptic words of wisdom strike Dase with a premonitary bass. Dase is moved by him to make a distinction between the mind and the supermind, the authentic and the passionate forms of knowledge. He realizes in his own mind that his soul is attached to a 'wheel of fire'. On his return home he enjoys a few days of familial joy. A grandson is born. He prepares his horoscope, bids farewell to Sudarshan, his wife's brother, who had helped the family in his absence and lavishes affection on everyone.

Sanatan is not a man of fixed attitudes. He is practical, physically aware and moral, but he is attached to his family and the functional world around it. He fights poverty with native endurance born of a tradition of unprotesting acceptance of faith, however painful it may be to cling to. He allows himself to be played upon by (perhaps) destiny, instead of trying to shape his destiny. Yet he does his duties with devotion and tries his utmost to lead a moral life till the moment for escape from the net arrives. He rationalizes his entrapment. But the primary recognition of the futility of worldly struggle has already dawned on him. Dase's conviction that poverty induces all debates of good and evil, cynicism and faith was shaken by Satpathy. But he had never imagined that he would be shocked out of his innocence by the same poverty-induced endgame. After his return from Dhavaleswar, he experienced a polarity in his functional reality. The distant shadow of the 1965 war, the election campaign, the Tripathy family's prosperity and marriage of their son, corruption, lies, the social rise of political manipulators contrastively exposes the squalor, poverty, disease and hunger and helplessness of Sanatan's personal world.

The first blow to his survival was the drying up of the trickle of money that had sustained him. When Raghu took his wife and son to his place of transfer, the postman never came again with a money order for his parents. Sanatan then sees his son Bata in bad company. Finally his wife and Jayi fall seriously ill and helpless, he watches them fade away. He could not serve them as he had no money to provide them wih proper food or medicine. His wife 'Tuku-ma' dies a victim (not martyr) of his poverty, his helplessness and his failed *purushakara*. The only link with his reality snaps. He sits in the crematorium, tired, defeated, lost, fallen:

> *After being ravaged by a terrible storm, the earth lies buried under a heap of broken branches and wet leaves on which the sun glints. A squirrel scurries over it, a sparrow takes off only to come down again. Dase's face looked like this storm-ravaged earth, empty, deserted, filled with wreckage, and utterly exhausted.*

The death of his wife and son is a turning point in Dase's biopsychic world as it is a climactic point in the thematic quest of the novel. The failure of the human agent to carve out his own niche, his personal reality, is complete in the case of Dase. His family disintegrates and is literally displaced. Sanatan leaves the ancestral home, the village, his sense-psyche involvement in places and people, and finally the iconic illusion of Lakshminarayan, serving whom, he had fed his family once a day through the years of his youth and middle age. Everything is left behind as Dase is removed from his reality and his compulsive obsessions, to his son Raghu's quarters in Madanpur.

The novelist, in order to resolve his own conflict between formal irony and formless fate, opts for the neutral maya, in line with the metaphoric nuance of the title of the novel: 'Yantrarudhani mayaya' (The Bhagavad Gita: 18:61). The human machine moved to activity by

God's power of illusion, functions according to its capacity for action: Sanatan's activities are now over, his reckoning closed. His attachment, his sensuous and motor-vascular functions and his conflicts, fears and agony now have come to a deathlike pause. But his incomprehension of his destiny survives the stasis of his soul. If destiny fulfills itself without releasing the non-comprehending soul from the mechanical prison of ignorance and maya to the knowledge of truth and final liberation, destiny too is a blind dark force of illusion. The author therefore reintroduces the catalyst, Profesor Satpathy, to lead Dase to unskin himself of the layers of *avidya* to his own *moksa*.

Satpathy takes Dase on a pilgrimage to the seats of esoteric wisdom which in itself is a rich, compensatory experience for his fantasy of taking his wife to Puri. In the company of Satpathy, the Dase body-machine moves out of the entrapment, eschewing the body by stages. The stages in progressively ascending order are: surrender, trascendence, bliss and liberation. At Dakhineswar, Dase is exposed to the human form of knowledge culled from the metaphysical quest of great men like Ramakrishna, Vivekananda and other philosophers. The essence of that knowledge is the immanence of the World Spirit or God where the will gets the impetus to activate the individual's soul. Recognition of that truth makes man feel humble. Dase after recognizing the truth forgets even to bless people who bow to him. He realizes the first lesson: humility.

He was on the verge of tears. He wanted to surrender himself completely— he would not mind if some one were to rush him to the top of a hill, he would not complain if someone flung him into the sea.

The next stage is attained at Manikarnika, the cremation-bathing ghat on the Ganga at Varanasi. This is the stage of transcendence, where reality appears like a perpetual flow. Time and eternity are beyond calendars, cycles, ages. The flow, the flux and the visions of reality afloat in the eternity of space-time appear dreamlike. Dase sees the bull (Sankaracharya's bull?), the florists, the shopkeepers yielding him the right of passage, and almost deifying him, giving him nature's flowers and fruit in royal ovation. Dase smiles, laughs like a soul moving up above the procession of faces, relations, animals and the biodiverse holistic order. He expands to fill the void of reality. He tastes the freshness of the new morning as if he had woken up to it after a long sleep never to sleep again:

After a long time Dase felt truly happy. The rusted iron doors in his heart
creaked as they were flung open. They would never be closed. To shut
them again, a host of ghosts, their eyes like burning cinders, would have
to labour hard on a drizzly night. Satpathy was now convinced that day
had dawned in Dase's inner space. There was no cause for fear.

On this morning, everything and all forms of life were beautiful
to him. He embraced the entirety of existence with uninhibited joy.
The motions of his physical senses suspended, he now moved on the
wings of extrasensory ecstacy savouring the fullness of being (like) a
disembodied soul.

The third stage attained by Dase is a state of bliss. This is the most
complex experience of light and shadow, body and bodylessness, illusion
and reality, dream and wakefulness, meeting, coalescing, interpenetrating
and consummating. What T.S. Eliot in the *Four Quartets* suggests—
the rose and fire in the oneness of bliss. In Vrindavan, Dase is agitated
by the relentless chase of a shadowy memory of Tuku-ma pervading
his body, mind and consciousness. Although the world has already
receded from his being, the rejuvenated Dase feels surrounded by the
unseen presence of his wife, making him full and empty, restless and
still. He can even meet the questions of the Professor with spontaneous
ease, stunning him with his wisdom, 'No sir. If you enter a zone of
light, you have to drag your shadow along.'

The Dase essence is now ready for the call of the flute. His wife
among the gopis, is Radha. In the second stage Dase is momentarily
identified with Krishna at Varanasi. Now Dase, at the call of the chief
gopi rushes to the Yamuna. The river, dark and deep, washes all layers
of illusions and restores him to nature. Dase in a somnambulistic frenzy
rides a chariot to the banks of the Yamuna, enters the water to the
accompaniment of the anklet rhythms of sixteen thousand gopis. In
the water Dase attains the bliss of yoga, union, transformed into the
creative energy attaining its own consummation, he then falls down
as if into a state of samadhi covered by bliss.

He is taken to Puri for the final confluence with the world-soul, the
goal and resting place of all life-streams. He is dumb, his senses indrawn
into the nadir after the zenith of bliss. He runs eyeless, speechless to
the temple of Jagannath; clasps the Garuda pillar amidst the sights,
sounds, jostling crowds, the penetrating air and the liquid sky pouring
on him from all sides. He is flowing, melting, drowning, falling into
the water of life, the ultimate receptacle. His clasp finally loosens, his

head sags. Listless, nerveless and absorbed, his inert body is taken to the sea shore, the reservoir of life, which according to the Bible is never full. All the rivers flow into the sea yet the sea is never full. The elements—earth, water, air, (ether) sky and the fiery stars wait in the visible darkness of the night, till the dawn, to receive the last breath. Dase breathes 'Jagannath' and lies on the sand, a ruined piece of time.

The four places that transform Sanatan in his final release, Dakhineswar, Varanasi, Mathura-Vrindavan and Puri are associated with the Indian metaphysical tradition. Dakhineswar is a seat of knowledge. Varanasi is a seat of renouncement and sacrifice of mundanity, being the space of Shiva. Mathura-Vrindavan stands for union and pristine joy. It bears the imprint of Krishna's *lila*. And Puri, the seat of Lord Jagannath, is the confluence of all divinities, knowledge and enlightenment. These four places raise progressively, receptacle-like Sanatan to receive the grace of mukti, the ultimate freedom which the individual soul gets merging with the energy of the universe.

Yantrarudha is an important milestone in the history of the Oriya novel. It restores faith in the divine order of things. The Oriya novel starts with a denial of the anthropomorphic universe in *Chha Mana Atho Guntha* where the human agent manipulates reality with cynical egoism. The other significant novels, *Matira Manisha, Paraja, Andha Diganta, Hida Mati, Satabdira Nachiketa* and *Amavasyara Chandra*, all show man as a bungling, graceless doer. Man and the universe appear in these novels as opposing agents of unyielding willpower resulting in man's fall. But *Yantrarudha* promises man a tenuous release ordained by a divine universe. In the modern world where the infected will confines man to a private enclosure, Sanatan Dase's passionless surrender to divine faith leading to his liberation is a comforting model. But the question still remains whether man is an agent or an instrument.

Chandrasekhar Rath's *Yantrarudha* is the first novel of a trilogy, the other two being *Asurya Upanivesha* (The Sunless Colony) and *Nabajataka* (The New Genesis). The trilogy is an intense metaphysical search for meaning involving man, society, God and the potential of the Indian superman. In the first novel man is an instrument on which the divine dispensation of the universe plays an ordained note. In *Asurya Upanivesha,* man is a doer, a manipulator of life where everything is vile, dark and evil. It is, perhaps, the darkest novel in Oriya literature leading man and society to the verge of tragic extinction. *Nabajataka* is an experiment in Rath's concept of the superman, who tries to modulate life on love, compassion, values of reconciliation and austere soul-force. But *Nabajataka* is abstract and philosophical, sacrificing fiction to authorial message. The trilogy, however, is a poetic quest for man's identity, purpose and validity in the Hindu universe.

Yantrarudha is not a quest novel nor is Sanatan Dase a quest hero. This is a thesis novel proving the Brahmanic soul of the universe, just and kind. It also establishes that the intuitive perceptions of scholars, philosophers and sages were true insights into the nature of reality. This novel can be compared with Herman Hesse's *Siddhartha*, the only difference being the form of the thematic quest. In *Siddhartha* we have a quest hero who moves out in search of the particular certainties of life from the temple-Ganga familiarity of his birth environs. He joins tantric groups, attends the Buddha's prayer and question-answer sessions but prefers not to follow others' perceptions; his quest is for the identity of man in his solitary encounters with reality. He goes to the other side of the Ganga and enters the world of attachment—love, business, competition and profit and loss. He returns disappointed recrossing the same river to time and historical sanctity. He discovers and recognizes the language of time and space, motion and stillness by his own dramatic encounters with reality, which finally becomes a part of his self and soul. He comprehends the binaries, the fatalities and also the mysteries to accept the world in its holistic order. Sanatan, on the other hand, has no quest, no choice to exercise. He only receives and endures the slings and arrows of reality till he is redeemed by the revealed form of knowledge of the ultimate reality in which he merges. *Siddhartha* causes conflicts by the western mode of logic and argument and creates a certain drama to achieve the state of enlightenment. Sanatan is exposed to the poetic metaphors as the images of terrestrial and celestial profundities dawn on him on his guided journey to enlightement.

Chandrasekhar Rath reinvents the metaphorical design of India's vedic core. This is a Hindu novel. A novel about the Hindu experience and vision of life.

Works

Among his numerous publications in different forms and genres the following are significant contributions to Oriya literature:

Novels: *Yantrarudha* (literally, the spirit that turns the wheel) 1967; *Asurya Upanibesha* (The Sunless Colony) 1974; *Naba Jatak* (The New Genesis) 1981.

Volumes of essays: *Dristi O' Darshana* (Vision and Philosophy) 1979; *Mu Satyadharma kahuchi* (Wedded to Truth I speak) 1977; *Kritadasara Swapna* (The Slave's Dream) 1981 (and four other collections).

Short Stories: *Samrat o Anyamane* (The Emperor and Others) 1980; *Anya eka Sakala* (Another Dawn) 1981; *Sabutharu Dirgharati* (The Longest Night) 1994; *Kramasah Gavira Nayee* (The Deepening River) (and eight other anthologies).

Poetry: *Tuma Pain Paksigana* (For You this Warbling) 2000.

Awards

1. Bisuva Recognition for Essays, 1963, 1967
2. Bisuva Award for Essays, 1972
3. Orissa Sahitya Akademi Award, 1980 (short stories)
4. Orissa Sahitya Akademi Award, 1981 (essays)
5. Sarala Award, 1981
6. Kendra Sahitya Akademi Award, 1997

Prafulla Kumar Mohanty

Man of Straw

Two trees—one banyan and the other a peepul, both equally old—had burst through a time-worn platform and grown into each other.

The double door of the temple lay behind the platform. Heavy and solid with knobs! You had to be really strong to push it open. It creaked noisily when it opened. The door led to a flight of two-coloured steps, and a neat row of stone pillars, carved with lotus flowers and figures of deities. Everything here flowed into and matched with everything else, like the rivers Ganga and Yamuna.

For four generations now, the idols of Lakshminarayan had been worshipped in the sanctum, with lamps and incense.

Every morning and evening, only a single gong was sounded here and a conch was blown. Someone chanted mantras inside the sanctum and offered worship, ringing only one bell. The evening sky washed clean by the witch-light of dusk, spread overhead. Flying across it a single bird, cut off from its flock, twittered from habit. In keeping the bird company, the sky above and the earth below made the creature even lonelier. It wasn't clear if it had become lost in the sky or the earth. But it kept piping as it looked around for its nest, because it was carrying food for its young. There was something of this aching loneliness about the mantra chanted in the sanctum and the feeble sound of the bell.

Sanatan Dase had been the priest of the Lakshminarayan temple ever since his investiture with the sacred thread. He was now going on fifty. But he did not look his age. He was also a man of very few words. That betel-stained smile gave the impression that he ate well and was content with his portion in life. Maybe he was the kind of man who thought to himself, 'Dying today, one is forgotten tomorrow. Why not make the most of life while one is alive. Let death overtake one when it does.'

And his eyes?

Greyish, and uncomprehending, like the glass eyes of Lord Lakshminarayan. They were unblinking, but their depths were hard to fathom. They saw everything, understood everything, but never once told you how much they had seen or understood. They could tell you a lot if only you knew how to read them. It was as if having found everything about the world, they said, 'So what? How does it matter?' But all this remained concealed in their depths. All one could see was the greyish colour of those eyes and their outward resemblance to the eyes of other ordinary people.

Everybody in the village knew and respected him. On festive days, offerings were made to the deity. Worship was offered when prayers for special favours were said to the deity. Dase managed everything efficiently.

That day it was well past evening as he closed the temple doors after laying the deity to rest. The son of Pradhan had sent an offering of sweets made of cream. These Dase carried in the fold of his towel. In the light of the stars, the temple, the trees—everything looked strange. It seemed as if they had huddled close to each other and dozed off. Soon they would blend completely into one another, lose their distinctness and become one.

Dase tucked the bunch of keys into his waistband and set forth.

His house lay at the other end of the village. It was getting late. Dase made his way along the deserted cart tracks.

Two generations of his family had provided the temple with its priests. Whenever this subject came up for discussion, Dase would say, 'Well, this is how God wants it to be.' But deep in his heart, he would tell himself, 'God Lakshminarayan is the lord of this earth. All these thousands of human beings depend on his mercy for their survival. It is He who provides for everyone and everything.' And that he, Dase, had the opportunity of being his temple priest was no small matter. Few were as fortunate as he. His father, Mukund Dase, who had died long since, used to tell him, 'Listen Sanei. For you, He is everything. Place yourself at His mercy and serve Him. He'll look after you.' No one ever called him 'Sanei' now. The postman, who occasionally carried a

letter addressed to him from his son's father-in-law, would get confused
and go around inquiring, 'Who is this Sanatan Dase?' Someone would
tell him, 'You don't know our Dase?' The postman would exclaim
'Oh!' as things suddenly became clear to him. Perhaps he thought, as
he smiled to himself, 'Does our Dase have a proper name?' The postman,
Sama Malika belonged to the new generation. He was fourteen when
he learnt the alphabet. His father, Balia Malika, had also worked in the
post office.

Everything seemed to have changed. Now there weren't many old
men in the village. Pakua Mishra, a toothless old man who was a few
years younger than Dase's father, called him 'Alei' whenever Dase paid
him his respects. Only Dase understood he meant 'Sanei' when he said
'Alei'. Others couldn't guess at all. It surprised Dase how his name was
being forgotten during his own lifetime. He found the situation not
so much sad as funny. He would tell himself, as if he had settled the
issue, 'Let it go. How does it matter? What's there in a name? After all,
one day this mortal frame itself will perish.'

A clump of bamboos stood midway between the temple and the end
of the village. Lengthening his stride, Dase reached it.

Muttering 'Astika, Astika,' he walked past the clump of bamboos,
striking the ground with his staff. This is where a cobra had bitten
Pradhan's brown ox. He muttered, 'Astika, Astika, Garuda, Garuda.'

From here one could glimpse the lights of the club-house of the
young men of the village. It bustled with activity till midnight.

The village was now full of educated young men. But the silly fellows
remained stupid. They enjoyed themselves loudly, stayed awake till
late at night, and woke up only long after sunrise. Dase thought, 'Do
these fellows care to eat properly? They eat like birds. At their time of
life they should be full of vigour and their skins taut to the point of
bursting. But look at them. Aren't they like dried fish? So lifeless, that
one can blow them away with a single blast of breath. Fools, why don't
they realize that no one can ever give up food and rest and live like a
proper human being. Well, let's leave them alone.'

A narrow stream of light flowed out of the club-house and lit up a
part of the village track. Dase stepped out of the deep darkness into it,
carrying his staff. The dirty towel on his shoulder in which he carried
the sarapulis now dripped with ghee.

You may not quite agree. But Bhalua Pradhan of the Pradhan
household is really a gem of a man. He loves good food and finds
giving others good food even more delicious. He knows what one

relishes. But his father. . . Oh, the man is a hardened miser, who won't even part with the dirt on his skin. These days he holds the annual Purana-recital only to compete with his son's father-in-law. Religion matters to him not at all. But for his son, Bhalua, I would not have got these sarapulis, though they are pitifully few in number for a large family like mine. Each member would get only a bite of the sweet. A wise man should never have a large family. But does one have a choice in matters like these? If one embarks upon a worldly path one begets children. This is maya, and who except the sage Suka has escaped its trap? Anyway, let's see. They would eat whatever fell to their share.

From somewhere a dog appeared and followed him. He gave a start and swung his staff. The dog, Baghua, as big as a colt, moved off a few paces. It was so strongly drawn to the buttery sweet smell of sarapulis that it wouldn't budge from his side. Trying to get away by taking long strides wearied Dase. He began to panic. A cold shiver seemed to rise from the ground under his feet and spread along his spine. Dase hurried, driven by fear.

He found many things scary. He was afraid of the bald Pathan living in the other quarter of his village. The tax collector, Brunda Nahak also scared him. The sight of the old man, Patra, from whom he had taken a loan and to whom he paid interest every month, filled him with fear. What scared him most was the anger which turned his wife into the blood-thirsty goddess Chandi. He lived in fear of everyone around him: his son, his daughter-in-law, his neighbours and his friends. In order to survive one had to live with fear. Dase had been a timid creature all his life.

He brandished his staff.

Scared, the dog retreated. So what if Dase knew the dog well? Didn't he also know the bald Pathan or his wife, his son Tuku's mother? Baghua was a beast, after all. Who knew if its greed wouldn't make it sink its teeth into his neck? Save me, O Lord Nrusingha.

Once he got past the embankment of the pond he would reach the safety of his own house. He felt as if the force which seemed to push him from behind, weighing him down had now relaxed its grip. Turning around, Dase noticed that Baghua had fallen back. It was busy playing another game, in which its partner was that stray bitch.

Oh.

Dase quickly figured everything out. Relieved, he smiled to himself, and walked on.

That Pundit Nilakantha gave himself airs because he had studied at Kashi, but at times he made truly insightful statements. He said that only four things really mattered in life: food, sleep, fear and sex. How true, indeed! Once entrapped by these, man can never free himself. They would hold him down like a mesh of roots.

As for Baghua, it was but a poor beast. The bastard was running after him for a taste of sarapulis. But the moment it glimpsed the sharp face of that bitch, it fixated on something else. The thought made Dase smile to himself.

Well, I must take Bauli to the veterinary hospital tomorrow. I'm told the new method makes cows give birth to bigger calves.

The idea struck him as very amusing. It made him laugh.

Presently he arrived at his doorstep. His wife opened the door and said acidly, 'You could have come after midnight. All the children have gone to bed.'

Not answering her question Dase said, 'We will take Bauli to the vet tomorrow in the morning. Here, take these four sarapulis. I brought these for the children.'

He thought to himself, 'Bastards! They are the same: human beings, cows and dogs.'

He felt sleepy. He went straight to bed after washing his hands and feet.

He turned on his side. Seated on the veranda, his wife tasted a piece of sarapuli. A kerosene lamp flickered near by. The midnight passenger train rattled past the village cremation ground. It was doomed to run along iron rails; it could never deviate from its track. All day and all night it ran breathlessly. There were windows on its body, and other openings. People and their luggage slipped in through these and spilled out.

Somewhere inside it, someone controlled everything; it was his hand which turned a handle that made the wheels roll, the lights come on or go out. The poor train had a terrible life.

It must have rolled past the club-house. Those young men there would now get up to leave, one after another. Thoroughly useless fellows. They looked so haggard, but they fancied themselves great lovers. Smoking bidis, they eyed nubile young women like lecherous tom-cats, each flashing his teeth under his moustache. But could they help it? Maybe, this is how they must behave at their time of life. In summer, even a dried-up ladies' finger plant puts out flowers and fruits. These fellows could not help dancing the way they are made to. Maya would

never rest until it ensnared them like flies in a spider's web. The lamp
burns itself out. And many a wretched insect flies into its flame and
perishes. But this has to happen for the world to go on. After all, women
are temptresses; men plunge into the pool of their charm and drown.

The lamp went out.

His wife asked, in a sarapuli-sweetened voice, 'Have you fallen asleep?
I have never seen sleep like this. Get up.'

'No, no. I don't feel sleepy. I am tired from running. I haven't yet
told you all that happened this evening.'

Tuku's mother came and sat down near him. Dase gave her a full
and vivid account of what Baghua did, making it as interesting as he
could.

'Eh, take care. Not so loud, please. When will you learn to be tactful?
Have you forgotten that your son and his wife are sleeping in the
next room?'

The morning next day.

A cloudy lazy morning.

Dase stood outside his house feeling oppressed by a strange sadness.
Suddenly the thought of Pundit Nilakantha crossed his mind.

Pundit Nilakantha read the Gita and understood it, but explaining
it to others gave him more pleasure. He had also studied other holy
texts. But to what end? He had five children, including the one born
recently. His property involved him in litigation. Because he liked fine
rice, quantities of it had to be brought from places as far off as forty
miles away. He was undoubtedly very learned. Then why did he behave
like an utterly ignorant person? The other day, his son Indramani
convened a meeting and talked a lot of rubbish. The father as well as
the son had big mouths. What is it he had said? Mice, monkeys and
dogs had been sent to the moon. And quite a few human beings are
now all set to travel all the way there. No doubt one lives in the benighted
Kaliyug. Or else, how could one get such perverse ideas? The moon
lies at a distance of two hundred thousand yojanas, and these fools
think they can get there. King Dasaratha had gone to the moon. He
came back after solemnizing a bond of friendship with the god Saturn.
These fools imagine they could get the measure of the infinite emptiness
of outer space riding a silly machine. Because you travel in that thing
taken from this world, it matters little if you travelled to the moon or
to Saturn. Reality would keep eluding you till you got rid of that silly
shell.

What sort of a learned scholar is that Pundit Nilakantha? What does he know after all? But then who knows anything? This is impenetrable maya. The learned and the fool alike have been trapped in this web of illusion. Even death is no escape. How did it matter? Sages like Vyasa and Parasar have gone before us. Millions and millions of creatures have perished. How did it matter if we have to go the same way?

Dase ran his hand over his belly, yawning. He called, 'Bata. Bring me water in a tumbler. I'll wash my face.'

Man, the Enigma

Dainty curls of locks and a shapely face
Like a polished bud the sandal paste on the forehead
Dark blue locks along its margin
Glow like emeralds bordering a diamond mirror.

It seemed as if the lines were plucked effortlessly from a tree. Dase never faltered or got stuck even once while reciting the eighteen books of the Mahabharata. A group of men would choose to sit on the bank of the pond at the other end of the village and listen to the recitation. Dase's voice reached them clearly although he read out the epic under an awning of coconut branches in front of Pradhan's house, a furlong away.

The way Dase recited the lines, Sarala Das' words seemed to yield up their meaning instantly and clearly. His listeners got carried away. They swayed when Dase did. They felt the five Pandava brothers were their own kith and kin and Draupadi was none other than their own daughter-in-law. Kichak and his hundred brothers were none other than the wicked people of the neighbouring village, Haripur. They deserved to be throttled and thrown into a fire during the next festival. Dase felt outraged when Kichak humiliated Draupadi in the King's court. When Draupadi entreated King Virata to help her, he would break down, his voice would choke with emotion. And when Bhimasen prepared himself for the duel with Kichak in the gymnasium, Dase would sit up, slapping his own thighs. His hands would lift the book he was reading. His voice would swell like a tide in the sea on a full moon night. His glasses would glitter, reflecting the light of the ghee-fed lamp. The kaniar flower tied to the end of his pigtail danced. So did his gold earrings. If one observed them from a distance, it would seem as if the reciter who read out the sacred text and his audience were swaying, caught in this tidal wave of feeling. Dase breathed life into the words. No matter how often one heard them, one longed to hear them again and again. Moved to tears, old Pradhan would smear Dase's forehead and chest with sandal paste. Old men and women of the village brought large quantities of sandal paste with them. Sandal paste brought great comfort to Dase in the summer months. But in their eyes Dase was then no ordinary mortal; he was transformed into a sage of the Dwapar era. The river of time would begin to flow backwards until it encircled Yudhisthir's palace in Hastinapur and stood still.

Rats had eaten the rice stocks of three years stored in old Pradhan's granary. Of his four sons, Hari, the eldest one, married and brought home a wife. But old Pradhan and his wife had been waiting in vain for a grandchild. It was in the hope of being blessed with one that he held these recitals every year. Doesn't he know that if one is not fated to get something, no one can pluck it off a tree and hand it to him? The fact is the old man loved to listen to Purana-recitals. In Patapur village grand annual recitals were held by his son's father-in-law. He spent lavishly on these occasions. In old Pradhan, the desire to hold similar recitals grew irresistibly. For seven years now, he had been organizing Purana-recitals in his own village. To listen to sacred texts being read out, villagers would come early in the evening and sit on old Pradhan's veranda. The respect with which they treated him pleased him immensely.

Old Pradhan was a simple-hearted man. He had recently had a pond dug in the village. People from five neighbouring villages helped themselves to the mangoes in his orchards. He would gift an umbrella to Dase every summer. Now everyone in the Dase household had an umbrella. Until Pundit Nilakantha became a man of means, every Sankranti, he would be the first to be invited to a meal by old Pradhan. Dase came too, accompanied by his two sons. It was again with Pradhan's financial support that he had conducted the sacred thread ceremony of these two boys. Pundit Nilakantha used to bring his son, Indramani, with him when he came for these meals. Now that Indramani was an educated young man, he preferred to stay away. That was but natural. After all, Indramani Tripathy was an engineer. He was on his way to becoming an important person. It would be difficult to imagine a man in his position coming to Pradhan's house to partake of a Sankranti meal. Everyone in the village treated Pradhan with great respect, expressed their devotion in different ways and lavished praise on him. When in the right mood, Pundit Nilakantha would comment sonorously, 'After all, what else would Pradhan do with so much wealth? Has it not been said, "If one earns money through rightful means one finds God?"' But Indramani, who had come home during the summer vacation this year, differed, and sneered, 'Old Pradhan is a fool.'

The forest would catch fire in the month of Baisakh. It got so hot no one could sleep until late at night. Ah, what a pleasant place Kakinada was! This thought absorbed Indramani. He found reading film magazines in the dim light of a lantern difficult. As he strolled around outside, the lines from the Mahabharata would reach his ears. Dase sang:

> You have the strength to conquer
> The three worlds, brother dear.
> Who makes you suffer like this now?
> It was my fault that I held back
> And did not give you permission
> To destroy the Kauravas.

In spite of himself he would soon be under the spell of these words. The cool light of the moon soothed him, and he made his way to the platform in front of Pradhan's house. Ah! What beautiful poetry! Stillness had descended on the listeners; they seemed to have lost their power of movement. They now sat like statues.

> He is Bhimasen, Yudhisthir's younger brother.
> Have you never heard of him before?
> One hundred and eighty pautis of rice satisfy his hunger.
> I was his cook, listen O King of Matsya!

Of course, all this had long been familiar to him. He had grown up listening to Dase's recitation of the Mahabharata. And yet, the words sent a shiver through him. He pulled himself out of the tidal wave of Dase's voice with a determined effort and told himself, 'Rubbish! A man endowed with the strength of a hundred, nay a thousand lions! Cock and bull stories! Meant to fool these poor wretches. Which one of these statements is scientifically valid? These are stupid fellows, all of them. Their bodies sway with ecstasy as they listen to the recital.' He looked at old Pradhan, hands in the pockets of his trousers. Enraptured by the narration, his eyes closed, the ecstatic old man seemed to be drinking in the words of the song. His face wore an expression of deep content. The fool! He could have got fantastic returns if only he had invested his vast wealth wisely. If he had grown fish in that pond of his, he would have earned thousands of rupees. But would the old fellow listen to reason? He said that growing fish for profit would enmesh him in sin. What nonsense! Again, he could have got all his land ploughed by a tractor. Why work your old exhausted bullocks to death. But the old man would retort that using tractors angered the goddess of wealth. Fine, let him not do so then. At least he could have given his sons an education. Given his wealth, he could have easily sent them to England, had he so wished. But money could not do everything; one needed a little intelligence also. These were peasants after all. They would never learn how to hold a pen properly. 'Anyway, it is superstitious people like these who have landed us all in such a mess,' he thought.

It seemed to Indramani that he was looking down from a great height at these pitiable creatures below. For generations, these fools had been rotting in a pit of ignorance. He was not one of them. He belonged elsewhere. He turned his face away in disgust.

Now Dase stopped singing, for he had no betel leaf left in his mouth to chew. He reached for a paan with his left hand. His listeners stirred and stretched themselves. In the last row sat Brunda Nahak under a bakul tree. Dase watched Indramani Tripathy, his hands in his trouser pockets, his eyes lowered, leaving very slowly. A few others, lost as they were in the faraway kingdom of Virata, turned their dreamy eyes in the same direction. Trousers were something of a novelty in the village; so was the act of getting up from the recital platform without a compelling reason. Slowly everyone made his way back into the world of the present. Dase, too, peered at him over his glasses, slipping it down the bridge of his nose. Old Pradhan would explain, as if he understood what Dase wanted to know. 'Indramani, Pundit Nilakantha's son.' Pushing back his glasses, Dase said, 'Oh.' But he thought to himself, 'How could a Pundit's son find all this so distasteful? Forget it. Times have changed. Who would listen to us. Sri Hari. . .'

The recitation began. Dase removed the peacock feather that he used to mark the pages and placed it gently on his left thigh. The listeners would become oblivious to everything else and focus all their attention on him. They were again borne off on the wings of fancy to the kingdom of King Virata. Everyone there was lost in the recital but not Brunda Nahak.

He kept gazing at the receding figure of Indramani Tripathy. 'He could never have received an education if I had not taken pity on a poor brahmin boy. He would have sat idle at home after school. True, his father was anxious to give his son a decent education, but wasn't he a good-for-nothing? Tell me—could he himself have gone to Kashi on his own if I had not persuaded the zamindar's son to help him out? Forget it. These people have such short memories. But one should not make an issue of such things as this.' The other day poor Pundit Nilakantha had come to him and implored him. 'Nahake. You know so many people who matter. Please get one of them to help my son.'

O, That was nothing! Brunda Nahak had been collecting taxes for twenty long years now; he had not started yesterday. From the collector to the clerk, he had kept everyone in good humour. 'I went to the head post office, approached the clerk and went with him to the headmaster of a high school. Oh, all this involved so much writing! The process was so long and so complicated! The matter of expenses was settled before Indramani went to Madanpur. Was it an easy thing to do? Could anyone else have managed to get it done? However, it must be conceded that the boy did well in his studies. But, don't you forget that I went to his school from time to time and put in a word in his favour to his teachers. "Please take care of this boy," I would say to them. Whatever I said to them did carry a lot of weight; they could never ignore my request, and they were the ones who decided everything. They made sure he was placed in the first division. Then the headmaster said that he would send Indramani to an engineering college on a government scholarship. I told him, "All right, send him there." If I had not said so, this fellow would never have gone this far in life. Anyway forget it.' Indramani had moved out of sight.

Nahak turned to look at the crowd of listeners. It was *Brunda Nahak*, no ordinary person, fixing his eyes on people. His eyes now rested on old Pradhan. He smiled to himself. This old Pradhan had almost ruined himself the other day; everything would have been over for him. The magistrate had come on a tour of inspection and set up camp. He had taken a good look at the rice fields and had inquired about their ownership. The question put the fear of God into old Pradhan. Palms joined, he had replied, 'Huzoor, all these belong to me.' The Sahib swung round. Old Pradhan would have been undone with a mere stroke of his pen. I winked at Pradhan. I followed the Sahib to his tent, and arranged supplies of chicken, fine rice, and ghee. Pradhan ran around and made all this available. What a narrow escape! Nahak's eyes scanned face after face: he had once mortgaged this man's utensils to buy him medicines from the Kabiraj. That man could not get his daughter married. Nahak found her a groom as handsome as a prince. That other man there...his house was about to be auctioned off. Nahak got the auction order cancelled by paying a small bribe. Someone came to him for a loan, someone else sought other favours. All these creatures had survived by his grace. Look at this Purana-singer, Sanatan Dase. The fellow shuddered whenever he caught sight of Nahak. 'The poor chap's pocket is always empty. Anyone else in my place would never have spared him. Poor Dase would have left this village long ago were it not for someone merciful like me,' he thought.

Nahak's mind had strayed far from the Purana. The moon had climbed into the middle of the sky. He paced, hands resting on his waist. Dase continued:

> You are handsome and graceful
> O mighty one
> For what fault of yours has fate been so harsh to you
> To hide from public view you have assumed a disguise
> Someone beautiful like the god of love
> So many graces adorn your comely figure.
> I only hope, king Virata fails to recognize you, Nakul.

Nahak said, in a tone of authority, 'Oh Dase. Let's stop here. We have done enough for today.'

Dase placed his thumb on the couplet and looked up through his glasses. The others also turned to look. A little subdued, Nahak now said, 'It is already quite late. How about stopping here—what do you say?' Dase looked down at the leaves of the pothi. He said, 'Only two more pages of the canto left.' People stirred, some got up and stretched. Nahak would not wait. He left, his wooden slippers clacking.

The recital came to an end with everyone saying 'Haribol!' Old Pradhan woke the children and distributed the offering of sweetened rice among them. Dase placed the peacock feather bookmark in the pothi and laid it on the book rest after carrying it reverently to his forehead. Then, in spite of himself, his eyes searched for Brunda Nahak. He felt relieved when he found that Nahak had gone. He was always a little nervous of him. Whenever Nahak came to him to collect taxes, Dase was never in a position to pay up. So Dase felt shaky and insecure like a debtor whenever he came to Nahak.

At last Dase rose to his feet. Sitting for so long had stiffened his joints and made them numb. The villagers got up and left one by one. While Haria Pradhan was packing some flattened sweet rice into a bundle meant for Dase, he wandered off to the baula tree and placed some crushed tobacco leaves on his palm.

Raghu Dalei's mother walked slowly. How long would she take to reach home? Dase knew how she got on. The poor woman had not eaten since the row she'd had with her daughter-in-law during the day. Dase learnt all about these quarrels from Tuku's mother, his wife. The old woman came here to avoid quarrels at home. But she was a sensible woman, always conscious of her dignity. Only ill-luck had led her to choose a bride for her son from a village like Haripur. She had received only a little education and so was unable to make sense of everything that was recited. So what? How many of those who came to this recital understood the scriptures, or even had the intention of doing so? Everyone had his or her own axe to grind. Take old Pradhan for instance. He had money. He wanted a brahmin to come to his forecourt and read out the sacred texts, and for all the villagers to assemble before his house. His wife came along and sat beside him even though in her heart she was not drawn to these things. Nor did she understand a word. How could she help it if everything went over her head? Nevertheless, she would sit through the recital, her legs outstretched, even when she felt very sleepy, for she was afraid of public ridicule. Her son and daughter-in-law followed her example. Haria thought this too was an auspicious ritual, like his marriage. He would set to work with great devotion. Gradually he began to understand some parts of the sacred texts.

The old woman from Banchha, the fisherman's house, came because her son forced her to. Her son worked as a peon, and earned a few rupees. He now wanted to be counted as a man of substance, a man like everyone else. 'Women from all the prosperous families go there; you go too. You must look presentable. No one is big or small in places like these.' The poor woman, a very simple soul, had to attend. No matter if she understood very little, she would carry a few champak flowers in a banana leaf to the place of recital. She would listen to Dase for a while and then doze off.

A group of young men taking the dewy night air would stop for a while and listen to the lines describing the wrestling between Kichak and Bhimasen. They would wander off after a time. One among them would eye the young daughter of Janaka, the cowman. Dase knew that the young men sat at the crossroads waiting for this young girl.

She too seemed quite pleased and excited at the attention she received. Her father had left home long ago, and she had lived with her mother since her childhood. They owned an acre of land—and they managed somehow. The poor woman came here in the hope that old Pradhan might take pity on the poor girl and find someone to marry her.

As for Brunda Nahak, fear drove him to where the Purana recital was held. An astrologer who had read his palm, predicted he would live for only another two years. He was one who would never earn merit at his own expense. Even in the holy month of Kartik he made an offering of only a brass two-anna coin. If he earned four paisa, he made sure that three out of the four was his profit. He came here because he would earn merit without having to pay for listening to the Puranas. If he had to pay, he would never have been seen anywhere near this place. Who could contradict what the lines on one's palm, forehead and horoscope said?

Well, why did not Pundit Nilakantha come here? His wife did, sometimes. She was a good soul. But her husband was an arrogant person. Just because you are a pundit, should you disregard the Puranas? The truth is he would come only if Dase was not doing the recital. He treated Dase with some contempt. The sight of so many people in the village treating him with such reverence was repugnant to him. Do you think you belong to a superior order of the brahmin caste, and we are inferior Samabedia brahmins? All right, don't come if you don't want to. The heavens won't fall if you don't turn up. The whole village attends the recital. How could someone like you, who is a learned person, stay at home on such a flimsy pretext? It is said the Mahabharata is full of nectar. Do the stories get devalued if I recite them? Your vanity deprives you of this nectar.

Haria finished making up the packet and called out, 'Everything ready, Sir.'

Haria was a worthy young man, and he had been told by his father that all these had been organized in order to make God bless him with a son. He had come to share his father's faith and had applied himself whole-heartedly to the task of holding the Purana recital. A very nice boy, Haria. 'Listen Harihara. You must arrange two milk cows by the time we get to the calf-stealing episode. Do you follow me? These cows will be gifted away. This will produce the desired result. Come closer and listen to me. That cow of yours will do. Look here. Don't hesitate. If you could persuade your father to make a gift of that cow, you'll make the brahmin happy. Take it from me. You'll be blessed with a son.'

He was going to bless Harihar, patting his head, when he heard old
Pradhan call out, 'Dase, you took rather long tonight, didn't you?'

'Oh, yes. Yes. I am leaving.' Saying this, Dase picked up the packet.
'Let me tell you Pradhan, only the very lucky are blessed with a son like
Harihar. God willing, you will be playing with your grandson this time
next year.'

On the way home, Dase thought to himself that thanks to this recital
his children would get supplies of sweetened rice for three months. If
only he could receive the gift of a cow, Tukua would get a little milk.
God! Everything is Thy will! . . . But is this worth anything? This could
never be the reason for which I come to recite the Puranas. Not so. But
talent is everywhere respected. Pradhan holds the recital because he
has to do so. One is of course entitled to one's dakshina and this small
quantity of sweetened rice. I say that I am totally disinterested when I
come here to recite the Purana. There is always a motive.

That way everyone practises some deception. Human beings are
by nature deceitful. Everyone is up to some mischief or the other.
There is no way one human being can figure out another. Why make
too much of the game of dice played between the Pandavas and the
Kauravas? We play more dangerous games than that every day of our
lives. Man is a stranger to straight talk. Every human being is a masked
cheat. Lilies bloom on the surface but down below there is nothing
but rotting mud. What a strange creature man is! He can be buried in
a piece of land measuring less than three cubits and a half. So fragile,
a gust of wintry wind could blow him away like a dry leaf. But what
arrogance, what capacity for deception! Even the gods are mystified
by these creatures.

The road was deserted. The moon was going down. It seemed to
Dase at that moment as if a lot of secrets were suddenly being unlocked
for him.

He stopped. He cleared his throat and brought out the box of ground
tobacco from a fold in his waistcloth. He put a pinch of it on his tongue
and said aloud, 'The One who has created all this knows everything.
If He finds something not to His liking how long will it take Him to
destroy it? Why should we unnecessarily trouble our heads over such
things? Hari Narayan.'

Dase headed straight for home.

The Rivals

Byaghrasya gotrasya. . . Sankuchana prabaray. . .aputrikaya Bhishma varmane. . .

Dase was on his way back from the pond, chanting this, *kusapatra* in hand. After offering oblations to the gods early in the morning, he chanted this all the way home. '*Aputrikay . . . Bhishma varmane . . .*' Oh, what a great soul. There had been no one left in the end to offer him oblation. Only because he had made a vow! He choked. He wiped his eyes with his wet towel, but he wanted to break down and cry like an orphan.

Sniffling, he came to his doorstep. He composed himself, clearing his throat and wiping his face, but the thought occupied him. 'Can someone really have a son like this? Oh, what a great man. He surpassed even gods in keeping his vow. Of course, why should he bother about an heir? Millions and millions in all ages would look upon themselves as his sons.' Dase entered his house. His heart overflowed with love and compassion today. He was more sentimental than usual. He went through his chores in a fit of abstraction. The deity was worshipped. His son went to school. He helped himself to a handful of sugared rice, Tukua seated in his lap. Everything was done as it should be, but his mind was elsewhere.

He spread a rushmat on the veranda and sat quietly, his head resting on his knees.

His mind went back to the rite of offering oblation and to Pundit

Nilakantha. Seated on a stone slab on the right side of the ghat Nilakantha offered oblation to his ancestors. His face was covered with a glistening black beard. On his body, as thin as a copper wire, lay his sacred thread. How beautiful he made pure Sanskrit sound! Pundit Nilakantha too offered consecrated water to Bhisma, his voice choked with tears.

'Oh my orphaned brother!' Dase felt like saying to him, and, in his heart, embraced him warmly. He kept his eyes closed for a time. When he opened them, warm tears rolled down his cheeks. These he hurriedly wiped.

Memories of the day his father died came rushing to him. That day, Dase was reading aloud the eleventh book of the *Bhagavata Purana* by his father's sick-bed since evening. Midnight. Drops of tears fell on the pages of the book and moistened them. But he went on. In the middle of his reading, his eldest son cried, and went back to sleep. In the evening, his father had signalled everyone to give him Ganga-jal. There was nothing to be done now. All one could do was wait for the end. The pause at the end of each canto filled Dase with an inexplicable dread. It was menacingly dark outside. He was feeling very lonely and nervous. He turned to look at his father who lay with his eyes closed. Dase returned to the book and went on reading.

The pensiveness that had oppressed him while pouring the water of the Ganga into his father's mouth seemed to have subsided a little. He went out to stretch his limbs. Dawn would break after two hours or so. In the adjacent room slept his wife and son. It suddenly seemed as if a shadow hung over everything. A little noise issuing from the room where his father lay made him hurry back. He found his father staring at him, as if he was waiting for him. Dase rushed to his bed. He thought his father looked up and gave him a smile.

'Would you give me a little chewing tobacco, Sanei?' Dase started. For three days his father had lain speechless, unable to utter a word. His voice was clear and resonant. No one who heard it would believe he had not eaten a grain of food for a month. Words failed to describe the hope which filled Dase's heart now. He started mixing some tobacco and a little lime and kneaded the mixture in his palm. But even as he was waiting, his father's face suddenly grew pale. As if he had not noticed the change, he offered the mixture to his father, who was unconscious. The mouth opened to receive the tobacco and the lime, but it did not utter a word. The eyes remained closed.

No. The end was at hand. Desperate, Dase grasped his father's hands and said, 'Father. What can I do on my own if you leave me. Won't I be orphaned?' His father's tongue was shrinking. He said, making an immense effort, 'Ja. . .ga. . .nna. . .th.' He went on whispering this name.

Dase called his wife. Together, they lifted the dying man and lowered him to the ground. A moment later, he stopped breathing altogether. A strange hush fell over everything. Dase stood still for a while. Then he covered his face, broke down, and sobbed like a child. Oh! What loving care his father had lavished on him when he was a child! As if he was a precious icon, to be dusted with a piece of velvet cloth. Now, there would be no one to feel for him in his times of trouble. Who would bother to console a wretched orphan? Dase opened his eyes. Grief gnawed at his vitals. Tears rolled ceaselessly down his cheeks. But he had no time for all this; he must hurry. The body would become impure if it was kept uncremated till daybreak.

No, he wouldn't let that happen. He wiped his tears, threw a towel over his shoulder and rushed out. What a crisis! Oh Lord Jagannath. Save me, Oh Lord. Bereft of all hope, I now turn to you, Oh my Lord.

Patapur lay close to his own village. All his relatives lived there. His father would invite them whenever a death anniversary was observed at home. But mother used to protest, 'Why do you feed our enemies? These people have grabbed our homestead, our landed property and forced us to leave the village and set up home here. What makes your heart overflow with affection for such rogues?' But his father would say, 'Blood ties never ever snap. Can you draw a line over water? The property they took away from me was no great treasure. All they took was a small parcel of land, which came down to me after our land was divided among several heirs. In my place, now they enjoy it. So what! Should this stop me from treating them well, inviting them?' Dase was deeply impressed.

When he reached Patapur, running part of the way, he found the doors of the houses closed. He went from door to door, calling. At last one of his father's cousins opened the door. Dase bowed respectfully to him and making a painful effort said, 'Father has passed away.'

'Oh. But what can a useless old man like me do at a time like this? Why did you take the trouble of travelling this long distance at night? Would it not have been better if you had waited till morning? Everyone in the village has gone away to do their priestly chores.'

'What!' Dase was shocked. 'I repeatedly asked them to stay back and wait for at least these three days. And they have all gone?'

He only said, 'Should we wait till morning and let father's body grow stale and impure?'

'You should not let that worry you, my son. After all you are alone. So things got delayed a bit. Wasn't my father's corpse cremated after it had grown stale and impure? Nothing can be done now.'

Dase turned around and left, striding along rapidly. But what was to be done now? He suddenly remembered Bhaiganana, his father's sister's son. He headed straight for Ratnapur, across the rice fields, looking anxiously at the eastern horizon every so often.

He walked on, head lowered, not bothering to notice anything around him. As he approached the village, he heard someone calling him, 'Who is it? Is it Sanei?' Dase started and looked up. Bhaiganana stood before him, a rope in one hand, a sickle in the other. Perhaps he was on his way to the hillock to collect rattan sticks.

Dase fell on his neck, and broke into a disconsolate wail. Bhaiganana understood. He asked, 'Did anyone from Patapur come?' Dase only shook his head. Bhaiganana knew they would do this. He left the sickle and the rope under a bush. 'Let those bastards stay home. Come with me. Let's go', he said. Dase felt immensely relieved. The two cousins set off.

The sky showed tints of red by the time they reached Dase's village. From a distance he noticed a few persons standing in front of his house. When he came closer he found that Ratna the cowherd, was preparing the litter to carry off the corpse. Ananta Pradhan accompanied by two men was present. Old Sibaram Dalei patted Dase on his head and back and said, 'You are like my son. Don't feel helpless. We the villagers will never allow the corpse to get stale and impure.' How generous these people were! Dase forgot everything else and wanted to throw himself at the feet of this old man.

Bhaiganana set to work single-handed. By the time the body was carried to the cremation-ground which lay at the outskirts of the village, the sky was light, but the sun had not risen yet. Old Pradhan had taken care to set up a pile of dry firewood. In fact, he had done everything that could be done without having to touch the corpse. With trembling hands Dase lit the funeral pyre. He came away, eyes closed. Old Pradhan had arranged two tins of ghee. So the cremation went off smoothly. Bhaiganana was strong, like Bhima. He had carried the dead body almost unaided. Dase had only given him a hand. Bhaiganana said to Dase, 'Sanei. You go home. There is no need for you to be here.'

The logs of wood caught fire. Five men from Patapur arrived. Bhaiganana rushed at them wanting to wring their necks and throw them into the burning pyre. He screamed at them, 'Get out of here, all of you. Or else, I'll smash your heads with this prod. You fellows made my uncle feed you. And when you were needed you disappeared, made yourselves scarce? And you dared to say that it did not matter in the least if my uncle's corpse grew stale and impure?'

The men from Patapur, poor fellows, stood apart, looking crestfallen and guilty. Their plight moved Dase to pity. These poor chaps were not rich merchants. After all, if they did not go out and earn in the morning, they had to go hungry at night. Ah, poor fellows! They had come running in the dark as soon as they received the news. What more could they have done? But he dared not put in a word in their defense when Bhaiganana was in such a fury.

Later Dase was told that Bhaiganana stood still for quite a while staring into the funeral pyre. Tears rolled down his cheeks. Some strange thought crossed his mind, and he flung the prod away, saying, 'Uncle. I won't let this stick touch your body. You were a great soul, a lover of truth. See, I have no one to help me cremate you. So, please allow the fire to consume your body.' As if his prayer was answered, the flames rose and reduced the corpse to ashes in no time. From Dase's back veranda, one could see the leaping flames in the light of early morning. . .

Dase sat, his head resting on his knees. He felt someone had tapped him on the back and exclaimed 'Father!' He looked up and saw Tukua holding out a paan. In a moment he was back in the world of human attachments. The face of this child made Dase forget all sorrows. He was his eighth child and the astrologer had predicted that he would be extremely lucky. Dase seated him on his lap. He put the paan into his mouth, sighed and looked across at the village track. His wife was watching him closely from behind the door. She could see that her plan was beginning to work. For all Dase's problems, she had solutions. She now quietly went back into the kitchen. For a time, Dase kept chewing a small piece of arecanut and sat staring vacantly into the mid distance. At last he said, 'Let us go to Pundit Nilakantha's house. I have not paid him a visit for a long time. Get up my dear.' He stood up, carrying his son in his arms.

He slowly made his way towards the pundit's house, holding an umbrella, a scarf thrown over his shoulders. On the way he ran into

Shyama Mallick, who saluted Dase, palms pressed together. Extremely pleased, Dase blessed him, 'May you live long. Are you going to distribute letters, my son?'

'No Sir, it's too early for that. Our work begins at 10.'

'Oh! How could I forget?'

At the crossroads a snake-charmer was showing his tricks to a group of children. Dase stopped there for a moment. Two huge cobras swayed, their hoods raised. The snake-charmer moved the lid of the box before them and sang in a raised voice.

> *Krishna is on his way to Nanda's house.*
> *Oh Lord Hari, but one cannot see the road in the dark.*
> *Masses of cloud hang over the city of Mathura, Lord Hari*
> *Lightning illuminates the path, Oh Lord Govinda.*

The children watched with unblinking eyes. A boy arrived, gasping for breath, and stood rooted, unable to take his eyes off the snakes. Equally interested, Dase stood amidst the children and watched the snakes.

'How well this fellow, the snake-charmer, has trained these vicious snakes! It's only fear of the snake-charmer that makes these two dangerous snakes dance side by side, or else they would have fought and killed each other by now.'

'Why should they attack each other just because they are dangerous creatures? But who knows?'

Dase moved out and reached the pundit's house after some time. The two young coconut trees in front of the pundit's house had put out new leaves. The narrow outer veranda coated with coloured clay looked spotless. At one end of it lay a matting of coconut leaves. This part of the veranda probably received sunlight in winter.

As Dase went up the steps, Indramani came out of the house. He saluted Dase. Dase blessed him clasping his hands. 'May you live long. Is your father home, my son?'

'Yes, he is writing something. Do sit down please. I will call him.'

'I can meet him later, there is no hurry. My work is not urgent. It is a long time since I saw you last. Won't your studies ever end?'

Dase sat down on the veranda.

'This is my last year. I have come home for the puja vacation. Father wrote to say that he would go to a conference in Puri for a few days and that it would help if I was home. Mother too was very keen that I come. Let me call father.'

His fair-skinned, smiling face, health and physique all seemed remarkably beautiful to Dase. It was such a son that mattered. The others didn't count.

Pundit Nilakantha emerged dressed in matha clothes, with a length of cloth printed with the name of God covered his body. On seeing Dase he smiled and said. 'What brought you here? Indra, send us the paan-box.'

The two settled themselves on the coconut leaf matting. Paans were prepared, and they fell to talking.

Childhood days were recalled. At last Dase said. 'Your son told me that you are going to Puri.'

'Yes, a conference where pundits and scholars from all over India will get together. Five from Orissa have been selected. I have been asked to write something and present it there.'

Dase got the hint. Truly, Nilakantha was a worthy man. He is someone who will surely make his mark and bring glory to his land. He said, 'Wonderful! This is a matter of great pride. When you are honoured, we all feel honoured. Tell me, when are you going? More than the conference, the opportunity to set your eyes on Lord Jagannath is what really matters. An auspicious day for your journey must be chosen.'

He had got used to carrying the almanac under his arm. Whenever he went out he never forgot to carry the almanac. He took out the kusha-grass bookmark, and opened the page. 'Today is Saturday. Tomorrow is Sunday. The day after that would be most suitable. The time of the day most auspicious for the journey would be after seven in the morning.'

Happy, Dase raised his smiling face, but there was no one before him.

'Did the pundit go away?' he wondered. 'Maybe, he had some urgent work at home.' It was not that Dase did not feel a little put out. 'Maybe this is how these pundits normally behave. Unless one is restless, how could he ever be a pundit.' The thought consoled Dase, and a feeling of brotherly love brought a smile to his face. The pundit reappeared and enquired, 'Did you find the auspicious hour, Dase? I found that there was no arecanut in my paan box, so I went in to get one. So, on what day should I leave for Puri?'

The words seemed absolutely sincere. Dase felt he had unnecessarily misunderstood the pundit. He now persuaded himself, 'Pundit Nilakantha really is a good man.'

The snake-charmer, carrying his boxes, passed along the village

street, followed by a large number of children. Indramani, neatly
dressed, went out. For his part, Dase suddenly wanted to go home.
He felt they should meet and talk shop some other time.

The pundit popped a few more pieces of arecanut into his mouth
and said, 'I have many things to do at Puri. We have just received the
first proposal of marriage for Indramani. Um. . .anyway, everything
will be sorted out once I get there.'

Since the matter of the auspicious hour for the journey had escaped
the pundit's mind completely, Dase decided not to raise it at all. He
said, 'Wasn't there a proposal from the village of Ramachandrapur
for Indramani? What happened to that?'

'Ramachandrapur? Oh, there were hundreds of proposals like that.
But how can I marry my son into such a family? Since everything in
this matter is decided by Lord Prajapati, no one can foresee the future.'

Shyama Mallick arrived. He said, 'Dase, I went to your house, looking
for you. No wonder I didn't find you home—you are here. There is a
letter for you.'

A letter? Few letters came to the village. Fewer still to Dase. A little
apprehensive, Dase took the envelope. The pundit looked on. Who
knew what it contained? Who had sent it? The fellow could have simply
sent a postcard.

The envelope carried an attractive invitation card in Oriya, neatly
printed, which said, 'An all-India conference of pundits will be held
on the first day of the month of Kartik under the auspices of the Utkal
Sanskrit Sansad. We humbly request you to attend the conference.'

The pundit coloured. He made an attempt to smile, but the smile
failed to appear. He said, 'Let me see. Is it addressed to you?' He
turned the letter over and read it.

As for Dase, he was at a loss: how could someone like himself get
invited to a conference of pundits, of all things. Had he received a
letter meant for someone else?

'Arre, oh I see. All this is the work of that Gadadhar. He is my
mother's sister's son and he works at the Sanskrit College in Puri.
Last year I had spent the panchaka—the last five days in Kartik—in
his house. Our Pradhan had sent me to Puri to perform the ceremony
of offering a pennant at the temple of Lord Jagannath. It is he who
has sent me this invitation.'

'Oh. That's it. A thousand such invitations must have been sent
out. Or else, how would they find an audience who would listen to
the speakers. Well, are you going to Puri? Let's go together.'

'Have you gone crazy, Tiadi, what have I got to do with these conferences? People like you should go there.'

Dase rose to his feet, holding the letter. The pundit, feeling a little uncomfortable, also got up.

On the way back, everything appeared strange to Dase. All right, you will go there and give a learned talk. You probably feel you are seated atop a tree. Then why do you turn pale when I get one of these invitations? Anyway, as you know, nothing is more mysterious than human nature. The other day, Pradhan's son said disparagingly that Pundit Nilakantha's stay in Kashi had been of no use. I gave him a tongue-lashing, as I felt as if he had slighted a member of my own family. Now I realize, I should never stick my neck out for a fellow like him, who can't bear to see anyone else prosper.

A jealous wretch. He feels tormented if I receive even a little honour. Little animals fight among themselves. If human beings did the same, what's the use of their learning? As has been said 'Fear your fellow human beings, for they are full of envy.' Why should you envy me? Why do such thoughts come into the mind of someone like you, who is a pundit. Shame on you.

No Return

'Fish makes a meal delicious as nothing else can. No amount of milk or curd can ever satiate the appetite like fish does. Oh Narayan.'

The cold was unbearably severe that day. The raw wind chilled the marrow. Having offered worship to Lord Lakshminarayan early in the evening, Dase was hurrying home where a guest was waiting for him. Dase had to reach early. The guest had arrived suddenly, unannounced, at midday, carrying some fish in a packet.

'Pundit. Everything fine?' Dase, who was standing on his veranda, turned around and saw Sudarshan, the son of his wife's uncle.

'Oh Nande, what brings you here? Come get in. Bata, get some water; your mamu, uncle, is here.'

The bundle Sudarshan carried might hold some balls of sugared rice. But in the packet there were seven excellent khainga fish. Wonderful.

So Dase came home early from the temple. Everybody ate early, and Sanatan Dase sat at a fire on the inner veranda with his children. After rinsing his mouth, Sudarshan Nanda fell to talking with his sister on the outer veranda.

'Come over, Nande and warm your hand here. Tuku's mother, bring me the paan box and send a toothpick through Bata. You Bata, go and get it. Jayi, my son, move aside and let your uncle sit on that low stool.'

'Oh, forget it. Let the child have it. Why make him get up. Don't move aside, my son. I'll sit on this coconut-leaf matting.'

Tuku's mother brought the paan-box. She too took her place by the fire and coated betel leaves with lime paste.

Dase took out a large arecanut and chopped it into small pieces. 'Who cooked the fish curry? You or our daughter-in-law?'

'She is a child after all. So one has to help her. How can one expect her to learn everything in a year.'

It took Dase no time to see through his wife. After all, who didn't relish praise, he thought. On another occasion, she would have said a few things in her daughter-in-law's favour. Anyway, what more could be expected from this stupid woman.

'Oh Nande. Does that fisherwoman Muktama bring you fish regularly?'

'Yes, she does. But she is getting old. Her two daughters-in-law sell fish these days.'

'Take this paan. I have put larger arecanut pieces in it. You'll have no problems, for you are a young man. You can crush the nuts. Let me tell you I've known Muktama for so many years now. Before I married your sister, I used to visit Ratanpur because my maternal uncle lived there.'

'Yes, your youngest uncle passed away last year. All his children have left the village for they are all working elsewhere. When we run into each other once in a while, we joke amongst ourselves.'

Tuku's mother got up slowly. Her eldest son was away. Her daughter-in-law had not eaten yet and she should not be kept waiting. She tied a paan in her saree-end and made her way towards the outer veranda.

Dase let out a sigh and said, 'That is but natural. I am caught in all this care and can't escape. I wish my son had amounted to something. But he is an utter failure. If I leave here for a day, the deity will go unworshipped. I told him, if you follow family tradition you bring your family a good name. Learn the priestly duties. But this did not appeal to him. A month ago he had gone somewhere to look for work. I hear that he has found a job which will fetch him fifty-five rupees a month. And there'll be something to grease his palms, too. Times have changed. Or else, why should someone choose to serve men when he could serve God? True, Lord Lakshminarayan would not pay him fifity-five rupees every month, but He would make sure he had enough to eat. After all, by His grace, I am able to support my large family. Arre, stop it. Why do you behave like this? These wretches will not let you talk in peace—go, to bed. Good-for-nothing idiots.'

Bata and his younger brother, Jayi, were fighting over a blanket.

They did not go to sleep when scolded; but they now huddled together under the same blanket.

Sudarshan Nanda, changing the topic, said, 'I couldn't get big fish. In the past the khainga fish they caught in the same place weighed as much as three bishas.'

'Don't I know that? That year, Nana had sent me off to my uncle's house. My eldest uncle, Jadu Mishra, was in the prime of his life. And I was only sixteen or seventeen years old. The things you hear people say about Jadu Mishra I have actually seen. His mother, my grandmother, was not good at preparing delicious cakes. She was a simple soul. She had two sons, Jaduni and Madhuni. She would grind six seers of rice and make two large enduri cakes in an earthen pot for her sons. Once cooked the two sons polished them off while chatting with their mother. What times they were, and how different the men who lived then. Think of the food they lived on! Did they peck at their food like we do these days? Even in his old age, my eldest uncle would never go without a non-vegetarian dish. Every morning for breakfast he had hot khai soaked in the milk of four coconuts. And if you served him nakshatra enduri cakes in hot sweetened milk, you would lose count of how many he swallowed. Oh, I have never seen another like him in all my life, who could eat and digest so much.'

Dase poked at the fire with a twig. Thoughts of his eldest uncle occupied his mind. He continued, 'Once he went to the temple of Goddess Bhagavati to eat roasted fish offered to the goddess. He liked it so much that he had to have roasted fish once every seven or eight days. And he must have a roasted khainga fish at least a forearm long. It also suited my grandmother fine. Even after he got married, my uncle would not give up this habit. Well, Nande, have you ever tasted roasted fish offered to Goddess Bhagavati? Ah, how delicious. Around this time of the year, large fire holes would be dug out, and they would take out burning faggots from these and roast three khainga fish of the finest quality on hot cinders. The taste of these was heavenly. They flaked off, because they were so brittle. Oh it was so delicious! That place is specially favoured after all. Even a simple fish curry cooked there will taste wonderful. The potatoes, plantains and badis in the curry would make it so thick if one threw the spatula into the pot it would stick straight up. Only one bhekta fish was enough to flavour three large pots of curry, and people would have a grand feast.'

Talk like this kept sleep away from the children's eyes. The two little boys listened with rapt attention. Sudarshan Nanda too, found it riveting.

'That year Nana took me to Banapur with him. It was there that I
saw how the goddess ought to be worshipped. Everything offered to
her—fish, balls of sugared rice—was fit for the palate of gods. As
you know, every deity has his or her preferred offering. Can anything
take the place of Lord Lingaraj's kora, Lord Raghunath's kakara or the
sarapuli for Lord Sakshigopal? The smell alone would fill half your
stomach, before you put these into your mouths. Blessed are these
places. And why talk of Lord Jagannath's mahaprasad! The gods descend
from heaven to partake of it. Nana used to take me with him to different
places. But I have never been able to go anywhere on my own, and I
think I never shall. He took me with him for I was his only child. Had
he been in my position, could he have done so?'

'Tell me, Dase. Did you have coconuts at Sakshigopal?'

'Of course we did. In everyone's backyard there grew coconut palms
and arecanut trees. They pluck coconuts with the help of a long stick.
Using coconuts they can cook four varieties of curries. Coconuts make
even a tasteless curry delicious. The woman at whose house we stayed
in Sakshigopal was a distant relation, an aunt. She came from a family
in the south. We spent half a day at her place. And what can I say about
the food she served us? After we had a wash, we were offered two
sarapulis each. They were so richly sweet, I found it difficult to eat
them. They dripped with ghee. Rice was served with mashed coconut,
a fish cooked with vegetables, and sea-fish curry. There was coconut
in every dish; no dish could do without it.'

Jayi's and Bata's mouths watered at the thought of the dishes
described. How delicious they must have been! So richly sweet and
dripping with ghee!

'Sudarshan wants to go back home tomorrow. He could not meet
Raghunath. I said he has sent his photograph. Looking at it is the same
as seeing him.' Tuku's mother made a fire in another earthen pot for
her brother. 'I looked for it, but could not find it. The boys just wouldn't
leave it alone. My daughter-in-law found it just now.'

The mention of the 'photo' made the children get up in great
excitement. 'What does brother's photograph look like?'

'Arere, then you have not seen it yet, Nande? Go and have a look.
What a wonderful machine they have invented? The photograph looks
exactly like my boy—the same eyes, the same face—isn't it a marvel?'

Sudarshan Nanda stepped on to the veranda. His sister showed
him the photograph, while Bata and Jai pushed each other and bent
over the lamp to take a good look. Every child in the village had heard

of the photograph of their elder brother. Groups of them had come to take a look.

Dase poked at the fire with a twig. He drew the pot of fire nearer and warmed his hands and feet. Memories of his uncle's village stirred. The people of Ratanpur were in fact troublesome fellows. They made fun of everything and everybody. And there was something peculiar about the way they talked. They looked like giants, but talked like women.

'Hey you J-a-a-d-u, there was no cho-le-ra this year.'

'How could there be cho-le-ra. We had no ma-ng-o-es this year.'

How stupid! These fellows regretted that there had not been an outbreak of cholera that year! Their village had been secured on all sides by mother Ratnamala. A very powerful deity she was. So this village had never had any outbreak of cholera. They always wished cholera to break out in the neighbouring villages, so that they would be invited to the funeral feasts there.

'Why are you smiling to yourself, Dase? Come over to this veranda. What are you doing there, all alone?'

'Leave me alone.'

Thoughts of his uncle crossed his mind again.

Maguni Sarangi was a distant cousin of uncle's mother. He was to attend the funeral feast of a client. That day Jadu Mishra set out early, after finishing his ablutions.

He had put on a new sacred thread rubbed with turmeric paste. He ran into Maguni Sarangi.

'You Ja-a-due. Where are you off to?'

'O-o-h, I am going to a funeral feast.' He arrived at the house of Maguni Sarangi's client and said to him, 'You are going to perform the funeral rites. Aren't you?'

'Yes, Sir. We are waiting for our priest Maguni.'

'Oh, Maguni Sarangi? But he is no more.'

'What? He was here only yesterday!'

'He is my uncle. Would I tell a lie? He died of cholera last night. I changed my sacred thread and put on a new one, because I carried his body. But your ceremony should not wait. Prepare everything. We should finish quickly.'

He collected the money and the rice and came home.

Later the same day, he met Maguni Sarangi.

'Why don't you die, Jadu,' Maguni Sarangi said.

Dase burst out laughing.

'What happened,' asked Sudarshan Nanda from the other end.

'Nothing in particular. Remembering things my uncle did made me laugh.'

The stories about his uncle went on, once more. There was a lot of laughter. For Tuku's mother these stories had become threadbare, too familiar through endless tellings and retellings. So she busied herself making a bed for her brother in the front room.

'Won't you go to sleep, Sudei, I have made your bed.'

'Coming. Dase is regaling us with stories about bygone days in our village.'

A lot of old memories came crowding into Dase's mind. It was as if a mirror was reflecting images of his childhood. He was not at all aware that Sudarshan Nanda had left his side in the meantime. . .The veranda of Santra's house was extremely narrow. Four children somehow squeezed themselves into this space.

He absentmindedly stirred the fire with a twig and made tiny sparks gleam in the ash.

Oh she was so guileless, she would come and say, 'Master, please give me some berries.' I would never have become a teacher if Nana and uncle had not asked me to. Oh, the six terrible months I had to spend teaching. . .she was hardly eleven or twelve at the time. Fair-complexioned and very attractive. How charmingly she would beg for the berries! Oh, these women's ways; they know everything from birth. But, why blame her? Did she know she was to marry me, or did I know she was to be my wife? The day Nana came to uncle's house and discussed the match, I never again set foot in her part of the village. Nor did she ever come to ask for berries. One day I ran into her when she was half-way up a small jack-fruit tree, eating parts of a ripe fruit. How could she get down? She stayed where she was, her face covered with the border end of her saree.

Dase broke into laughter again.

How everything changed! The same girl bore eight children. But fate took four of them away from us.

Tuku's mother walked back and forth along the upper veranda, a kerosene lamp in hand, which lit her face up from time to time. But in this face Dase failed to trace the lineaments of the one that had eaten berries. The bunches of thick curly black hair which had hung over her ears once upon a time were no more. Anyway, everything passes. Why should this be an exception? And yet, how time had flown! It seemed like yesterday. He was a groom seated in a palanquin, on his way to get married. The hu-han sounds made by the palanquin-bearers echoed in his ears even today. But the past had vanished like a dream. Everything passes into oblivion like this. As they say, 'The lowest branch on a coconut palm is dropping off, the uppermost branch is laughing. The branch in-between says: "My turn will come soon." He was already fifty. How much time was left to him? Your time is also running out, how long are you going to live? The fruit is ripening. Soon the stalk will lose its grip, and then a slight gust of wind and the fruit will drop. Nothing can put it back on the branch again. Oh Lord, everything happens according to your wish. Man is engulfed by maya. It is as if he is borne swiftly across alien fields and forests at midnight in a palanquin. No one knows where the demon-bearers that carry the palanquin will take it. Man dreams so many dreams, dozing cosily inside. Open your eyes and you will see that all about you is darkness. The hu-han calls made by the bearers sound eerie in the dark. Oh God!'

Dase cleared his throat and reached for the box of chewing tobacco.

Truly, life is a strange affair. It flows on like a rapid current. It always flows down. It can never rest until it loses itself in that vast expanse of salt water. Not that it can choose its course. There is someone who makes it dance, controls its movements. It does not have the power to take even one step backwards. Life is but a relentless forward movement. After all, we all die. Nobody escapes death. So why be afraid?

'Are you going to sit there all night?'

If these words had been addressed to him a little earlier, Dase would have said, playfully, 'Wouldn't you like to have some berries today?'

But now he felt terribly oppressed. The 'hu-han' sounds rang in his ears. It became clear to Dase that the demons that bore the palanquin would never retrace their steps; they would go on and on.

He mumbled, weakly, 'Coming.'

The End of All Journeys

'Listen to me, Tuku's mother. You must not get upset over this. Patra's son took his parents to Puri, but why should you take them as a model? They are rich, after all, God has blessed them with wealth. For them, making a pilgrimage is no great thing. I don't understand why you should sulk and refuse food. Go, get up and have something to eat. Doesn't Lord Jagannath know that many suffering beings like us want to have a glimpse of him but can't, fettered as we are by care.'

'This is nothing new. This has been my lot ever since I married you. All you do is to get me caught in a web of cares. For these twenty long years that I have been running this house, have I ever stepped beyond this doorstep? Someone like Kanchi, the oilman's wife, went to Puri to see Gobinda Dwadashi. Isn't my lot worse than hers? So many get to go. There will be so many shops in the fair. Everyone will buy something. What a cursed life! I could never buy myself even a few bangles from Puri!'

Dase sat pretending not to hear his wife's words exuding grief, anger and bitterness. The sky was completely covered by a dark cloud. It had been drizzling, but now a gust of cold wind brought a cloud burst and with it torrents of rain. It was a hot, steamy grief that had remained locked up inside for too long, the grief of being obliged to accept a life of deprivation after a life of comfort and affluence; of not being able to fulfill her aspirations; of losing her children.

But Dase thought to himself, 'Oh, women are all alike. The darshan of the Lord is the least of their concerns; all that interests them is eating delicious food and buying trinkets. This is what makes them eager to go to Puri.' The thought made him smile; but he said nothing.

From the room inside came the sound of sobbing.

A sheaf of palm leaves lay on his thigh. Dase sharpened the tip of the stylus by rubbing it on the floor and tested it by pressing it against his cheek, but his mind was elsewhere. It was difficult supporting a family of eight in these hard times. The prasad from the temple gave them their first meal of the day. And as for the other, Dase would often say, if he was in a good mood, 'Maybe times are difficult, but the Lord provides for us. When He does not, we do! Let me tell you how. The day we come by a little money it's the Lord who looks after us that day. On days on which we get nothing, we go quietly to bed on an empty stomach. Tell me is it the Lord, or we ourselves, who sort things out on such occasions?'

On winter mornings, Dase with his back to the sun, copied out on palm-leaves the text of *Keshab Ramayana*, and the *Sarala Mahabharata*. The characters were small, neat and pretty like brinjal seeds. Three lines to each leaf resembling garlands of kaincha beads. Not a single word would be crossed out, and not a single line would go aslant. Once the full text was copied out, Dase bound the leaves into a volume in deerskin. He made a little money by selling it. People from all the neighbouring villages bought these volumes. Everybody who had a little money liked to have a set of these volumes copied and bound by Dase. Even though printed books were available, people continued to cherish and treasure these. They would say, 'After all, the printed book came only yesterday. And can it ever be the same as the palm-leaf? It is unique, after all.'

The tip of the stylus was being tested by being pressed against his cheek, but Dase's heart was no longer in the copying. Deep inside, he was disturbed and restless.

Everybody was so keen to go to the Gobinda Dwadashi festival in Puri. But was it their intention to acquire merit? Each idiot was merely following the herd. That year, everybody in the village had trooped off to Patapur to watch a Badipala. They had stayed awake there all night, enjoying the show, leaving their own villages deserted and empty. Not even a kitten had mewed when they came back the next morning. A commotion in Pradhan's house greeted them. Someone had broken into his granary and stolen all his rice. And old Patra fainted when he discovered that his money-box was gone. He was one who never went to sleep without the box kept securely under his pillow. Yet he too had come under the spell of the Badipala. Served him right. Like them, these wretches too think that marvels are taking place in Puri and that they must not miss them. These stupid women leave their meals half-eaten and rush to the village street if a woman acrobat arrives. And could such as these travel to Puri with the intention of seeing the Lord? To wash their sins away? And who does not have money these days? What strange times we live in! Six pa's of rice sell for a rupee, and the rascals grow rich overnight. If we had a few rupees wouldn't we too have set off for Puri? But luck will never smile on us, and we'll never be able to go to Puri. Fine, so be it.

He heaved a deep sigh.

Dase picked up the stylus and busied himself in the work of writing on the palm-leaf. He managed to fill two to three leaves with writing. He had copied out the song in praise of Lord Keshab. Suddenly a fight broke out among the boys and there came the sound of crying from inside the house. 'Bata, I know you are incorrigible. You will beat them to pulp.'

'Hey Bata come here. A scoundrel like you should have been born in a scavenger's house. Why did you take birth in mine?'

His wife's voice, still heavy with bitterness, followed, 'Why do you hate that child so much, you tell me? He went to bathe long back and hasn't returned yet. These two who stuffed themselves with food are fighting now. You blame Bata for everything no matter whether he is home or not.'

Dase was silent. He had got used to the commotion the children made. These boys had always been like this, but look at her, she could not keep them under control. What kind of a mother was she! If that girl, our daughter-in-law, was not around, this woman would have been worm-eaten long since.

Thoughts of his daughter-in-law softened him. He told himself, 'Well, boys will be boys. But my daughter-in-law is a gem of a girl. This stupid son of mine, her husband, never stays at home. He plays the pakhauj in the Bhagabat-room late in the night. His family responsibilities never bother him. But I will not live forever. Well, he can't escape. He'll have to shoulder his responsibilities when I'm gone.'

Smiling to himself, Dase took off his glasses and put them carefully into a cover. The palm-leaves were tied up and put away. He put a little chewing tobacco into his mouth, and went out to the front veranda. Kanchi Teluni's house, which his house faced across the village path, was locked. She had gone off to Puri. And half the village had followed suit. Why should they not? A day like the Gobinda Dwadashi came but rarely. Only the most fortunate got the chance to set eyes on Lord Jagannath on an auspicious day like this. There was no question of going to Puri alone. And I would need not less than a hundred and twenty rupees to take the whole family there. Anyway, the less one dwelt on the matter, the better. Dase paced the veranda slowly, his hand stroking his belly.

Pundit Nilakantha was in Puri too. He is a learned man. Not for nothing did he go to Kashi. There was money in his pocket now. Every morning after a bath he would cover himself with a shawl, on which he would throw a scarf printed with the names of the Lord. But, for most of his stay in Puri he would enjoy being the guest of other people. A proposal for his son Indramani had come from Puri. This would keep him busy. Why would he bother about the festival of Gobinda Dwadashi? After his son marries into that family in Puri he could always go there and see Lord Jagannath. The Lord would not run away; He would always be there.

Gloom descended on Dase. He saw Bata returning home, weeping. Raghu, his eldest son, followed him, shaking with rage.

'What happened?'

'Get lost, you scoundrel. If you go on like this, one day you'll drown. Look at him, father. See how his hands and legs have swollen.'

'Let him be. He is thoroughly spoilt. What can we do about him?'

As soon as Bata stepped into the house, he was dragged back to the forecourt by Tuku's mother, who said, 'See for yourself, would anybody hit even an enemy so cruelly? Look how bruised his back is. It's bleeding. Nobody denies that you are his elder brother. But why must you beat him black and blue? Why couldn't you just scold him?'

Raghu's fingers had left reddening welts on Bata's back.

Since this happened all too often, Dase said nothing; he only fixed his gaze on Raghu, who said: 'Won't he get completely spoilt if he is not punished? If you mind him I'll never ever touch him again. I won't care whatever happens to him.'

Dase kept quiet. But Tuku's mother flared up and said, 'Let him get spoilt. What have you all done? Have you become scholars or officers? If he remains alive, he can beg for alms and get on somehow. How will we gain if you beat him to death?'

The quarrelling, the noise: this was part of life. Dase threw a towel over his shoulder, picked up his walking stick, and made his way along the village street. He had nowhere in particular to go. He merely wished to get away.

His life seemed an utter waste. Someday I will pass away, worn out completely by wordly cares and worries. Anyway, why should I bother about what happens to others. After all, is anyone another's personal possession? Who is one's own, after all? Everyone will suffer the consequences of his own karma and die. There is nothing anyone can do about it. Pakua Mishra died. And death was deliverance for him. Had he lived any longer, he would only have suffered. He lived a full life, and breathed his last in the sacred month of Kartik. This fate will overtake everyone. Everybody will die alone; no one will keep him company. But maya keeps everyone under its spell as long as there is life—that is the source of all one's problems.

Walking absent-mindedly, Dase found himself on the lane leading to the temple. The lane ran through the Bauri quarters past the rear of the temple.

He had come rather early. So what? It would be nice if he could spend some time in the forecourt of the temple. He felt his sacred thread to make sure the keys were in place. Then he walked on slowly.

The houses in the Bauri quarter had low, sloping roofs. The place swarmed with pigs. Heaps of bamboo from which baskets were made lay in front of every house.

What? Had even Brunda Bauri locked his house and gone off to Puri. Let him go. Why shouldn't he? Just because he is an untouchable? Hadn't Dasia Bauri become immortal as a devotee? What simple souls! Absolutely untouched by feelings of pride or vanity. Their minds unsullied. Selfless service is their creed. Surely, it is they who are truly learned. We who pride ourselves on our superior caste, commit thousands of sins.

A dusty, dark-skinned Bauri child played with a plump piglet. He gently stroked its head, and it sniffed him all over.

This little boy's heart is pure. But, alas, he is doomed to live all his life in squalor. What can he do? Karma decides everything. He can never escape the consequences of his karma. Was there ever a more virtuous person than Nala, the king? Think of what he had to suffer. He was to be crowned at daybreak, but karma had decreed otherwise. And Ramachandra had to spend fourteen years as an exile in a forest. But what a funny thing this karma is! Hasn't the Lord himself said. 'I am the one who acts through all creation. There is no alternative to me.'? It is He who resides in us and directs all our actions. Where does this thing known as karma come from; and why should we suffer the consequences of our karma? Thus it is He who acts, and He who suffers. Where do we fit in? What is the point of so much worship, so many rites and ceremonies? The poor little soul has to slip through the net and merge with God. This now brings us back into the picture. But these are very complicated matters, and are beyond us. No one has penetrated these mysteries, which have defeated even great sages like Suka and Sanak.

How dirty the backyard of the temple is! I must tell Sania to do something about it. The idiot has been granted land for keeping the temple premises clean. And the fellow doesn't do even a shred of work. All right, he needs some talking to.

Dase opened the temple doors and entered the premises. Everything was quiet. Only a light breeze blew and a little sunlight fell on the steps of the Natamandir. Dase settled himself, leaning against a stone pillar. He would have loved to close his eyes and take a nap, as he did on such occasions. But today, he simply did not feel sleepy. Thoughts pestered him. 'Everyone had gone to Puri to see Gobinda Dwadashi.' But only he could not.

Soon his eyelids felt heavy. But the same thought kept echoing in his mind.

Pradhan had a large family. Because he travelled to Puri, others in the village joined his party. It must be quite a crowd, with so many people carrying their bags and boxes. . . You will reach the station all right. But will the train take so many? Old Pradhan must grease the ticket-sahib's palms. Only then he'd let you enter. Oh don't get into that buggy. That's more expensive. Oh what a press! Hey Raghua. . . Bipracharan! Hand the child in through the window. Kanchi, get inside, carrying the box on your head. The train will leave soon. You Brunda. Don't you worry about touching a low caste here. The train is leaving. Has everyone boarded it? Hey, has Baraju got in? Keep a watch on the box.

. . . The clamour, the sound of the engine. Soon all noises subsided. There remained only the sound of the wheels clacking. Brunda Nahak talked about how he once slept through an entire train journey. The train stops. Block the door. Don't let anyone else get in. If you do we'll all die of suffocation. Hey, hey, that's a helpless old woman, heave her into the buggy, or else she will fall off and die.

. . . See how old Pradhan dozes. And you thought he'd have looked after everyone. Oh, so many from different places are in the buggy!

Not a single one was a known face. But we all stand here, jostling against one another. No one bothers who is high or who is low. All are Puri-bound pilgrims. A silken thread binds them all and pulls them forward. The many have now become one.

. . . The cry 'Jai Jagannath!' echoes and makes everyone's hair stand on end. How anxious everyone is! They bend to have a glimpse of the blue disc at the top of the temple from the train window. Oh Lord Hari, the deliverer of the fallen. Wash away the sins of millions of lifetimes through this one glimpse of Your blessed pennant. Overwhelmed by feelings of devotion everyone wipes tears of joy from their eyes. The soul is purified. 'Glory to Lord Jagannath'—the voices of people in the train rise in unison, rending the skies.

. . . Take us to the Garuda pillar. We can't bear to wait. To have a dip in the sea? Let's go, Pradhan. Oh, how the sea roars. The waves and the foam! Waters from all the holy places flow into this. This is the king of all holy places. Duck your head in its water and your body will be made holy. Well, let's go. These waves will intoxicate you. So break yourselves free and come away. Quick!

. . . Take the dust of the Badadanda—the Grand Road—and put it on your forehead. The feet of millions of holy men have trod on it. The wheels of the chariot Nandighosh roll over this. Roll on this dust. This is no mere dust—it has been marked by the feet of gods who descended to earth. Rub this dust all over yourselves. You will earn more merit than a dip in the holy Ganga.

. . . Oh, what a crowd! There are heads wherever you turn your eyes. Hey Kanchi, come away from that shop. You won't be able to tear yourself away. The trifles will trap you and loosen the silken thread that binds you all to the Lord. Look up and behold how the pennant of the Lord flutters gaily. Get on, get on. Jai Jagannath. The Meghanad wall is visible at a distance. Uh, can't this stone wall move away. For one who is the master of the fourteen worlds, moving this stone wall should be child's play. Move it, Oh Lord. Let this wall disappear and let the wretched of the earth enter the premises of your temple.

Ah, I have arrived at last.

Now I am near the Aruna pillar. There's the flight of twenty-two steps. The natamandir, the Garuda pillar lie beyond the Lion Gate. Oh, Lord Jagannath, I am saved. O mighty one, Oh round eyed one. Oh deliverer of the fallen, may I breathe my last with my eyes fixed on this blessed sight. Break into dance, all of you. Dissolve, fade away as you dance. O, Lord Hari, O Lord Jagannath. . . .

Daylight was failing when Sania came to sweep the temple premises. He stopped dead when his eyes fell on Dase, who lay crouched on the floor, fast asleep, his head resting on his towel. A tear clung to the corner of his eye. His body trembled. Was he ill? Sania wondered.

'Master, why are you sleeping here at this hour of the day? Are you feeling unwell?'

The teardrop trapped under the lids rolled down when Dase opened his eyes. He looked about him, confused. He closed his eyes, leaned againt the pillar and stayed still for a moment.

'Oh Sania. Sweep the temple courtyard, will you? Oh, I feel feverish. I'm shivering. Let me get up. Oh Lord Jagannath. Have mercy on me. Oh-Oh.'

The Gift

'You are buying many things today, Dase?'

'. . . Oh, Brunda Nahak! What brings you here, my son?'
Dase had deposited the holding tax the day before yesterday.
Had he forgotten some other dues?

Old Patra said, tying up a packet of cumin seeds, 'Dase will be away from home for a month. So he must buy rations for his family.'

A smile spread over old Patra's chubby coal-black face. The teeth under his long feline whiskers were black from chewing paan. A single gold tooth glittered.

'Is that so, Dase?'

'Yes. The money-lender from Madanpur will perform the ceremony of rudrabhishek at Dhabaleswar. I am going there.'

'Of course you should. Or else how would you make a living? And you must be buying all this on credit. I am sure what you have bought would cost at least fifteen or twenty rupees. This has to be repaid, after all.'

'Do you take him for the same old Dase? Times have changed. He takes nothing on credit these days. His son sends him money every month.'

'That's quite true. Dase no longer needs to buy things on credit. All I meant was. . .maybe he did, and this time, he won't have any problem in repaying his debts. After all, Raghunath works as an orderly under a sahib. In a sense, he is even more powerful than the sahib himself, for everybody has to present his petitions and grievances before him first. How come someone like me, Brunda Nahak does not know this? Well, Dase. I hope you'll not forget us. Your son now serves a big officer. A word from him, and your luck may turn.'

'Let's leave everything to God. Please bless my boy.'

Dase counted the items and paid the money. It did not escape his notice how Brunda Nahak stood aside respectfully and made way for him. He looked back before reaching where the road turned, and saw old Patra and Brunda Nahak exchanging meaningful glances, bringing their faces close together. He was expecting this and felt amused. He felt a little scared, too. It seemed to him as if his old, familiar ties with them had been severed. When a calf grew horns, its master would hesitate before getting too close to it, and pat him cautiously from a safe distance. Until now, Dase had needed their pity, sympathy and help for his survival. Now that he could stand on his own legs, it was but natural that they felt somewhat jealous. Even a little unhappy.

Maybe I am wrong. Has my son become a top official? All he does is send some money home to help us make both ends meet. Can we now afford expensive clothes, or have we built a stone house? Earlier, most of the time we went without a meal a day. Now we can have two. That's all. You fellows unnecessarily make something out of nothing. The fact is, you find it unbearable that someone like Sanatan Dase, who never got enough to eat earlier, now enjoys two square meals a day. This looks like a crime to you. Someone else's well-being scares these rascals.

I know, money is all powerful; it brings you status and honour and decides who is big and who is small. Why blame these fellows. Look at Tuku's mother. Since the day Raghunath started sending money she hasn't allowed her daughter-in-law to lift even a piece of straw! She now endlessly sang the praise of the same Raghunath, whom she earlier called a good-for-nothing. Whoever earns money becomes the provider. Can I tell him off now as I could do before? Why should I? After all, he is the Bhagiratha of the family, one who would offer oblation to the manes.

Back home, Dase arranged all the packets neatly. Jayi, Bata and Tukua surrounded him excitedly.

'Hands off! Don't open the packets. Their contents will get mixed up. Listen, Tuku's mother. Get some containers. Empty the packets into them here.' Bottles, tin boxes, clay dishes and pots, and bamboo baskets were brought over.

'Why can't you forget that old Patra? You are no longer buying things on credit. Why should you accept whatever stuff he sells you. Look at these rotten red chillis. They have turned black and are full of seeds. Why didn't you go to Ganesa's shop? Yesterday I sent Bata there to buy some cumin seeds. They were of excellent quality and without a single grain of sand. Arre, stop it. Keep your hands off the mustard seeds. I give up. Bata, my dear, take these boys away.'

His wife's reaction set Dase thinking, 'I have long been taking things from Patra's shop on credit. Just because I can now pay cash for my purchases, do I go to some other shop? Have you considered how old Patra will feel? Is this done?' But he chose not to say a word to his wife.

'Take care. Don't let things get out of hand. Tomorrow is Monday. I'll be back three Mondays after this. Sudei will be here. Your uncle is like your father. So you'll be all right. Well, Tuku's mother. Where is your brother? It's now getting dark.'

Tuku's mother was busy peeling small onions.

'Will you take proper care of yourself over there? Make sure you have your meals on time. You are weak. It worries me to hear that you'll have only one meal a day, which you will cook yourself. May Goddess Mangala make this month pass smoothly and bring you back safely. Our daughter-in-law is expecting a child. You'll be absent, and her husband too is away from home. If something happens, who'll manage everything? How can I nurse her in the lying-in room and look after these boys at the same time?'

'These worries make me wish I didn't have to go. Our son left his wife in our care when he took a job away from home. What would he say if things went wrong? He may say, why did I choose a time like this to go there? Couldn't I have waited a little?'

'Anyway. God will look after us. What would you do if you were to be around. Only it may not look nice if there is no man in the house at a time like that. In any case, our Sudei will be here. Raghu is no stranger to the problems of this house. If you go there, you'll earn one hundred and fifty rupees. How could one forgo a chance like this in these difficult times?'

'How could you leave this boy to play all by himself in the village lane. It's the hour the cows come home. He could be injured if a cow attacks him,' saying this, Sudarshan Nanda came in, carrying his nephew in his arms.

'I know. That Bata is incorrigible. He must have left him and wandered off. Why did you take so long? Your brother-in-law was looking for you.'

Dase was wiping his legs with a towel after a wash.

'Stay with your mother, my son. Let me go.' Saying this, Sudarshan went up to Dase.

'No. No. I was just asking idly why you took so long. It was only because you agreed to stay here during my absence that I am able to go. Or else, would I have dared to make the trip? Listen, I leave the deity in your care. Make sure the temple door is securely locked before you leave, for there are a lot of precious jewels and valuables. There is no limit to man's greed. We'll all find ourselves in the police lock-up if someone steals them. The children also I leave in your care. This Tuku is a troublesome child. You must take particular care of him.'

'Don't you worry about all this. I'll manage everything. Will you surely come back after a month? You know how much work I have got to do back home. True, my three brothers are there, but still. . .'

'All right. You have a wash and then we will go to the temple.'

———

'Aren't you sleepy Dase? You are tossing about. It will be some time before daybreak. Try to get some sleep.'

'No. No. The cock has crowed already. I must start early. A distance of twelve miles has to be covered. Having finished his bath, the Marwari would be waiting for me. Oh why do you leave the bed when it's so cold!'

'Let me walk you a part of the way,' saying this, Nanda washed his face with water from a jug.

'Why do you make such a noise when you rinse your mouth, Nande? Take it easy. You will wake the children. And you'll hurt yourself if you clear your throat so hard.'

'Is it already time to go?' Tuku's mother emerged from the adjacent room. She had had a wash hurriedly and carefully arranged everything Dase was to take with him. Some flattened rice, some molasses in a packet, a jug, a bunch of twig toothbrushes, a neatly folded cloth and a towel, a patri, sruba, srucha, a tuft of kusha grass, the paan box, the snuff-box, a small bottle with a little coconut oil in it.

'I have put all these in your bag, Sudei. Since you'll stay here you won't need your bag. You'll have it back when your brother-in-law returns home.'

Dase paced up and down the veranda in front of the bedroom. He so much wanted to see the children before he left.

He could not go inside, for his daughter-in-law also slept in that room. The door was ajar, so he could see that the wound on Bata's left leg had not healed yet. A shard had pierced his leg when he was frolicking in the pond. How skinny he had become lately! His bones stuck out.

'I have put everything in this bag. In this bundle I have put your shawl, and Sudei's blanket.'

'Why did you pack the blanket? Sudarshan might need it.'

'I don't need it at all. You are travelling to a far-off place. Suppose you need it?'

'All right. Hand me the bag. And my walking stick lies in that corner. Bring it to me. Come Nande. Throw something over yourself. Well, Sudei will see to everything. What else? Take good care of our daughter-in-law. May Lord Lakshminarayan protect her.'

Dase looked up and called out, 'Sri Lord Durgamadhab' thrice.

'Let's go. Nande.'

They set off.

Tuku's mother followed them as far as the front veranda. Dase turned to look back at her before he stepped into the village lane.

Tuku's mother said, 'Take care of your health.'

Dase and Sudarshan walked together as far as the canal at the outskirts of the village.

'Let me turn back from here.'

'Well, yes.'

'Will you be late?'

'Of course not. It's not such a long distance.'

'Don't worry about the children. I am here to look after them. I'll write to you.'

'That's fine.'

Dase watched Nanda melt into the morning mist.

Dase held up the border of his dhoti and stepped into the water of the canal. Oh, how deprivation corrupts human nature. If I had money, would I have ever torn myself away from my children to make this trip? And when my daughter-in-law is in such a condition? How greed has blinded me. I was getting on somehow, wasn't I? Money is the source of all evil. Man runs wildly after money until death overtakes him. Will money take you to heaven? It can't extend even the least bit of happiness. You feel miserable if you don't get money, and if you come by it somehow, others feel miserable. Isn't this strange? The earth yields whatever man eats and wears. What are these minted copper and bronze coins doing then? You can't do without them, and they change their appearance from year to year; those stamped with the queen's head and the head of the old man went, in their place came coins with a hole in their middle. And they have been replaced by other coins. They are like fish scales. We had been taught as children that there were sixteen annas to a rupee, or sixty-four paise to a rupee. And now we are told there are a hundred paise to a rupee. Times are changing. Greed has poisoned every heart. Money and women. These drive people to commit sin. That drunkard was going to throttle Santra's son just because he was wearing a gold chain. Take the case of old Patra. Does he ever sleep at night? He smothers his fears by singing at the top of his voice. When day breaks, he sets about making money. You stupid fellow, will you take your money-box with you when you breathe your last? Or do you think your children will throw it into your funeral pyre? Do you know they will pull the gold ring off your finger before they burn you. But you understand nothing, and run after money like a crazed man. O Hari.

Across the canal, a dusty cart-track ran through the bushes. Dase sighed and hurried on. The track was deserted and uncannily quiet. Afraid, once or twice he stole a nervous glance over his shoulder. There came the faint sound of a dog barking near the club-house on the other side of the village.

It must be the dog Baghua barking from the veranda of Subala's house. Was he barking at thieves? Hasn't the night ended yet? He felt as if his legs were giving way. He stood still. Just then a cock-crow reached his ears, piercing the stillness around.

Oh, the day breaks at last. It seems so eerily quiet here among these trees. Shame on man. How desperately he clings to life! His love of life is matched by his terror of it. If only one could overcome this love and this terror, one could become a yogi. All one's problems would disappear.

The Marwari will pay out one hundred and fifty rupees to me for a single month's work. The fellow rolls in money. The richest man in this area, the sum of a hundred and fifty rupees is small change for him. But before the money reaches my hands, it has already been decided what it would be spent on. Around forty will be spent in repaying my debts and thirty in buying sarees for Tuku's mother and her daughter-in-law. The thatch on the rear wing of the house has rotted and collapsed in a heap. Repairing it will surely cost some money. A hundred rupees have been accounted for this. The balance—fifty rupees—will slip through one's fingers like water; one would not even notice when all of it was gone. Money is a fickle mistress after all. Here today, gone tomorrow. One can never have enough of it. What can a poor man do?

What about the babus who ride around in motor cars in Madanpur? Don't they have money? Surely they do, but they also have to spend a lot to keep up appearances. As has been said, the bigger the bamboo, the hollower it is inside. They must be entangled in worries just as we are. Can anyone ever have enough? If you run after money you'll never stop running. Getting five rupees will make you long for twenty-five, and if you come by twenty-five, you'll die to have five hundred. No matter how much you have, you'll never feel satiated. And yet, one can't do without money. True, chewing a coin will not fill your empty stomach. But, if you haven't got this round thing, you'll get nothing to eat or wear.

The yogi wanders about, a begging bowl in hand. He neither cares nor craves for money. He is content if he finds something to eat and something to throw over his body. In fact this is all one needs in order to remain alive. Then why are people so desperate to earn money? Is this merely an obsession? No, these days the ability to earn money is what matters most. Only money will enable you to get what you want in life. Can you set your eyes on the deities in Puri unaided by a panda who stands guard at the temple door. Can you get past him? If you want to live a proper life, you have to have money. If you haven't got it, you die unregarded, uncared for. What a strange world we live in. Copper and bronze coins have more value than human life! Money is all powerful. But should we then spend our whole life guarding a money-box like old Patra? That fellow does not want to spend anything on food or clothing for himself. A veritable Jaksha indeed! Ghosts will enjoy that hard-earned wealth. What's the point in saving money like a bee who collects and stores honey. Enjoy whatever you earn. But why forget that old Patra gets pleasure out of what he does. If we call him a fool, it's perfectly possible that he thinks we are stupid. Go on guarding your money-bag, you old fool. Money will bring you salvation. How deluded the fellow is! As the poet says.

> You have set up a home, full of valuables you have amassed with care
> But the day your soul leaves your body, you'll be called a ghost.

Dase now stepped off the cart track and took the metalled road. It was already light. He stopped, put a little chewing tobacco into his mouth, and resumed walking. 'Namo Narayan.'

Initiation

'**O** honoured one! We haven't seen you for the last two years. Young men these days have lost all respect for gods and brahmins. I wonder what made the Mahajan send for you this year. He is such a skinflint he won't give anyone even the dirt on his skin. I think he must have been pressed by his old mother into inviting you. His late father was an excellent person. Ah. Not a single Baisakh passed without a brahmin being invited over. You yourself came a few times, didn't you?'

Sanatan Dase had already spent five days at Dhabaleswar. That day it got dark by the time he returned to his room after having offered over three thousand bel leaves to the deity. He had had his meal, and was seated on the front veranda of the house. The gardener by his side was talking about his work.

Two houses stood on the embankment of a tank near the temple. The lame gardener had been living in one of them for the last thirty years. The other was meant for guests.

'Yes. Suruja's father, Haribhagat was a very good man. But can one come here unless Lord Dhabaleswar wants our presence? So, the gentleman who comes here every morning is Gangadhar Satpathy? I don't know him well. But he is someone who fills your heart with reverence.'

'What a man! He is like a god in human form. A man untouched by wordly attachments. God has denied him nothing. All his sons are doing well. In his time, he too was very highly placed. He wasn't what he is today. He was one who never stayed in one place for very long. He has visited places beyond number and has been to all the holy places. But now these things don't hold any interest for him. He comes here every day and sits in that spot on the eastern side. On occasion, if he feels like it, he stays the night here. He leaves instructions at home that nobody should disturb him. He never talks to anybody, only smiles if you pay your respects to him. The other day the minister came here. And, you know, no one who comes to Madanpur can think of going back without a darshan of Lord Dhabaleswar. Does one dare do otherwise? A temple like this is not to be found anywhere else in this world. The Lord ordered Nandi and Bhrukuti to lift this huge mountain up a little. With their hands they split this hard gigantic rock in two. Usually, mountains split vertically from top to bottom. Have you seen a mountain split from one side to the other along a straight line? The linga rises in between the two halves. And of course, you see this tank flanked by two steep hillsides. Again, no human hands dug it out. This place is the abode of deities and overflows with divine bliss. I would not dream of disparaging Lord Lingaraj of Bhubaneswar, but nowhere else has a supreme deity chosen His own abode and prepared it for his residence. Why are you looking so thoughtful, master? Is something worrying you?'

'No, I'm all right.'

'Yes, what was I saying? The minister came. At that time electric lights were installed here. These steps were worn out and had been repaired. Something happened, which one should have witnessed with one's own eyes. Just after he finished offering worship to the deity, the minister's eyes fell on old Satpathy, who was standing in a corner. The minister went straight to him, fell prostrate at his feet and said, 'Sir, you are here!' Everyone looked on, amazed. Who is this man at whose feet even a minister throws himself? Later, they learnt that the old man had taught the minister when he was a student at a college in Calcutta. The minister and all the important officers stood respectfully around him. But his only response was the old familiar smile. An amazing person. No one has got the measure of him. He has become old, but glows like a flame. I am awed by him. But I am intrigued by something. He spends such a long time talking to you every day. Believe me, he never talks like this to anyone else. Let me go. I left the curry on the fire. Let me see what has become of it.' The gardener limped back to his house.

Are you the only one who feels awed by him, you fool? Do you suppose I am any less terrified in his presence? How terribly inferior I feel when I sit beside him! He makes one realize that one has learnt nothing even though one's entire life was spent struggling in the net of wordly cares. But Satpathy is a veritable treasure-house of learning. I must have performed some good deeds in my earlier life; or else how could I have the great fortune of meeting such a person! Today he said, 'Worldly attachments are our own creation. Just as a spider gets entangled in the web it produces from its own body.' How true! But is it so easy to dismiss what one sees, and what man longs to have even at the cost of his life, as an illusion? It is true, wealth, women, children are all bound to us through ties created by maya. But how much courage is needed to sever these bonds? No, sir, such a task is beyond people like us. The parrot stuck in the hunter's glue wriggles and flaps its wings desperately to break free, only to get more hopelessly trapped. Its exertions are futile; they only leave it utterly exhausted. Maybe one out of a million breaks free and flies off; but only because its wings are strong or the glue in the hunter's trap has dried up. The old man was a professor. He has toured all of India. There'll be few holy texts he has left unread. How convincingly he explained the Gita to me the day before yesterday. Of course, we understand the Gita a little. But this kind of learned discourse is beyond us. 'The passage from old age to death is no different from that of childhood to youth.'—Who would disagree? 'The body will be reduced to ashes, but the indestructible soul enters another body.'—This is also true. These are things we have been reading and listening to all our lives. But the doubts remain.

Satpathy Mahasaya said that we lacked faith. But how can we accept this? Do we ever lack faith in any deity? 'But that sort of faith in a thousand deities is no faith at all. What we need is boundless faith in the brahmatva and ekatva.' But how is faith different from devotion? Isn't Lord Jagannath Brahma, and is there anyone who does not have faith in Him? We see all the deities revealed in him. He is the prime mover, the source of everything.

Satpathy Mahasaya said some wonderful things. He said, 'Consider the strange figure of Lord Jagannath. He has no legs, so He is immobile. He can never come to your rescue. He has no hands; so He can't act. He has no ears, so He can't hear you no matter how loudly you call out to Him. All He has are large round eyes shining like the sun and the moon on a face black like a cloud. He does nothing but look out of his sanctum. One's dharma then is to do what these eyes can see.' Oh, the more I think about these things the more lost I feel. They

sound wonderful but they also make me feel guilty. It seems to me as if in attempting to penetrate these mysteries I am trying to get the measure of God. Satpathy's clever way of relating one thing to another leaves me numb and speechless. Maybe, we have no need for this knowledge. Is God a machine that you can take Him apart and figure out how the parts work? Whatever you may think, He'll appear before you in a form you wish to see. Can we ever understand His ways? We must simply have faith in Him and act. After all, He is the prime mover. As has been said, 'He is the root of all creation.' Only the poet Jagannath Dase can write a line like this. One thing I must admit—Old Satpathy explained such difficult things in such simple terms, smilingly. His words are music to my ears and they would make one's heart overflow with faith.

'You' don't exist; neither do 'I'. He alone pervades the world. Everybody is the abode of the Lord. So whatever you think, say or do has to be ultimately attributed to Him. Once you realize this, variety and worldly attachments will melt away. The distinctions between self and the other will vanish. The home and the world will merge. One will no longer covet the fruits of one's action. Life will no longer be affected by either joy or sorrow. One will be in the world but not of it, like a drop of water on a lotus leaf.

Words to this effect do greatly appeal to the heart. But what's new in all these? They only repeat what the scriptures say. To grasp them, all one needs to do is to apply one's mind a little. But the problem is, where does man begin? Life in this world rarely gives one time even to breathe. No matter how sincerely one wants to focus all one's attention on God, one gets distracted. Thousands of worries come crowding in and make the mind their home. What can one do? The mouth craves tasty food, the children, good clothes; and even if half the world is offered up to one's wife she is still discontented. And all one's time is spent supplying these needs. Man is a helpless creature.

Look here, you have to feed and care for your body as you feed and care for a horse. Or else, do you think it will run for you? The mind is the master of the body. The mouth swallows food; but who savours the taste: the tongue or the mind? If the body enjoys good health the mind remains cheerful. The body is ruled by something else. How can the scriptures be wrong? But isn't it puzzling that one has an existence apart from the pain and pleasure experienced by one's own body? It's difficult to accept such a thing. How can one part the water of the ocean and see the floor beneath its depths? Every time you try to part the waters they flow back. One's life will be spent churning the salt water to no purpose. Only one who can dive into the depths, holding one's breath for long, can reach the bottom. But how many of us can do so? Most of us are content to splash about on the surface.

Dase heaved a sigh. The hills caused darkness to descend early. The silence of the place had something mystical about it.

'I have to go, master, because I have to get a bucket of water. I must buy a good clay pitcher from the weekly market. It is difficult to manage without one.' Every time the gardener put his limp left leg forward, the bucket hit the ground and made a metallic sound. He went off to the tank.

A few large rocks lay scattered on the peak of the bare hill which rose on the other side of the tank. Among them, a male jackal set up a howl which echoed through the gathering twilight. Twenty jackals or more followed suit and began howling. Then everything went quiet, suddenly. Dase felt lonely and vulnerable. He looked about him, a little scared. He had to admit to himself that he was indeed frightened. How shameful this desire to live is! Why be astonished if children fear the dark, when someone like me, an old man, feels scared when it gets dark or lonely. All this because man is scared of death. But why bother? Who is immortal? Who will not die one day? Death will come to me. So what? The world won't come to a halt if one passes away. So, why be afraid?

Dase sang a few lines from *Manobodha Chautisa* in a loud and ringing voice.

> *O mind, do as I tell you.*
> *Let's go and gaze upon that comely black face.*
> *How long do you think you'd last?*
> *What would you take with yourself when the soul flies from this shell?*

'Master, we were taught this *Manobodha Chautisa* long ago. I remember the verses, but I never sing them. If one reads these lines regularly, the mind will soon rise above wordly attachments.'

'You are quite right.'

'Please go on singing. I'll be back in a moment after putting this bucket of water away.'

> *Your wife will purify her body.*
> *And along with your kith and kin,*
> *Perform your funeral rites.*

'How very true! I needlessly torment myself for those I consider dear to me. There is no one you can really call your own. Each one goes his separate way. This world is but an illusion. Everyone is on his own. One is told that everyone is responsible for his own karma, that no one should bother about the other; that one should renounce the world and set the mind free. But one is again advised that if you have a family, taking care of them is your supreme duty, your dharma. How terribly confusing all this is! Which road to follow, which to reject? Oh. But the fact is, when one lives among one's fellowmen, one is bound to follow what they do. Because man dares not live alone, he finds it convenient to live in a group. Is that not so? Fear of society drives man to toil half his life to raise his children. The other half is spent in the hope that they might come to his rescue when he is old and worn. And add to all this the power of human attachment. If one does not have the right to call someone "his own", he, like the beast in the jungle, would also be free from the responsibility of rearing his young. Maya has cast such a spell over man that his heart melts the moment his eyes fall on his children. Take my own case. Doesn't it warm my heart to see Jatia in a new shirt? Doesn't it gladden my heart to see all the members of my family sitting together and sharing delicacies? How could this fail to please one? They have issued from my soul, after all. But a learned man like Satpathy Mahasaya tells me all this is an illusion.'

'Once you get drawn into this, you can never break free. However, this does not mean you renounce the world and become a sanyasi. That would amount to a defeat. You must perform your duties as a householder but your mind must remain focussed on Nilachal, the abode of Lord Jagannath. You have raised a family, and every member of it has a claim on you. They'll stake their claims and you must distribute yourself equally among them. But they have a right over only what you accumulate by exercising your bodily faculties. Make sure that your soul remains beyond their reach. For example, no matter how many guests come to your house, you make beds for them on on your veranda or wherever but you never let them sleep in your puja room. It is all true, I admit. But the mind partakes of the body. Can we think of it as a separate entity? Can this body do anything on its own if the mind does not guide it? This had given old Satpathy pause. Then, smiling, he said, "The mind of which you speak is like a sense-organ. There is within you a finer conciousness. That's called chitta. One must keep it untainted. No matter what goes on outside, it should remain calm, undisturbed"—I haven't been able to grasp this yet. But Satpathy Mahasaya has given me a few nuggets of wisdom. Only another pundit like him can understand what he says. His words will pass over the heads of people like us. He made another interesting observation. Human nature is replete with animal faculties. In some respects, there is no difference between human beings and animals. But there is one important distinction; the beast in a jungle turns savage because it enjoys absolute freedom, whereas something called "conscience" tames and controls the beast in every human being. But one should never forget that a tamed animal is an animal all the same. It'll become violent if it is not provided with food, and grow wild. Let me give you an example: A cowherd drives out a herd of hungry cattle every morning. Leaving them to graze in the pasture, he relaxes under a tree, playing his flute. Just like him, throw some food at your hunger, worldly cares, keep them busy and concentrate on purifying your chitta. To completely ignore these cares would be as great a mistake as getting thoroughly ensnared by them.'

'How wonderful! This remains indelibly printed on the mind. What a profound thing to say! A pundit in the true sense of the term. Can that Nilakantha compare with a man like him? Can there be a comparison between a majestic queen and an ugly one-eyed woman? Anyway, Satpathy Mahasaya gave me examples from his own experience. But does he understand the lot of people like us who do not have enough of anything? We lack money and will and our understanding is limited. And let's not talk about our knowledge or wisdom. Take his example of a cowherd grazing his cattle. That's if only we had pastures. We only desperately drive our cows from one parched field to another. When do we have time to play on the flute?... Its awfully difficult for us, sir! Please understand. Of course, as you say, God is much remembered at the time of need. As worries keep increasing and man feels more and more helpless, to that extent he will depend solely on God if only he is awake within himself. But once he dozes off there is no chance of knowing where maya will drive him from here.'

'I am a bit late, sir, but you are still seated here! I thought I could eat something and be done with it. You get wonderful breeze here. If you sit quietly for a while you will surely fall asleep. Oh, Hari, Hari!' Patamali, relaxed leaning on the other wall of the veranda.

He continued, 'You will get the reply to your letter by tomorrow. The distance is nothing, one can just walk down. But once you post a letter it takes three days to reach there.'

'True. I do feel a little worried at times. Nobody, in fact, belongs to you in this samsara. But there is no way out of getting entangled in maya. The daughter-in-law is in an advanced state, the son is not at home. Of course, Nande is there—he is my brother-in-law—but then he too is a young man. What does he know? In such a situation like this, I came here for a little money. Well, everything is Lord Dhabaleswar's will. Let Raghunath be blessed with a gem of a son. He will tonsure his head here.'

'Is it just this? Take it as done. Nobody's prayer has ever been turned down here.'

Neither spoke for sometime.

'Well, Sir, I am an illiterate person. No reading or writing have I done. Serving Lord Dhabaleswar is my dharma. I have been wondering if I could ask someone a question but I haven't. I could ask Satpathy Mahasaya but I am scared of him. . . The thing is, whoever comes here has something in mind to ask for. They invoke a lot and supplicate. I am a little puzzled. I have been here for more than thirty years, sir. Never has a desire crossed my mind to pray for anything. I don't know why I fight shy of it. You come here to see the Lord. But how odd it is to ask about your needs the moment you meet him! And you come with a plan. What is this, Sir?'

What a question of profound wisdom the fellow has really asked! Dase was struck dumb for a while. Then he looked at Patamali, the gardener, and said, 'Satpathy Mahasaya was saying the other day that four types of people come here—those who are in deep danger, those who have an enquiring mind, those who have desires to fulfill and those who know. The Lord knows everybody's mind and grants them what they deserve. Hasn't it been said, "One's Lord is as large as one's mind!" And the rest who throng here come merely by force of habit. There is no meaning in it. No profit and loss either.'

'True true, sir!'

'Do you know Patamali, you alone are blissful. You do not have the thousand tangles we are in. You did well by staying out of this samsara. You would have got into meaningless turmoils.'

'No sir, how could a learned person like yourself say so! What is my calibre after all? What can I tell you? But sir, even if you do not get into samsara, does samsara let you go? I've been here since my boyhood. But can I swear and say that sin hasn't entered my mind? I am a disabled person, sir, its not easy to have a family. But I couldn't stay alone. I have a distant cousin. I raised her son and daughter as my own. Did for them whatever I could. The boy finished his education and got a job. The girl is married and happy. Strictly speaking I do not have any samsara, and yet I have one. I have worries. Worries will never end as long as one lives. But, as it seems, all these haven't touched Satpathy Mahasaya. He has, and yet hasn't, a samsara. That's the core of it all, sir! He alone is blissful who can extricate his mind from samsara. The rest are ignorant like us. . .'

Arey hey! This fellow I see is a pundit! How did I rate him as a simpleton? Now he has taught me quite a lesson! He says the right thing. The very thought of samsara has to be rooted out of the mind.

He said, 'What you said, Patamali, is in fact the purest truth.'

There was a soft, cool breeze blowing. Patamali babbled a few odd things to himself and dozed off leaning on the wall.

There were a million stars above the hill. What doesn't the hill bear. Summer, winter and rains had descended on it for hundreds of years. But it is pure to the core. It has parted and made place there for the self-manifest Shiva.

This reservoir is no less. Everybody draws water from it. Its waves are only on the surface. Its depth remains unmoved. Unperturbed.

I stayed in this room for a month. Now I am ready to go. The room will continue as before. Life too is like that. Why make it more complicated by bringing in attachments and delusions?

The jackals howled to indicate the first half quarter moon of the night. It echoed and re-echoed from all directions and Dase could not continue to be seated. He got up.

'Hey Patamali, go to your room. Ho, hey, do you hear me! get up!'

'Oh look how I dozed off. It is the quality of this breeze. It is already late sir, you too better go to sleep!'

Patamali staggered to his feet, walked unsteadily into his room and bolted the door inside.

Dase muttered to himself: O Lord, ferry me across, I am so ignorant.

When shall thy pennant lift the fallen
I drift in the waters of samsara, ferry me across

Let thy will prevail.

Procrastination

'**W**hat did you buy for your children? You went off at noon and came back after dark. You must have bought many things.'

It was the last day of Dase's month-long stay at Dhabaleswar. He made the offering of fruits to the Lord early, because his client could not wait for long on an empty stomach. After Dase was paid his dakshina he came to his quarters, had his meal hurriedly and set off to the Madanpur market. He spent a long time there, and by the time he got back it was already night. Patamali the gardener, limped into Dase's room as soon as he arrived.

'What can one buy? Only the rich baboos can shop in markets like these. You have to pay to just touch the goods here. Oh, how expensive everything is these days! A cotton towel cost five rupees. And a shirt, seven. You have to pay twelve rupees for a saree. What can one buy? How can one survive?'

'But I can see that whatever you bought has been chosen with great care. These clothes have been woven properly. The fibre will not shrink when they are washed and these will last at least a year. If you are not careful, you buy clothes that are no better than fishnets, woven with filaments from a spider's web.'

'They did show a lot of those to me. But if you put one of them on you can't be sure if you're wearing anything at all. They are as transparent as water and conceal nothing, you only disgrace yourself.

'You are quite right. If you sneeze hard, these clothes will split down the middle on your body. And come to think of it, they cost a lot.'

'But do they lack buyers? All the shops are crowded with customers who want to buy them. And their noses touch their foreheads at the very sight of coarse cotton cloth. They picked up fine clothes and paid large sums. Anyway, forget it. I felt I threw a lot of good money into water. Let me tie these things up in a bundle. I have to leave for home very early in the morning.'

'You are leaving tomorrow in the morning then? I had grown so used to your pleasant company this past month. Now life will be lonely and dull once again. But what can be done? We must all submit to fate.'

'That's right. Can man do anything on his own? Everything is the doing of providence. Lord Dhabaleswar willing, we'll meet again. Can you get me a piece of string from your house? I have to tie all this up into a bundle.'

'Let me check.'

'Oh, let me get out of here. I long to go back to the children, whom I have not seen for a month now. Of course, Nande must be looking after them. But I have no news of my daughter-in-law. Tuku's mother is not very capable and has had to shoulder these responsibilities. I leave everything to the all-merciful Lord.'

'Will this do? I have another, but I think that's too thick.'

'This is perfectly all right.'

'Let me make the bundle. Is that all, or is there more?'

'No, that's all. I have not put the tumbler in the bundle because I need it for my ablutions. There is room for it in that bag. I'll put it in when I set off in the morning.'

'Have you cooked your food today? Will you go to bed on an empty stomach? Let me get you some flattened rice. Soak it in water and have it.'

'No, why should I have flattened rice at night?'

'But you have to cover such a long distance on foot tomorrow. How can you go to bed without having something to eat? Someone brought me a few nice bananas. Let me bring you a couple of those. Add a piece of nabata and have your meal.'

'All right. I'll do as you say. The way you put it makes it difficult for me to refuse. I should take this from you, for who knows, we may never meet again.'

'What a thing to say! How can I give anything to you. There is neither a taker nor a giver; we all share things that belong to the Lord.'

Dase went to the back of the house to have a wash. He was not conscious of it, but he was actually very hungry. When someone lovingly offers me a handful of flattened rice, why should I say no to him?

Suddenly he remembered Gangadhar Satpathy. His body was like a length of copper wire and his nose as straight as the blade of a sword. Every morning, by the time he reached the sanctum after bathing hurriedly old Satpathy would already be seated in a corner, his legs crossed under him. His eyes would be focussed on the point between the eyebrows. Dase would stop dead. It seemed to him as if the soul of the mountain sat absorbed in deep meditation. Taking a deep breath, he would tiptoe to the seat of the Lord and place the plate of puja offerings before Him. He would begin the worship, taking every care not to disturb Satpathy Mahasaya.

This thought absorbed Dase as he bent to wash his hands and feet.

'Bring some clean water with you to soak and wash the flattened rice.'

Dase washed hurriedly as if suddenly waking from a dream.

'Place it there. Let me have a bath.'

'I think the nabata may not be sufficient. It was all I had.'

'Oh, don't worry. I'll make do with it. Leave it over there.'

Patamali the gardener closed the front door behind him and limped off.

While bathing Dase experienced feelings of wonder, affection, awe and reverence as he tried to understand Satpathy Mahasaya.

Dase entered the house, wringing out the wet dhoti and wiping his face with it. He hung it to dry on the two nails he had driven into the wall on the day of his arrival. He was sure it would dry during the night.

Although I spent one long month here, only thrice did I get the chance of talking to Satpathy Mahasaya. How could he spend so much time meditating? I think he would have clarified my doubts if I had asked him to. But my courage failed whenever I approached him.

Anyway, why should a small man like me worry about big things. Why should a petty ginger-trader worry about the price of a sailing ship? God decreed that I should be denied intelligence. Wrote on my forehead that all my life I would be racked by care. What's the point in trying to get deeper into the mystery of life? Satpathy Mahasaya is a learned man, after all. He knows everything, understands everything and engages in reflecting upon the nature of the soul. He has no wordly worries to torment him any more. Blessed is he who is free from all care. One who is wealthy and has many children cannot be counted among the truly fortunate. One who has enough for his needs and the time to direct his thoughts towards his soul enjoys real bliss. All the ties that had bound the venerable one to the world have now snapped; only the soul waited to fly from its cage of flesh. Oh, to have done so in this fallen kaliyug is indeed a great achievement. He is truly a great soul!

How sweet this banana is! And how fine these grains of flattened rice are! Patamali eats well. Why should he not? He has no family to worry about. So what if he is lame? He must look after his body well, mustn't he? You may despise your bodies for you have become learned pundits, but everyone needs food for their bellies and clothes on their backs. This poor gardener eats whatever little he manages to get through his hard labour. He is not doing anything wrong. He is doing the right thing. It's a different matter if one finds nothing to eat, but why should not one feed oneself if one comes by food? How can this lead one to be caught in a mesh of attachments!

Oh, it is quite tasty but some grated coconut and fresh creamy curd would have made it really delicious. Not that it is not tasty now. . .

Satpathy Mahasaya is a very learned man, and gives such wise counsel. But if he had been a needy person like me, burdened with a large family, could he ever have become what he is today? Fate was kind to him. Think of life as a ladder with fourteen rungs. If at birth you are already on the tenth rung, how long would it take you to climb the remaining four? If you had been one of us, who find ourselves standing on the wet ground, you'd still be here below, your feet rooted in the soil. And grass would have grown on your back. You have achieved a lot, Sir. I salute you. May God never make you a poor man! As has been said: Oh God, never make me a poor man. For a poor man is everyone's enemy. If you are poor, all your time is spent in trying to find food for the belly and clothes for the back, Oh Lord Jagannath!

Dase rose to his feet. After rinsing his fingers, he sat down and opened his paan box, feeling cheerful, and relaxed. The thought of Tuku's mother crossed his mind as he went on chopping arecanuts. Hadn't he spent a lifetime with her as his life partner? The poor woman was doing her best, wasn't she? It was she who raised so many children. How can I find fault with her? Will it be fair if I call her the source of all my worldly care, the root of maya and renounce her? Why talk big? Can I even dream of leaving her? She is trapped in worldly worries in the same way as I am. She never planned to ensnare me in the web of wordly care. The poor woman has done her duty ever since she married me. Can leaving her to her fate now be called a sacred duty, a dharma? Bata, Jayi and Tukua are all still very young. I have to toil until they are able to look after themselves, take responsibility for their lives. How could I look upon them as strangers in order to save my own soul? Since I have brought them into this world, I have to take care of them, don't I? It is a sin to treat your children as strangers after you beget them. True, one struggles a lot to raise them. But so what? Should I for this reason abandon them to their fate, renounce the world and become a sanyasi? Let's not bother our heads with these things, for they really don't matter. It is one's karma that decides everything. After all, can we forget that we are family men? All the members of a family have to face joys and sorrows together. Once the children grow up, I'll go to places of pilgrimage with Tuku's mother. I have long been planning to take a dip in the holy water of the Ganga. We must go there. After that we'll leave everything to the Almighty. He may save us or destroy us. His will be done.

Patamali's rush-mat rested against the wall in a corner. Dase unrolled it and spread it on the floor. He laid his head on the bundle, using it as a pillow. He felt the money in its paper packet in a fold in his waist cloth. Then he bolted the door from the inside and blew out the oil lamp.

It would be around midday by the time he reached home. Tukua would be playing in the front veranda. Who knows, he might have grown skinnier. One couldn't make out the things he lisped. 'What's the matter Jayi? Your sister-in-law has given birth to a baby boy? Very good. Tuku's mother has grown thinner, too. Here, take this money. . .'

Dase's eyelids drooped into sleep. A herd of jackals began howling from the peak on the left. Dase felt restless. But sleep soon overtook him.

—

'Master, Dase. Wake up.' Patamali banged continuously at the door, shouting. Muffled sounds came from inside the room.

'Master, please get up! Wake up please!' the gardener said as he pounded on the door. It was quite a while before the doors opened.

'What was the matter, master? I've never heard you talk deliriously like this. Oh how loudly I called you! I must have called you at least a hundred times.'

'Oh Lord Gobinda! Oh what a terrible dream I saw! It was so sinister and full of bad omens.'

'What did you dream?' Patamali sat down at the edge of the rush mat.

Dase sat up, stretching his legs as if he had been resting after back-breaking exertion.

'I dreamed that I was marching aimlessly through pitch darkness. I had to cross a river on the way. What a river! The waters were menacingly dark. Water wherever I cast my eyes. Tuku's mother clings to my shoulder. Soon the others hold my hands and legs tightly. I can't swim, and I sink into the water, and desperately rise to the surface, throwing my hands and legs about. They cling to me like creepers no matter how desperately I seek to shake them off. I shout at them angrily, gasping for breath, but to no avail. Just then in the starlight I see someone crossing the river in a boat some distance away. He looks like our Satpathy Mahasaya. I call out to him loudly. But he rows away, paying no heed. I grow weary shouting. Big black waves like those that rise in the sea at Puri surge towards me. The stars disappear behind the clouds. I shout desperately, more loudly than before. Oh what a terrifying river! See, how I break into cold sweat. . . It seems someone from the boat pulls in the fish caught in the line and laughs. When that sinister-looking man pulls the line up my Tukua rises to the surface, the bait in his mouth. He is lifeless. Oh Lord Hari, Oh Lord Gobinda!'

'Don't you worry, master. These things mean nothing at all. Go and uproot a small plant and throw it away before you rinse your mouth.'

'Let's go. It will be some time before daybreak. But I know I won't sleep again.'

'The night is over, master. See, it's already dawn.'

'Let's get ready then.'

The Horoscope

'Do you get my point, Dase? It is no longer necessary for me to stay here. By the grace of God our daughter-in-law has safely delivered a baby. That was worrying me. How could I leave her in that state! Now you take care of your grandson and let me go. I wrote that I would return home after a month. Now it is a month and a half.'

'O ho! You are always in a hurry. Shortly we will observe ekoisia, the twenty-first day of the baby. Then you can go. You are already like this. Ahead are the days when you will settle down with a family. What then? Come on, sit down. . . Arey Bata dear, get the mat here for your mamu. Let me note down the time of the baby's birth. We will get the horoscope made. I will approach Nilakantha Pundit. He'll do it.'

Dase sat in a corner of the outer veranda. The *Panchang* lay open on the coconut leaf. There also lay a sheaf of horoscopes written on palm leaves rolled in a piece of cloth, smeared with turmeric. On a small narrow palm leaf, Dase was noting down the particulars of the baby's time of birth.

Nilakantha Pundit may not readily agree to do the job. But why? Is he going to do favours free? He will be paid hard cash. So. . .

Dase wrote and thought.

'You've brought the rush-mat. Well, spread it here. You sit here, Nande. Let me finish my work.'

'Listen. I've spent so many days here. I had to overstay because you went through a difficult patch. Or else, I would have left much earlier.'

'All right. This is also your home. You are not staying at a stranger's house. Of course you'll go home. We'll hold a Satyanarayan Puja on the day of the ekoisia of the baby. Go the day after that, I won't stop you. It's only a matter of a few days. Today is Tuesday. The ekoisia falls on Sunday. Can't you stay on for four days more? Why are you getting so restless? You are a funny man.'

'I'll certainly leave on Monday, and nothing you say on that day will stop me. All right, now let me know what the child's day and time of birth tell us.'

'The boy was born at a very auspicious hour on Monday. I am sure his horoscope will be a good one.'

'Why don't you cast it yourself. Why approach that Pundit Nilakantha? All you have to do is scribble on a palm leaf.'

'Fie, fie. How can I bring myself to cast horoscopes? The astrologers are children of the planets. It's inauspicious to set one's eyes on their faces. You will get nothing to eat if your eyes fall on them. Are astrologers true brahmins? Not one of my ancestors in fourteen generations was an astrologer. Pundit Nilakantha wants to give up casting horoscopes. But how can he? This has been his family trade for seven generations. He comes from a family of astrologers. So they are inferior brahmins.'

'Are all these horoscopes in this bundle our children's?'

'Yes. This contains two of mine, two of your sister's and one each for every child. Once a famous astrologer had come to Patapur. His brilliance was legendary. He'd look at your face, make calculations using nothing but his fingers and foretell your future. My father got him to cast another horoscope for me. That is why I have two horoscopes. My father was not happy with the horoscope of his daughter-in-law, so he got another one cast after the marriage.'

'Whose horoscope is this new one?'

'Put it back. That is Tukua's horoscope. He is our eighth child. He is therefore the luckiest in the family. If God gives him long life, he'll grow up to be a great man. Pundit Nilakantha, who is not the type to praise anyone, said while casting his horoscope, "Listen Dase, this child of yours will bring you fame and prosperity. See, three planets occupy favourable places in his horoscope. Jupiter is in the fifth place." If God grants him a long life he'll make this house see good times. You must all bless the boy.'

'Only a lucky man is blessed with a large family. Let me tell you something. First tie these horoscopes into a bundle and put them away. A dispensary has recently been set up in our village. A doctor who works there tells us that the government is trying to control the population growth. He says famines occur because too many people are born. He organized a meeting in the village the other day, and talked some such rubbish. But who'd pay him any heed? Don't we come across these things in the newspapers?'

'Yes, people get perverse ideas when their ends are near. Why should a man say such silly things unless he has gone crazy? You fool, can you control the processes of birth and death? These have been decided already by what is written in the book of Chitragupta. Whatever you may say will not increase or reduce the growth of population.'

'But the doctors have developed methods to control births.'

'To hell with those methods. Immoral people become shameless.'

'You Sudei. Come inside, for a moment. I want to tidy up the room in the lower wing. But I can't reach that sika. Unfasten it for me.'
Sudarshan Nanda followed Tuku's mother into the house.

What strange things present themselves as time goes by. Truly it is said, 'There is no end to surprises as long as one lives.' People are increasingly drawn towards sin. The horrifying Kaliyug approaches rapidly. Tell me, how can you control birth? Again, just because you people want to live in comfort and eat well, should no one else be allowed to take birth? Will you then murder embryos for your self-interest? Wretches, you believe it is you who beget and raise children. But you are terribly mistaken. Someone else is responsible for creating and sustaining human beings. Could anything happen against his will? He gives birth to you, He rears you, and it's He who will bring death to you. Your ignorance will never allow you to understand these things. Just because there is not enough food, you'd torture people by keeping them from marrying? You have invented so many machines. Why don't you invent one which can make the soil yield more food? Shameless wretches! Do you cut a child's head off because you can't find enough oil to rub it with?

Tell me, do you know when great men will take birth? You useless fellows do not give them a chance to come into the world. Does it matter in the least if millions like you exist or perish? You fellows worry that there won't be enough food or enough space for people. Do you suppose a God who has provided for fifty-six crores of creatures will ever abandon these human beings? Has all your learning, your education not equipped you to understand even this?

We are old-fashioned people. I have five sons by God's grace. If Yama, the god of death, had not taken away three, I'd have seven sons and a daughter now. You may say that I'm unable to support them. But who feeds them? Neither me nor you. It's Lord Lakshminarayan who provides them food. You buy your only child a new shirt or a tricycle, and I admit that I can't do this because I have a large family. But so what? Should I prevent a human being from coming into this world? I don't claim that they'll perform amazing feats or become great men when they grow up. But no one's life is worthless; we can never find out what divine purpose is served when they are born. A mango tree sheds five lakh leaves over five years, before it begins to bear fruit. Will you lop off its branches because they spread too wide? Should you prune the mango tree and make it look like a palm with only a few branches at the top so that it'll bear a few healthy fruits? Do you realize how many millions of trees and fruits you are killing in this process? Out of every mango fruit would have sprouted a tree. But you have no need for so many trees. But who are you, and how can your needs matter? Are you the lord of the universe, do you make it move?. . .

'You haven't finished tying up the horoscopes yet. What are you thinking about?' asked Sudarshan.

'I was pondering over what you just mentioned.'

'How would thinking help you now? You didn't stop and ponder when it'd have helped you.'

'Why should I have bothered, tell me? Should one ever let such thoughts into one's head? Only what fate has decreed will happen. Birth and death are both beyond our control. Crores upon crores of animals take birth, don't they? Doesn't their population increase? That reminds me of something very interesting. Children these days are taught many new things. Bata read about a sea creature. If all the young ones from its eggs survive, in three years' time the sea would be full of them and there'd be no space left for anything else. There would be crores and crores of them. But the creator has set a limit to their growth. All living beings function within such prescribed limits. The number of children in the case of human beings does not exceed seven or eight per person except in rare instances. If one is unable to support his children, the creator will certainly find some way for their survival. You will find that one day human beings will become like banana plants that bear fruit once and then die.'

'You have a strange way of putting things, as always. You can never change your old way of looking at things and can never understand these new ways. Well, wait. I'll get you a few paans.'

Maybe what these people say is true in a sense. 'His pocket is empty, yet he longs to get his son married with pomp.' Is it right to have eight children when one does not have the means to support even one? Is it right to blame fate for one's own mistakes? Not having been raised properly the children will end up begging for their survival. But how can one escape having children when one gets married? Will maya allow men and women to stay away from each other? The need to raise a family is as powerful as hunger or thirst, and must be satisfied. But what these people say cannot be dismissed lightly either. At least the earth will not be covered with human beings running around like pigs. The creator has made provisions for animals, but the case of man is different, for he is endowed with intelligence. Who knows if this again is not part of God's plan? Maybe God wants humanity to destroy itself little by little.

But which of these two views should one accept? One holds that it's better not to bring a child into the world at all if he is going to suffer all his life from want and deprivation. But the problem here is that one thus prevents a soul from taking birth and realizing itself through human life. There'll always be rich and poor. Poverty can't stop a human being from fulfilling himself. Only the most fortunate get the rare opportunity of human birth. And salvation can be attained only after a human being passes through thousands of births. So, this human form is precious beyond measure. This is why one should allow everyone to take birth, no matter how painful their lives are going to be. These problems can never have a solution. Everything can be interpreted both ways. Do this or that. In the end you realize no one knows anything: they merely continue to shout. The world is full of cares. Who enjoys being tormented by them? You are yourself stuck in the mud. Why drag a few others into this mud-pit? And consider that terrible dilemma which confronts you. . .the scriptures say that after death the soul enters another body in order to suffer the consequences of its karma. But the heart remains unconvinced. It feels that everything ends with death, there's nothing beyond it. But if that is true, why should the soul strive to do good, and take another birth? Forget it, these are very complicated matters. Why should we trouble our heads with them? Let others try to sort these things out. Fine, we now agree with you. We don't have the energy to prove that this is right or that is wrong.

'Here, take this paan. It has more arecanut pieces.'

Sudarshan Nanda handed him a paan, and himself sat down. He picked up on what was being discussed a moment before and said,

'You must have heard what happened to Nidhi Mohanty of our village. He always behaved like a know-all. He went and got himself operated on by a family-planning doctor. At the time he had two children—a son and a daughter. When he returned after undergoing the operation he was the talk of the village. He was the the new doctor's constant companion. He was something of an advertisement. Shortly afterwards, a deadly fever claimed the lives of both his children.'

'Oh, what a terrible punishment of fate for the man!'

'Now, whom could he blame? It was he himself who was responsible for this calamity. He had cut off his own tongue, as it were. He ran around a lot, desperately spent money like water. But he was beyond help. There is no point in sticking your tongue out to lick the treacle after it has flowed down from your palm to your elbow. He was such a handsome man. He is now pale and haggard. You won't recognize him if you run into him.'

'A stupid man. Got carried away by this rubbish and now there is no one to continue his family line. He'll never set eyes on a son or a daughter again. The pity is, there will be no one to raise libation to the ancestors of seven generations.'

'This Nidhi Mohanty was a man of great influence. He's about my age. Just because his father left him some property, he treated others as if they were flies. He would boast that the commissioner was a close relative. He always talked big. A born braggart. He would take a pinch of cannabis and talk endlessly. But he is strangely altered these days. He now spends all his time at home, saying nothing. . .'

'The fellow was deceived, wasn't he? I knew his father, Ratnakar. He was a good soul, a religious man who gave freely. How much money he spent when this Nidhi was born! For him, my uncle chanted the name of Lord Gopal a thousand times every day for a year. Nidhi was born after so many vows and rites and fasts. And see what came of it all. No one is left in the family to offer consecrated water to the manes. Fate is all powerful, Nande. You'll not agree with me now, but you'll come round later.'

'Quite. Quite. What's the use of so much property now? He will adopt someone from another family and make him his heir. What kind of son would he have? A son in name only.'

'Listen, Nande. The world is a strange place. Think of our Raghunath. It seems like yesterday. Nana was not that old when he was born. Overjoyed, he said, "Oh, this child is like Bhagirath for my family. May Lord Raghunath bless him with a long life. You'll shave his head at the temple of the Lord at Odagaon." It seems like yesterday. But how fast time flies! Now Raghunath has become a father, and I am setting down the details of his son's birth. We must sing the glory of the One who brings all this to pass. So many things occur before our very eyes. These children grow up so rapidly, all one can do is to watch wonder-struck. The wheel of time rotates and clinging to it like insects and flies, we too keep moving. Can pitiful man ever penetrate the mystery of birth, get its measure, or bring it under his control? Tell me, can we even explain how grass grows?'

Nanda continued to chew his paan, eyes fixed on the void above. Moments passed. Dase tied up the horoscopes and put them by. As he threw the towel over his shoulder and rose to his feet he said, 'Listen to what I have to say after much reflection. The burden of man's sins is getting too heavy. So heads will roll, and the time of annihilation draws nearer. The cunning which helped man in every battle so far will now lead him to disaster. He'll destroy himself by exploding bombs. Birth control will also finish his race. Do you suppose Kalki, the lord of destruction, will take a visible form? He'll devour everything, himself remaining invisible just as the fear of Kokua finished the descendants of Yadu. Man these days is gripped by a nameless terror. As time goes by, you'll witness strange and perverse happenings.'

Nanda found the whole thing somewhat odd because Dase declaimed, pointing his index finger at him, as if warning him.

'See how Jayi bothers Tukua and makes him cry. He wants to put on this printed shirt.'

'I'm wearing mine. He has soiled his. Now he wants to put on my shirt.' Bata rushed in and complained.

Dase stood for a while, staring at Bata.

'Well, why don't you give it to him? Let him put it on for a while. He'll give it back when his own shirt is dry. Please give it to him. You Bata, my dear, please put these things away. Go. . . Nande, let's go to the shop and take a stroll. We must finish our work early, because we have to go the temple.'

The Rule of Fate

'The marriage of Pundit Nilakantha's son Indramani will be held on the tenth day of the bright fortnight in the month of Baisakh. He will marry Ila, the daughter of Mahapatra from Puri.'

'Ila or Pingala? What sort of strange name is this?'

Dase looked at his wife over his glasses. Then he read the programme. 'Mangalan, the bridegroom's procession. Look at the cards Pundit Nilakantha has had printed. How beautiful they are!'

'Let me see. I couldn't learn a single alphabet in the whole of my wasted life. See how the letters glow as if they are made of gold. What is this? How nice this painting of the holy pitcher is!'

'Yes, Looks exactly like a real pitcher. You, Bhaiga. Go and get me a jug of water to drink. You are a big boy. Why be so curious?'

'Oh leave me alone. These wretches won't let me look at it in peace.'

'*Om Sri Prajapataya Namah... Dear Sir*', Bata read aloud leaning over his mother's shoulder. From the left side, Jayi pointed with his finger, 'This letter is "ma", that one is "kha".'

Little Tukua crawled into his mother's lap and began pulling at the card.

'Tukua, please give it to me. You won't? Well then, we'll no longer be friends with each other.'

'Don't give it to Jayi, Tukua. Don't give it to him. Come, play with me, we'll cut out the figure of a deity from that card.'

Bata carried Tukua in his arms. Jayi followed them, weeping.

'Why did you bring water in this? Where is the other jug?'
'I couldn't find it.' Saying this, Bhaiga, too, ran inside.

'Tell me, is this how someone invites a guest? Shouldn't he have come himself? Turmeric paste and rice paste should have been distributed. Didn't we send turmeric paste and rice paste to the houses of people we invited to Raghu's wedding? Is Pundit Nilakantha such a rich person that simply sending out a piece of coloured paper would do for him? Turmeric and rice paste are auspicious. Again, no woman has been called to take part in the rite of handi mangula.'

'Things are done differently these days. Who cares for old ways any more? You were a child when you got married. When people marry now, they bring their brides home with them. It's a good thing. In the past one had to wait for years. Do you think Pundit Nilakantha will not invite us properly? He is a sensible man. He'll never forget to send us the sacred arecanut. Our families have a longstanding relationship and have been exchanging gifts, too. I'm sure, he'll send us arecanuts and invite us properly. There are still five days left. True, his son is an educated man of the new generation; but the father belongs to our generation. Will he forget propriety? But who knows?'

'What gifts will one give these days? Four coconuts cost two rupees now. There is a large pumpkin in the backyard. We could send that as a gift. A basketful of brinjals, and a piece of yam could be added to that. We must begin getting these items together one by one from now, so that we don't get into trouble when the time comes.'

'Well, let's see.'

On his return from the temple in the morning Dase had been busy tidying a stack of palmleaf texts. He had unwound the thread binding the sheaf, and was placing each leaf on a wooden stand. A plate containing a mixture of burnt coconut shell, turmeric paste and coconut oil lay near him. He dipped a piece of cloth into the mixture and wiped the palm leaves clean with it.

'Do you think you'll be able to clean all these, dry them and tie them into a bundle today?'

'No, no. I'll clean just this one bundle. The rest I'll clean tomorrow. Please get me two paans. My mouth feels sour.'

'We've had no betel leaves at home since morning. We got a bundle the day before yesterday in the afternoon. How long could it last?'

'Well, then, bring me my box of chewing tobacco. I haven't got it in the fold of my waist-cloth.'

'It'll be tomorrow by the time one is able to locate it. One can find it only if you always remember to keep it in the same place.'

When his wife left, Dase thought that gifts had to be arranged. The month was coming to an end. The money his son had sent was beginning to run out. After all, Nilakantha's son was getting married. Will it look nice if we go there empty-handed? Hadn't he, for his part, visited them with many gifts at the time of Raghu's wedding? We should give him something. True, there's no question of our being equals. But we must give whatever we can afford. Fortune now smiles on Pundit Nilakantha. Thirty years ago he was a non-entity. On returning from Kashi, he had wandered around in search of clients. He was then reading 'purusha' as 'purukha'. No one in the village employed him as a priest for they feared that performing a rite according to Vedic principles might cost more. . . But look at him now. Fortune had favoured him at last. How proudly he walked, the owner of extensive lands and a pucca house! A fellow like Brunda Nahak, whom I timidly avoid whenever I run into him, never forgets to salute Pundit Nilakantha. The Pundit would only touch his chin with the curved handle of his walking stick while blessing another. His son is an engineer. No one in the village now dares to say a rude word to him.

This Nilakantha would be about two years older than me. We went to school together. He was so dim-witted, he couldn't utter 'Vishnu' even if you thumped his back. Must have described circles on thousands of palm leaves to make his hands stable. Even so, his handwriting was as clumsy as the scratches made by a cat's claws. And he must have worn out three headloads of white chalk practising the alphabet on the floor. Arithmetic had always been beyond him. But when he took to Sanskrit, there was no stopping him. . . One day the zamindar visited the school. The two of us were chosen to welcome him. My task was to garland him, and Nilakantha's was to recite a shloka. The zamindar was so impressed with him, he insisted on doing him a good turn. The headmaster explained everything to him. Nilakantha received a scholarship of forty rupees per month. Or else, could he, or his father for that matter, have met the expenses of studying in Kashi?. . . After that, no matter how many shlokas I recited no one bothered to give me a scholarship. I left school and took up my father's priestly duties. Nilakantha's father, Gopal Tripathy, would often come and sit at our doorstep. Nana used to call him whenever there was a festival at the temple of Lord Lakshminarayan. He always waited eagerly to be called. And see, his son is now a famous pundit, and a rich man. We stayed where we were and remained mere temple priests all our lives. Maybe, my life could have taken a different course. But no, that never happened. The planets determine one's destiny. If they wish to make someone a learned man, he becomes one. Or else, no matter how desperately you exert yourself, you achieve nothing at all.

His son Indramani is extremely lucky, too. True, he worked hard at his studies. But luck smiled on him. He got a scholarship just after he finished his examinations. Things suddenly fell into place. Our Raghu, for his part, amounted to nothing at all. A blot on the family name. But, come to think of it, what has Indramani become after receiving such an education? And does Raghu starve because he remained uneducated? After all, it is he who supports such a large family like ours. There is no point in pondering over all this. Nothing is mightier than fate. I would have sent him to school if he had taken an interest in his studies. But the stars upset my plans; just when I was going to enroll him in a school my daughter died. That was my first experience of the bitter loss of a child. Everything went awry. Raghu ended up reading in a tol. But even there he didn't apply himself to his studies, and wasted all his time. His younger brothers followed his example and lost all interest in their studies. What a shame! Our son now does a peon's job, which is done by the lowliest of the low. And our family survives on the money he sends us every month. Anyway, what can we do. . .

After completing his studies, Indramani became a big man. His social position allowed him to marry into a rich family and his in-laws look up to him. And how unlucky we are! Its all best forgotten.

Why torment oneself with these thoughts? And what's the point in blaming one's fate?

. . . A band from Calcutta had reached Madanpur. They would come with the bridegroom, in a glittering procession. The whole village had been invited. The invitees included Indramani's friends who were all officers and government employees. The marriage would be celebrated with dazzling pomp.

Why bother? Things will not remain the same forever. Should we torment ourselves with envy just because someone else is prospering? Hasn't it been said, 'Time's ways are peculiar?' Who can foretell what's going to happen to a human being? What a man aspires to do or to become means nothing at all. Unless the powers above will it, man can do nothing, for he is utterly helpless. No power on earth can erase what has been inscribed by fate. Therefore, whatever is fated must come to pass. Fate will make everything serve it, fall into line. Even the most powerful human being has to submit to its dictates. A warrior like Dasrath, who could have subdued the whole world, lost his life pining for a son whom he had exiled to the forest. This is what his fate had decreed. We believe we can determine the course of our lives through our own efforts. Had Indramani not studied seriously, if he had not worked hard would luck have smiled on him? But the fact is, he was fated to study and work hard. So he succeeded. Even if he had wanted to, he could never have remained ignorant, or become a peon in Madanpur. One's fate is everything; it determines everyone's portion in life.

'Here, Father. Mother has sent your box of chewing tobacco.'

'Why are you running away? What's your mother doing?'

'I don't know.'

'This idiot can never stay still.'

Dase tipped a little tobacco into his palm and lost himself in thought once more.

Well, doesn't man see discrimination and unfairness everywhere? He feels he always deserves much more than whatever he comes by. It seems to him that others who are his equals, and those inferior to him, have received more than their due. Jealousy and discontent fill his heart, but these offer no solution. He needs to console himself. Belief in fate solves half his problems; it compels one to resign oneself to what seems unfair. If this fails to work, one resorts to the fruits of karma, and suffers the consequences of one's actions from one birth to another. Again, if this does not do the trick, heaven offers the last resort. If you think you haven't been rewarded for your talents in this life, heaven holds out hope for you. . .

Or is this 'fate' thing a ploy to make the poor and weak meekly accept their lot so that they will not envy the wealthy? Who knows? These riddles are beyond us.

Do you then claim that there is nothing called fate? Of course there is something called fate. When young, one tends to dismiss it. But buffeted by adversity, one learns to believe in its existence. . .Tell me, what harm had that Santra's daughter done anyone? Oh, what a beautiful girl! She glowed like a flame on her wedding day. And her husband was so handsome! Tall and well-built, he was somewhat dark, but his features were finely moulded. But look at what happened to the couple. In a week's time everything was over; the girl became a widow. No matter how much people persuaded her father, he did not get her married again. Tell me, won't her whole life be clouded with despair and futility?

Fate brings someone down with a thunderbolt, and makes someone else a king overnight. Someone remains childless even after giving away gifts and holding thousands of yajnas. And the house of another swarms with children, who are uncared for and neglected. Who makes these strange things happen? I, for one, think that man is utterly helpless. He is powerless to do anything.

Someone else makes us move like machines.

What does fate mean? Isn't the course of one's life decided by God? While making pots the potter puts clay on a wheel, throws a handful of water at it, and moves the wheel. He presses the clay between two fingers as it rises, and gives it a smooth rim. Then he removes the pot from the wheel with the help of a thread, just as one severs the umbilical cord. This pot is dried in the sun, and then baked in the kiln. When he sells it off, the potter taps it hard and says, 'You can cook two seers of rice in it; the other one will hold a seer and three quarters of rice.' The smaller pot looks even smaller. When the potter taps it to show how well it has been baked, the sound it produces is not impressive. After all, it is the smaller of the two pots. Is it responsible for its own size? The potter did whatever he wanted to do. But, for his part, he too can't make pots of the same size. Similarly, someone is born in a king's palace and someone else takes birth in a beggar's hut. Someone is born so clever that he understands everything in a flash, can take in a book with just a single look at it. And another is born so stupid that he is not even fit to mind a herd of goats.

Not merely is one's life-span predetermined, his portion in life is decided before he is born. The course along which his life is to flow can never be altered. At times one might get the impression that no one is directing the course of one's life, so one can move in any direction one likes. It's exactly at this point that disaster strikes and brings a man back to the groove. From time to time fate reminds everyone of the limits they must accept. Someone else has to be caught by the scruff of his neck and made to see that he has to take to the high wide road. The main thing is, one has to submit to God, the real mover. All our problems fade away when we rest content with whatever He has granted us. The feeling that the others have got more than what one has torments everyone from their childhood. Make do with whatever little you have got—that is the right thing to do.

All of us stand on different rungs of a ladder. No one is at its top, nor is anyone at the bottom rung. If someone is above you because he has more wealth, you are above him because you have a larger family. Everyone's portion in life is thus a mixed fare. Looked at from this angle whatever you see is but an illusion. If you take everyone's share of sorrows and joys into account, you will realize that all are equal. One who lowers his head and lets the surging wave pass over rises above the high and the low. He finds joy in every experience. He discovers the meaning of existence. After all, everything is part of the divine sport of Lord Jagannath.

'You are still cleaning that leaf. Will it take the whole day?'

'I have nearly finished cleaning it.' His wife's words made Dase start. He began to rub the leaf with the mixture faster.

'Come and have your meal. Today is Monday. So I won't eat fish or meat. I'll just have the bhog. How long will you make our daughter-in-law wait for you? She eats only after you finish your meal. Come.'

'All right. Let me clean this leaf. I'll join you.'

'Raghu has sent word through that boy from Dalei's house. . .'

'What does he say?'

'His mother told me in the backyard that Raghu now finds cooking for himself troublesome. He will come this month and take his wife and his son with him. He has already rented a house there.'

'Won't it be difficult if he takes such a little child with him? Can't he wait for another two months? How can a tender baby stand this heat? He should take the mother and the child to Madanpur when the rains arrive.'

'What you think does not matter. I knew all along that this girl was not as simple as she seemed. She must have cast a spell on Raghu last time, for he talked rudely, flinging his words at me. He lost his temper for no reason at all. If Tukua went to him, he treated him like a stranger. And you think he'll listen to you?'

'You talk as if you know everything.'

'I am not a fool like you. You only gape at everything, dazed, and unable to make out anything.'

Batia entered the front room, calling, 'Sister-in-law says that food has been served.'

'I am coming. Let me tie these into a bundle. Or let me leave them lying here. Keep a watch over the children. Make sure they don't touch these. Let's go. Oh Lord Narayan. Oh Lord Jagannath.'

Life Beyond Death

'Who is so ill-fated that he would accept that girl as a daughter-in-law? What a dangerous girl she is! She can make up a story in a moment. So young and so wicked! How unmanageable she will be when she grows up!'

Addressing these words to Dase, Tuku's mother emerged from an inner wing of the house, paan box in hand. It was already dark. The children had assembled in the front room after an early meal. A cheerful Dase was picking his teeth and listening to his children gossiping.

'Who are you talking about?'

'That Kuma, Hari Panda's daughter.'

'Oh. The daughter of Haria Panda? Her father is a terribly jealous fellow. Why, what happened to her? Hand me the arecanuts, I'll chop them.'

'Have you brought that Berhampuri khaira?'

'Give me a pinch of it. Let me smell it. . .'

'What a nice smell, Can I have a little, Mother?'

'You want some?'

'Mother, I too want some!'

'Go, gobble up all that khaira, you snake-faced idiots.'

'Hey you. Put that khaira back in the paan box. You know it smells nice. Why smell it over and over again. Now, tell me about that Kuma.'

'She came to our house. It's all right, one may come visiting. You should seat yourself, talk a bit, then leave. Why should you barge into this room and that and ask what is stored in this box, and what in that?'

'Some people are like that. They can't stand anyone's prosperity. They are full of envy. Haria Panda is one of them.'

'Listen to the whole story first. She entered the bedroom and sent her eyes about it, searching every nook and corner. That blue tanank, which is kept in a corner. . .'

'You should say "trunk", mother, not "tanank".'

'When her eyes fell on it she sat down near it. She caressed and, stroked it fondly. Then she asked whose trunk it was. I felt like saying it was not her father's, but I only said it was ours, that Raghu had sent it. She said that they had a much bigger trunk than this in their house. It was blue and very strong. Her sister had taken that trunk to her in-law's house and her father says he'd get another two—no, four—such trunks.'

'Why didn't you ask her to shut up and tell her, "Your face tells us how rich you are." Four trunks or eight! As if they cost nothing!'

'There is more. She twisted the lock and asked, "What have you kept inside it? Have you put all your worn-out clothes in it? It's a good thing to put all these in one place, rather than let them litter the house." What could I say to this? Then she caught sight of Raghu's empty bottle of scented oil in the recess in the wall. She took it down, sniffed it, and said, "My brother uses this kind of oil. No, the oil he uses smells nicer than this. I'm sure this costs only a rupee or twelve annas." I felt like giving her a piece of my mind. But I thought that she'd soon get married and leave her father's house. Why tell her anything? One cannot change her nature.'

'You are useless. You are always very clever only after the event. If you had given her a piece of your mind, the girl would have learnt a lesson. It'd have done her a world of good. It would have taught her how to behave in her in-law's house in another village. Well let's forget it. They are all like that. . . Oh, the betel leaf will tear, don't roll it up any harder. Give it to me. I'll have it. It's a ripe leaf, very tasty. The old man chose these leaves carefully and persuaded me to take one kada in place of a half.'

'Father, give me a few pieces of arecanut.'

'No. Don't eat arecanuts, they produce phlegm. Just have a few. It won't do you any good if you pick up these bad habits at this young age. It's said, "One who earns a hundred rupees can afford a little arecanut, and one who earns a thousand can afford a paan." We took to this habit when we were little children. It's not a good habit to pick up.'

'The girl raved about her elder brother. What does that Haria Panda's son do these days?' resumed Tukua's mother.

'What can that fellow do? He is utterly worthless. Yesterday, while returning from the market someone told me that he was going to join the army, why shouldn't he? He is two years older than Raghu, after all. Raghu has become a father. God willing, he may soon be blessed with another child. That fellow is still a bachelor. His father is a shameless person. At this age he has a child every year, and his grown-up son remains unmarried.'

'Tell me. Will he really join the army? Won't his mother stop him? After all, he is the eldest son, one who offers oblation to the manes. How could his mother let him go? Think how we feel about Raghu living only six kosas away. Where has a war broken out that they are sending their son over there?'

'A war is going on in China, which is near the Himalayas,' said Bata in a manner that indicated he was very knowledgeable.

'This god-forsaken war has pushed up the price of everything. I wonder how we can survive in times like these.'

'The Chinese soldiers are fighting with huge guns. We don't have them. We got them from America and England.'

'Haven't I seen a Chinaman? There is one in Madanpur who makes false teeth out of bones, and his talk sounds like the chatter of a monkey. What battle can such round-faced idiots give? If you feel their faces with your fingers you can't find the trace of a mouth, eyes or a nose. There will be no war. Only people like Haria Panda's son, Satrughna Panda, who are wandering like mangy dogs, will now get something to eat. Sahibs, military officers have set up a camp at Madanpur to recruit people who want to go to war.'

'Our teachers in school were talking about this. The recruiting office has been set up in the school. If someone is selected, they send him for training. Mother, tomorrow is donation day. I'll have to give something to the defence fund.'

'Didn't you make a donation a few days ago? You and Jayi gave eight annas to the fund? Why are you asking for money again?'

'Tell your teacher or I'll go and tell him that we can't give any money. We can't afford even two meals a day. If we keep making donations we will be beggared. Tell me, can one milk money from a cow? Dalei wanted to send his children to school, but he couldn't afford it. Do you think schooling is a joke? Paying for your children's clothes and books would break anyone's back. And add to this all kinds of donations!'

'This is not like the donation for Ganesh Puja. This is what the government is raising from all of us to help our soldiers in the battlefield.'

'So what? Would we have refused to give if we had the means? We haven't got the money; so how can we make a donation? Where would we get it from?'

'But everyone is giving. We must. Um-um-um.'

'Why are you growling like a cat with a fish in its mouth. Why are you getting so impatient? We'll see when the time comes. . . How much do you have to pay?'

'Four annas.'

'All right. I'll give it to you. Take it from me when you go to school. Now hand me the box of chewing tobacco that's by you.'

'Oh, keep quiet, all of you. Someone is on the outer veranda,' Tuku's mother whispered, and everyone fell silent. Moments passed. They heard a rustling sound. Clearing his throat, Dase said, 'Who is there?' No one answered. Tuku jumped over the paan box and settled himself in his mother's lap. Jayi and Bata snuggled up against Dase. Bhaiga came running in from the other room.

'Who's making that noise, Mother?'

'Stop. Keep quiet.'

Dase didn't like this exchange of whispers between mother and son.

'Oh. Why is this boy so scared? Aren't you a man? You howl because something made a slight noise. That's nothing. It could be a cat or a dog. If it is a person wouldn't he say something?'

'Look here. It was not that. I am convinced it was a man. I even heard him breathing heavily.'

'Don't imagine that thieves are breaking into your house in the evening. Tell me, why should a thief take the trouble of breaking into your house?'

'It may not be a thief. Maybe it was someone else.'

'You mean to tell me it was a ghost, then?'

The children now sat huddled against the wall in a heap. They stared wide-eyed. Just then came the rustling noise again.

'Now listen to that.'

'Bhaiga, bring me my stick from that corner.'

'Don't go. Last night when Dalei's daughter-in-law went to the backyard, some creature rushed past her. It gave her such a fright, she's now down with high fever. She raves deliriously. First open the door a crack, and peep out.'

Dase stuck his head out and burst into laughter. He opened the door wide, struck the veranda with his walking stick, and said, 'Hoosh,

Baghua. Go away. You are all so scared by a mere dog? The poor thing was scratching its lice-bitten ears. And you heard the sound of footsteps, and human voices. Stupid.'

'All right. Now bolt the door and come inside. . . Fine, this was a dog. But did Dalei's daughter-in-law encounter a dog? That sisam tree is certainly home to a ghost.'

'Rubbish. It's all so fanciful. Why? I have never ever encountered a ghost. However, I must admit that one day I had a strange experience. I had gone to the backyard. The ground was dappled with moonlight. It seemed to me as if it was already daybreak. I looked around. I thought I heard someone groaning. I was carrying this staff. With this staff in hand, I fear nothing, because a coin burnt in the fire of the yajna held last year in Harihat has been planted on its head. Have a look, if you like. No witch or evil spirit ever dares come anywhere near it. I, too, made a noise. The sound ceased but soon it came again. I picked up a stone and threw it in the direction of the sound. Some creature fled heavily towards that tree and appeared to dissolve into it.'

'That was very daring on your part. The ghost spared you only because you are a brahmin. Otherwise it would not have been unresponsive when you threw a stone at it.' All the children were wide awake now. They stared unblinkingly, listening in rapt silence. Tuku's mother continued.

'But don't you do something like that ever again. There are some ghosts who would not care for anyone. I have heard my grandmother say that she had seen one such with her own eyes. It rides the air. It has a head as big as a large basket with the rest of its body tapering off. It's feet always remain a cubit above the ground. If you ever cross its path, you are finished. It will swallow you whole. True, this is something I have heard from others, not seen myself.'

'But consider your own experience. We would not have believed it if someone else had told us about it.'

Whenever the topic of ghosts came up, Tuku's mother would repeat the same old story. The children had heard it several times already, but they never tired of listening to it again.

Bata said, 'Have you actually seen one yourself mother? Tell us what happened.' Tuku's mother forgot that she had recounted this story to them not less than fifty times. The children, for their part, forgot that they, too, had heard it at least fifty times.

'O, what an experience that was, my son! Whenever I recall what I saw, I get goose pimples. I was a young woman then. Your father was not at home that day. Raghu was a small child. My mother-in-law was no more. Father-in-law used to sleep in the front room, where we are all seated now. I had to get up a little before daybreak when it was still dark and finish the morning chores. After all, I was the daughter-in-law in a brahmin household. There was no way I could venture out once it got light. That night I lay asleep with my son by my side. Suddenly I woke up with a start. A bright moon shone out of cottonwool clouds covering the sky. It felt as if the night was coming to an end. I picked up this brass pitcher, put a twig into my mouth, and made my way to the pond through our backyard. You know how far the pond is from our house. But as long as we did not have a well in our own backyard I had to go there every day to bathe. There were no houses on the way which lay through a dense forest of jajangi trees.'

'Why don't you tell us where you ran into the ghost?'

'Have patience. I am coming to that. When I stepped onto the village path, everything seemed uncannily quiet. But since I had already come out, I thought I must go on to bathe. When I went as far as Sindura's house, it suddenly burst out of a corner, dressed in immaculate white.'

'Wasn't it a ghost?'

'Listen. Don't interrupt her. She is talking and you must listen to her quietly. Why do you ask whether it was a ghost in the middle of the story?'

'When I caught sight of it I thought she was the old woman from Sindura's house on her way to the pond. I was not supposed to say anything to anyone. So I pulled the end of my saree over my face, and walked on without fear. But something bothered me: Why should the old woman not recognize me and not talk to me, and why was she walking along that untrodden wilderness among the jajangi trees?'

'I'm scared, mother.' Bata admonished Jayi, saying, 'Why should you feel scared? After all this is only a story.'

'I was feeling a little nervous, but I was still far from being really frightened. I put the pitcher on the bank of the pond and went to the field to relieve myself. The old woman was now out of sight. It was at this time that I felt oppressed by a nameless fear. It was eerily quiet all around. I rose to my feet, took the twig out of my mouth and threw it away after scraping my tongue. I took a quick dip, filled the pitcher, and came on to the bank, not bothering to squeeze my wet clothes dry. The ghost, which lay hidden somewhere nearby, now suddenly emerged. On my way to the pond it had walked on my left side; now it walked beside me on the right. Covering my face with the end of my saree, I had walked along the path. I got up some nerve when we neared the village, and assured myself that there was no reason for fear now. Just when we reached Sindura's house, it crashed against me. I collapsed like a felled tree, and everything went blank. That ghost has its haunt there. It only gives people a scare, but it never harms anyone. That is why it allowed me to live when it had me completely in its power.'

'What happened next, mother?' said Bata. His mother had fainted and he couldn't rest easy until he found out what had happened to her after that.

'I lay there unconscious. Back at home, my little son screamed and flailed his arms wildly for he was terribly hungry. Father-in-law, who tried desperately to soothe him, was furious. "It's still dark. Where did that girl go so early? I'll give her a piece of my mind when she returns!" Just at this time, old Dalei came out of his house and said, "What's the matter, Dase?"

"Strange! Where has my daughter-in-law gone when it's so dark. The brass pitcher is not to be seen in the house. She must have gone out to have her bath. I have been keeping her child amused for a while now. She is taking too long."

"I heard you complain. So I came to tell you this. From somewhere near Sindura's house there came a jingling sound and it seemed to me as if someone wearing ornaments had fallen with a crash. I thought it could be your daughter-in-law."'

'At the time I was covered with ornaments. They must have tinkled and clinked when I fell in a faint. Old Dalei and the others came running and found the brass pitcher a little distance away from where I lay unconscious. They carried me home. I came to my senses after a time and narrated everything. Father-in-law scolded me. That same day I went down with high fever and was bedridden for six long months. Many vaidyas and gunias, had to be called in before I was cured.'

'That was brought on by the shock. If the ghost had really wanted to harm you, it could simply have drowned you. Why should it have allowed you to walk that far?'

'See mother, how fear has sent Tukua to sleep.'

'Tukua got scared and you think you are all brave fellows. Go to bed, all of you. You shouldn't stay awake at night after you eat. The rice will rot in your stomachs. Take these boys away and put them to sleep.'

'We are scared.'

'Why? Mother is with you. Get up and go to bed.'

'Hold Tukua in your arms, Bhaiga. Let me get up. The beds have already been made. Go to bed all of you.'

'Leave the lantern here. There must be another one in your bedroom. Why take this away?'

Dase held the tip of his walking stick against the light and examined it.

One of its screws had loosened.

The coin planted on its head might work itself loose. Thirty-three crore gods had been invoked in the fire of the yajna, in which this coin had been burnt. No ghost or evil spirit ever dare come near me as long as this is with me. Anyway one can't believe half the stories people tell about ghosts. It's the human mind that creates most of them.

The other day, on a full-moon night, someone came and reported that the old woman from the mason's house had thrown off her saree and was stark naked in her backyard. All of us, still bleary-eyed, ran out to see what was going on. We found that the old woman had really flung off her saree, which lay a little distance away, and was swaying, moving her hands and legs crazily. . .

It was a summer night. Everyone slept on cots in the open. Someone suggested that we go and find out if the old woman was sleeping in her house. We went in and found her in her bed, fast asleep. Who was that woman, then? You must admire the guts of Sundara's son. He dashed into the backyard, wielding a cudgel. He discovered that it was nothing but the wind shaking a young date palm, near which was placed an earthen pot coated with quicklime. The sight made everyone laugh heartily. But if that young man had not dared to enter the backyard, the story would have got exaggerated and spread far and wide.

But what had Tuku's mother encountered? Can one claim convincingly, that such apparitions don't exist at all? They do exist, but just as we shun dark, deserted places, they avoid places which are bright and crowded. So we run into them only by accident, and rarely. But do human beings wander about as ghosts when they die? If this was the case, the world would be crowded with ghosts, and one would bump into them everywhere, even at midday. Maybe human beings are reborn as animals or ghosts depending on their karma. Satpathy Mahasay said something very profound the other day at Dhabaleswar: 'This offering of oblation to the manes is a matter of faith; it has nothing to do with evidence or proof. We believe that manes exist, and that they inhabit a particular sphere. If they are gratified, one's family flourishes. For this reason, once every year, a son offers oblation to his deceased father and grandfather. Life would be impossible if death was the end of everything. Human beings would be in the constant grip of fear. So human relationships continue even beyond death, and it takes seven generations for them to dissolve. Doesn't this instil some hope in man? Or else life would become terrible.'

'I agree with you, sir. We have created the sphere of the manes to comfort ourselves. But the truth is, there is nothing beyond death. But to assert a thing like that one needs proof. The point is, no one really knows anything about these matters. Some believe in the manes, others don't. That's all. If you say all this is merely a matter of faith, let's not forget that we see Brahman in a log of wood. It has been said, "You worship this pillar, and even in this you'll discover God." Certainly manes exist in a subtle form. Or else, would the Lord himself have told Arjun, "I'm present in the manes and I'm called Aryama." You are a learned person, sir. Your ways of expressing things will always be beyond ordinary people like us. However, we are honest people. Our ancestors have offered oblation to their manes for the last twenty-seven generations and this has not discredited them. The skies won't fall if we follow their example. We should not deny the manes their share of offerings, claiming that they do not exist. Arre, the dasami falls on the day after tomorrow!'

'Listen, come here.' Dase called his wife.

'What do you want?'

'Come over here.'

Tuku's mother came in and asked testily, 'Tell me, what's the matter?'

'Father's death anniversary falls on the day after tomorrow.'

'I know that. So what?'

'All I was saying was that we must get some leaves from the jack-fruit tree in Santra's backyard—we also need four banana fronds. Many such items have to be arranged by tomorrow.'

'Of course these will be arranged. You have run out of kusa grass. Let me remind you now. Don't make a fuss later.'

'You are right. The first thing I must get from somewhere tomorrow morning is kusa grass. Well, we have time for that. Have the children gone to bed. . .let's get up now. I was just pondering. . .'

'Forget it. You're always brooding.'

Mother and Wife

'Didn't I tell you? Seventeen days of this month have gone by. Do you still hope he'll send us money? You got upset when I warned you then, but are you convinced now? I can always tell how things are. I can even count the feathers of a bird in flight. How can he fool me?'

'You are an utter fool. Read his letter. He writes, "Nana, this month my younger son fell ill and I had to spend a lot of money. . .so I couldn't send you any. Please manage somehow." You don't spare a thought for the ailing child, and you blame your son for failing to send you money.'

'Don't tell me that the child is down with some serious illness. The bangle-seller told me yesterday or the day before, that he saw my two grandsons playing on the road and that he sold my daughter-in-law bangles worth a rupee-and-a half. And how can I believe that the children are ill? If someone doesn't want to send money, he'll always find some excuse or the other.'

'All right. Let him not send any money, if he doesn't want to. There's nothing to worry about. He has only just begun to earn. And I have been supporting such a large family like ours for forty long years by the grace of Lord Lakshminarayan, haven't I? If he is in difficulties, let him not send any money and let him look after his own family. We'll be content if he lives happily. After all, his salary is only fifty-five rupees. How can he survive?'

'When he was home last he himself told me, "Mother, my job fetches me a few rupees on the side. At least four or five rupees come into my hands daily. Or else, how can I send fifty out of the fifty-five rupees I receive as my salary every month?" It was only because his wife and children were here that he never forgot to send fifty rupees every month. Now his family is no longer staying with us. Why should he bother to send us any money? I'm sure he'll never give us any money. Here, I'll tie a knot in my saree end. I don't care if he forgets us all. All my children have now grown up. So why should I drop to my knees before him and beg for help? Tukua will be eight in the month of Baisakh this year. And in a few years' time, he too will be able to look after himself when he's picked up a few things at school. These days one does not have to travel long distances to find a bride for a son as one had to in the past. If God keeps him alive and well, dozens of girls will be offered to Bhaiga by their parents. He can then marry whomever he likes.'

'Don't worry. I am not past work yet. If I could raise Raghu, I certainly can help settle the others in life. The thought that a son like Raghu could do this, hurts me.'

'Has brother sent a letter, mother? What does he say?'

Bhaiga now looked big and strong like his father. He had taught himself how to perform priestly chores. On occasions when Dase did not feel like going to the temple he asked his son to offer worship to Lord Lakshminarayan. Raghunath took up a job. So it would fall to Bhaiga to carry on the tradition of priestly duties at the temple.

'What'd he say? He writes to say that he will not send money this month, nor afterwards.'

Tuku's mother answered the queries made by her son as tactfully as possible. For his part, Dase listened to them in silence.

'Is sister-in-law behind what brother is doing?'

'Everyone is like that. When you get married and set up home you'll do the same thing. Once you set eyes on your wife's face the rest of the world will cease to matter. As for your old parents, you would want them to die as early as possible, for that'd be a great relief.'

'Just because one son behaves like this, do you think everyone else will follow his example?'

'I have seen it all, my son. And the lessons have been learnt. A mother carries the baby in her womb for ten long months, then raises him, and goes through all kinds of hardships to settle him in life. But the son becomes a complete stranger to her the day he marries, for he finds a new mother in his wife. Whatever she now whispers into his ears becomes as sacred and indisputable as the words of the Vedas for him.'

A little embarrassed, Bhaiga said, looking at the wall, 'Don't think it happens like that. Not so easy.'

'Well, your time to take care of us will come one day. I have kept some flattened and sugared rice in a basket on the sika. The others have eaten. There's a little curd in an aluminium saucer kept in the recess in the kitchen wall. Have that as well. Or wait. Let me prepare it for you. You'll not find these things. All of you are useless, like your father. A thing might be lying under his nose. Yet he'll run around, looking for it and never find it.'

Bhaiga followed his mother meekly, like a good boy, scratching his head. Bata, Jayi and Tukua were fast asleep after their midday meal. But God knows how they sensed that mother was going to give Bhaiga something to eat. They woke up, got together, and went down to the veranda of the inner wing of the house. Dase in the front room, could see everything that was going on.

Batia leaned over, hands resting on his knees, and asked, 'What's this, mother?'

'You stuffed yourself with this and went to sleep. And now you want to find out what it is. Wait. Your elder brother hasn't eaten yet. Let me give him some of this first. Now you all come running to me when you feel hungry and pester me. But who cares for his mother once he gets married?'

The same topic would come up again and be elaborated on. Dase knew this would happen. So he paid no attention to it and opened his son's letter again and went through its contents.

What had happened to the boy's handwriting? Every letter now had a tail at least a cubit and a half long! *I salute my revered father a million times.* May God give you a very long life, my dear son. May Lord Jagannath bless you with success in all your efforts. *The younger child has been ill for the last seven days. I took him to the government hospital. I was told that government employees got free medicine. But that's a lie. Perhaps the important people do not have to pay for medicines. But these benefits are not for people like us. I bought an injection. Going to and from the hospital in a rickshaw also cost a lot of money. I brought my son home two days ago. He is a little better now, but is still on medication. I so much wanted to send some money— if not fifteen rupees, at least ten—home. But even this much was difficult to arrange. Try to get by somehow. My wife sends you and mother her respects.*—Dase smiled to himself and thought, 'Shameless fellow. Says my wife.' He folded the letter carefully and put it aside. What's the matter with the child? He turned out to be frail and sickly. The poor child is in such bad shape. And this stupid woman learnt from some bangle-seller that he was playing on the road. That bangle-seller is an old wind-bag. Of course, he has to tell a few sweet lies to women to get them to buy his stuff. Anyway, forget it. Women are like that. It is said: 'They are with you as long as you can put money into their hands; you stop doing that, they turn away and completely forget you.' Take the case of our Raghunath. She lavished praise on him as long as he was sending money. See what happens when he couldn't send money just once?

Get lost, you foolish woman. Why should he give you money, tell me? God has blessed him with children. Will you come to his rescue when he finds himself in trouble? No, no, you'll never do that. All you want is to milk him dry. Why should it matter if he stops sending money? You hear same story everywhere, in all families. The son sets up home on his own the day he gets married. Since we are brahmins we are expected to live together. Living together and having one hearth for all suits only those families who have land, because they become poor if they separate and parcel out their ancestral property. As people like us have no land, we manage to get by somehow. It's fine if our son wants to perform his filial duty by supporting his old parents as best as he can. But he commits no sin if he feels it is beyond his means to do his duty to us. What is Indramani, who is now a big shot, doing? But the Lord has been kind to his father. He now has land, and lives so well that he looks young for his age. He is a clever person, one who knows the ways of the world. He explained to me, 'The times have changed. One's children can never live in peace if we cling to them like leeches and suck them dry. They don't have to be told, for they are not unlettered fools. They'd look after their parents, if they really felt like it. Indramani tells me that the sahibs never live with their parents after they get married. They marry only after they are able to earn their own livelihoods.' What if he is a learned pundit? He can never resist the temptation to show off. No one would deny that he has asked his son not to send him any money. But don't forget that he made sure Indramani looked after his younger brother Chandramani and his sister. Nilakantha would now not have to bother about the expenses of raising these two. The rest of his children are still very young. So he does not have to worry about them at all. So doesn't it amount to the same thing in the end? It's all the same if you hold someone down to kill him, or tie him up to do him in. Our sons are good for nothing.

Or else, wouldn't they have stayed with Raghu and received a little education? If Raghu could not help his brothers in this way, how do we get by if he fails to send a little money every month? After all, he is no pathan or phiringi that he'd leave his family and set up a separate home after his marriage.

The words reached his ears. 'She'll be everything to you. One look at her face, and you'll not care for heaven, earth or the nether world. We'll see how much your mother will matter to you then. Who knows if I'll live to see that day.'

The words made the children, who were now no strangers to the facts of life, fidget. Bhaiga, his eyes lowered, continued to eat in silence.

Dase thought, 'Tuku's mother is right. People really change after they get married. Women are enchantresses, after all, for they have mastered all the four arts of seduction. But why say that they have mastered these arts? Nature endows them with these skills when they take birth. When men set eyes on them, they come under such a spell that nothing in the world matters any more. And they melt like wax. How strange all this is. Someone who was an absolute stranger a moment ago becomes everything in the world to a man. Think of our old Pradhan. He is a very pious man now, who does good deeds and helps the needy. But I've known him since he was a child. He would run around naked catching phirikas even when he was a big boy. A black ram was very fond of him, and he would take it wherever he went. This ram had already been pledged to the goddess by Pradhan's father. The day it was sacrificed before the goddess, Pradhan, his face covered in tears and snot, ran like mad through the village, bleating like a sheep. He refused to eat, left home the next day and went off to his maternal uncle's village. Amid all this, he never said a single harsh word to his father. But when he got married, the same Pradhan made his father's life miserable. One day a quarrel broke out and Pradhan did not hesitate to give his old father a blow or two. The shock drove the old man to bed. He never recovered from it, and died. We all knew his son was close-fisted, but we had never expected that he would do such a thing. What a terrible thing he did, under his wife's influence! Women are like a strong intoxicant, which when it hits you, blots out your sense of right and wrong. They even make sages lose their balance.'

'You want a piece of this?'

'No I had my midday meal late and haven't digested it yet. Put it away. I'll have it later, if I feel hungry.'

Bata, Jayi and Tukua came running in, wiping their mouths. They ran out on to the village track.

'Hey, Bata. Where are you taking these two? It's still hot outside. Why must you go out at this hour?'

'We are going to play on the veranda of Gopa's house.' Saying this, he ran away.

Bhaiga walked towards the bedroom after rinsing out his mouth. Tuku's mother followed him, carrying a fan. She would fan her son to sleep.

Dase felt amused.

Disappointed by her eldest son, this old woman now nurses the hope that her second son would look after her. These women really can't do without some support. All their life they have to placate one and please another in order to get by. Life is not possible without women who are at the same time the source of all mischief. They are at the root of all the conflicts and quarrels—it's they who are at the core of the Ramayana and the Mahabharata.

They are pitiably weak creatures. Like creepers they wind themselves around you. But soon their grip tightens and they crush you to death. It is said women are enchantresses. God has given them the power to bewitch men. Or else, would anyone bother to so much as look at them? Creation itself would have ceased to exist. Didn't a group of young men stalk the daughter of Janaka, the herd, wherever she went? However, the poor girl sought some relief by getting married to one of them. This is how the world goes on. Everyone wants to enter family life by setting up a house, complete with a wife and children. And maya, in the form of women, keeps the world going. In their different roles, as mother, wife, sister and daughter, they keep men entangled in the coil of earthly desires. They know the art of getting cream out of water. If they did not possess this skill the world would have seemed unreal, eerily empty. The world would hold no charm for men if women did not fill their hearts with desire. It is they who make men love life; it is also women who lead them into a snare and undo them! Strange creatures, these women! Strange are their ways! Looked at from one angle a woman seems so innocent, so vulnerable, as if she would collapse if you did not support her. Looked at from the other, she reveals herself to be a veritable python, which winds itself tightly around the victim, pulverizing him. We, stupid fellows do a funny thing. We say, protect women from men who surround them on all sides like tigers on the prowl. They are defenseless doves. Fools, they are the tigresses. There is no man who can ever give them the slip. You always hear them wail 'I am defeated,' but in reality, it's they who always win. Everywhere, in their role as defenseless, vulnerable creatures, they cast a spell such as would cripple warriors like Sumbha and Nisumbha and finish a warrior like Birochan. They make demons like Mandargiri, who could shake a mountain, sag. Men, like demons, drink the bewitching beauty of Mohini with their eyes, but not a drop of nectar fell on the leaves spread before them.

Oh, these women are the deadliest weapons in the hands of Lord Vishnu. To make sense of their nature is to understand Lord Vishnu's maya. Hasn't it been said, 'The nature of women and the fate of man are beyond the grasp of deities, not to speak of mere human beings.' The one who takes the whole creation as his playground, uses these women to play hide and seek with us. When man is young and energetic, these women come from nowhere and encircle him. In the game they play with man, he discovers that all his escape routes are blocked by women who link hands. But it is easier said than done. They circle you all the time, trying to suck you in like eddies in the river Mahanadi. 'Gho gho queen, your feet are under water, gho gho queen, now you are waist deep in water. Gho gho queen, you are chest deep in water.' In this manner, you will drown slowly and finally disappear under water.

Take Hanuman, the great wrestler of the Treta yuga, and a great yogi and devotee. Even someone like that was defeated by Surasa, the demoness. The larger he grew in size, the wider her mouth became. Defeating her was simply impossible. So, if one cannot win using one's strength, one has to use one's wits. Make yourself small, enter her mouth, and let her believe that she has swallowed you up. Happy, she'll close her eyes and gulp you down. But she'll soon discover that Hanuman has slipped out of her nostrils. If you think you can ever deny them their share, you are utterly mistaken. They long for worldly attachments; so yield your body to them and let them savour the pleasure of family, wealth, and fame. But make sure your soul slips out of this net somehow. Or else they will devour you completely and their fiery hunger reduce you to ashes.

A cow must eat grass. So she must be taken out to graze. Leave her to wander in the field and relax under some tree, playing on a flute. If you let her go hungry for long, one day she will sink her teeth into your body and tear a piece off. If you want to save your soul, offer up your body. Let them have this worthless thing of clay. You'll lose nothing by giving it away but again, it is easier said than done.

Dase put a little chewing tobacco into his mouth. Eyes closed, he sat leaning against the wall for a while. He moved his hand gently over his head and smiled to himself. He thought to himself, 'What's the point of dwelling on these philosophical matters? They have nothing to do with real life. Tell me, who doesn't know that women are enchantresses? How many have been able to stay away from them? As a form of maya, she is a blind force, irresistibly powerful. The poor soul can only watch helplessly, like someone who is lame. Of course, the body and the soul must remain together for creation to be possible. However, both will go far, if, as in the story of Trinath, the lame points the way to the blind who carries him on his shoulder. But, such is the influence of the blind that the lame one's eyes will grow dim and he'll see nothing. He'll end up falling into some ditch.'

'Why sleep in this position? If you are feeling sleepy lie down properly.'

'Oh, why did you startle me? Get me a jug of water. I'm thirsty.'

'Would you like to have some ukhuda?'

'Well, bring me some.'

The Five-yearly Vote

'**D**rink it slowly.'
'First take the cup and hold it. I'll go out and look at the two motor cars that now stand in the middle of the village square where we have sankirtans.' Saying this Bata put the cup down on the veranda, and bounded away in a flash.

Picking up the cup, Tuku's mother said, 'It seems there'll be another election. Or else, why would motor cars come to the village? This farce will now go on for quite a while. Trash!'

'Mother, I want to go and have a look at the motor cars,' Jayi said, whining, and tugging at his mother's saree.

'Why didn't you say so when Bata went off. You could have gone with him then.'

'I'll go.'

'Go, who's stopping you? Go now. Let me sweep the floor. Bata will also be there. Go.'

Rice was on the boil. The bhog, which Dase brought from the temple now and then, would not be enough. Something else had to be cooked in order to have a proper meal. The children were all playing outside after their meal of puffed rice in the morning. It would be quite late by the time Dase returned from the temple. Tuku's mother swept the floor, munching a handful of puffed rice.

Ever since that beggar's daughter left the house, a heavy weight seemed to have been removed. We'll get by somehow. That crafty woman cajoled our son into leaving us. She's so cunning you can never tell what move she'll make when. A man like our son Raghunath clings to her day and night. What a shame! But what can he do, after all. She turned him into a sheep by casting a spell on him. Anyway, let her do whatever she likes. I don't care. I'm not a helpless woman. Lord Lakshminarayan has blessed me with another four sons. I don't have to throw myself at her feet and beg for help.

She put another handful of puffed rice into her mouth and made her way to the upper veranda, broom in hand.

Oh, how much dust their feet bring into the house. You sweep once; in no time, the place becomes dirty again.

Oh, what have they got against the edge of this veranda? I must have plastered it with mud at least a thousand times. But before two days are out they break it up. How does one control this herd of monkeys. Look, how badly they have damaged this part of the veranda.

If I had seen which of you did this mischief I'd have hung him upside down.

'We are going to have an election, mother, an election. They are distributing pieces of coloured paper near their motor cars. Look at these.'

Tired from running, Bata was gasping, unable to speak clearly.

'Tell me, who has damaged the edge of this veranda?'

'I don't know. Oh, how wonderful that motor car is. It has four big wheels—one here, one there, another here, and another there. Yet one more wheel is fixed to its body. So many people have gathered there. Someone is singing from inside a machine. Keep these pieces of paper with you. I'll go and get a few more.'

'Hey, have you seen Jayi? He went off to be with you.'

'No, I haven't.'

Bata ran off.

Tuku's mother turned the pieces of paper, looking at them closely. Her right hand held the broom.

Look! The same pair of oxen again. What happened that year is going to take place again this year.

She folded the pieces of paper and put them on a cross beam.

Where did Jayi go? He is already nine or ten, but as timid as ever. Poor Tukua was asleep. If he had been awake, he would have enjoyed all this fun.

Tuku's mother went down to the lower veranda. Rice was cooking in the fireplace. She must go and see if it was cooked.

Tukua woke up, and, as soon as he opened his eyes, he called his mother.

'Have you woken up, my dear? Wait, I'll be with you in a minute. I'll give you some puffed rice.'

With Tukua busy eating puffed rice, his mother happily set about finishing all the household chores. When she worked undistracted, she did so at a pace no one could match. In no time she could cook seven different curries to go with the rice. But the poor thing was worn out having borne eight children. Not that she looked thin. In fact, she was quite plump. But these days she found it difficult to stand up. She had to place her hands on her knees for support. Her back grew stiff if she exerted herself a little. Despite this, she did manage to do all the housework. After her daughter-in-law left, she had had to do everything—wiping the floors, keeping things in order, cooking, fetching water from the well, and sweeping the large courtyard and the long veranda. Work like this could break one's back. But she managed it all.

When she had entered this house as a bride, she had brought seven cartloads of things. She was from a wealthy family, the only daughter in a family of four brothers. Their big stone house had so many wings that your voice would not carry from one end to the other. Her uncle's paan pouch was full of so many kinds of spices. Adorned with brass studs and decorated with many coloured pictures, the pouch was so heavy it wasn't easy to lift. Her father and his three brothers would sit in the cutcherry, chatting, and chewing paan. From the kitchen all manner of dishes would be sent over to them. . . Their mother would get impatient and worried, for she feared there'd be little food left for her sons after her grandchildren had had their meals. She had been blessed with these four sons after she had showered a hundred thousand champak flowers on Lord Mahadev. What hadn't she gone through to have her sons! They hadn't eaten although it was so late. She would pace up and down restlessly all over the house, walking-stick in hand. The cutcherry was out of bounds for her. So she would send her grand-daughter there. Tuku's mother was the little girl Kuni, then. 'O my dear Kuni, go and call your father and your uncles that they must eat now. The rice left at the bottom of the pot has gone dry and is full of grit.' But the brothers were too busy talking to listen to her.

Kuni would go to the cutcherry munching some cream or sweets, or some toasted rice coated with sugar. Her eldest uncle would make her sit on his lap, knead perfumed khair and paan on his palm and give the mixture to her. She could not remember for how long she had been chewing paan. The cutcherry would be littered with the brass utensils in which food had been carried there. Three to four water jugs would be lying in the room. Some people from Ratanpur would be there sweet-talking the brothers in the hope of getting a little money from them. Kuni would forget all about her grandmother, and enjoy herself, seated in her uncle's lap, chewing paan and reddening her lips. A sweet smell of sandal paste rose from her uncle's body. His hair was gathered into a top-knot and champak flowers were tucked in his ears. There would come the sound of someone tapping softly on the door. Who was it? It was none other than grandmother. She would open the door a crack and say, 'It is getting so late. Why don't you all get up and come in. The women in the house have almost collapsed like doors unhinged. And don't forget that one of them has just delivered a baby. How can you be so inconsiderate?' The four brothers would hurriedly rise to their feet. Eldest uncle would say, 'Why did you not send a word through someone, mother? Why did you take the trouble of coming all the way here?' The four would follow their mother into the house.

'Does anyone care if I send a word through somebody? I sent your beloved daughter, the little princess, to you. See what she did! She stayed back to chew paan and snuggle up to her uncle.' Uncle would pat his niece's head and lie to his mother, 'She did in fact call us, but we were so absorbed in our conversation we paid no heed. We have a gem of a daughter, haven't we?'

His words would make his niece blush.

However, she did not receive the same affection from her father, who petted her but rarely.

The four brothers would go with their mother to the kitchen veranda. The much washed stone floor was a shiny black. Rice in four large plates would be placed before four seats made from jack-wood. There would be a large fish head by the plate of one uncle. Beside the plate of the other would be a silver dish containing cumin seeds and a handful of large green chilies fried in clarified butter. After his meal, father had to have a huge enduri cake, fresh from the earthen pot and steaming. His elder brother insisted on a potful of milk covered with thick skin, red like lac dye. This had to be boiled with powdered ginger wrapped in a piece of cloth, and sprinkled with a little ground pepper. Before he began eating, he would dip his finger into the milk pot to make sure it was neither too hot nor too cold. Only then would he think it was fit to drink. He would seat his niece on his left side. Two of his brothers would sit a little apart. Father would be seated on his right side. In the middle would sit grandmother, a fan in hand. Sundry topics would come up in the course of having their meal; there would be much laughter—anyway, why dwell on all this?

How times had changed! Things came to such a pass that men like these had to grovel before others for help. After the brothers died, that wonderful house had fallen to pieces. Raghu and his ill-fated brothers, whom death soon snatched away, were born by then—the brothers would send five rupees through a man every month for her paan expenses. Once every two months, the bangleseller would give her bangles and collect the price from her uncles in Ratanpur. First, her father's elder brother passed away. Then, in the space of only three years one after another, the other three died. They had built such a large house, but now it lay in ruins.

Maybe because she was all alone, memories of the past kept haunting her.

She had had a bath before she started cooking in the morning. She had no time to have a wash after finishing the household chores. Her hands and feet were covered with dust.

A strange nameless grief gnawed at her heart. The more she tried to compose herself, the more oppressive it grew. Tears rolled down her cheeks. She was wiping them with the end border of her saree when Bhaiga came in.

'Mother. Mother. Where are you? Tukua, tell me where is she?'

She collected herself with an effort and replied, 'I'm here. What do you want?' Her sorrowful voice, wet with tears, made Bhaiga, who had strode in triumphantly to boast of some great deed, freeze.

He hurriedly got off the veranda and went up to his mother. He saw tears in her eyes.

'Mother, you are crying!'

'It's nothing my son. Memories of times gone by returned to wrench my heart. Where have you been for so long?'

Assured that the matter was not serious, even if not quite natural, Bhaiga now began. 'There will be another election this year, mother. Two or three political parties will fight their battles here—you know, two motor cars came early in the morning. After a while they were joined by two more. It's beyond me to describe the fierce battle of words which followed. It was like a Badi Pala. The two cars that came earlier were handing out leaflets in the square when the other two cars stopped at a distance of only forty feet from them. A member of the second party put his mouth to a machine and began shouting. The loud noise echoed through the whole village. Everyone came running. Now someone in the party that had arrived earlier began shouting.'

'Yes, I heard some strange noise. It must have been made by those cars.'

'You are right. We had great fun. They raised flags tied to the top of bamboo poles and sang songs. One of them, his face painted, even danced. A contest between the two rival parties to attract a larger crowd began. Now something interesting happened: a man got on to the top of the motor car which had brought in the second party. Two large bundles were placed on either side of this man. He took out handfuls of sugar-coated lozenges and gave them away. In no time he was surrounded by a noisy crowd of children, who were soon joined by grown-ups. See, I have brought four lozenges. Taste one. You'll find it smells exactly like an orange.'

'You have them. Give two to Tukua.'

'I have more with me. I'll give him some. Why don't you have one?' She got up, taking a lozenge, which Bhaiga was holding out before her mouth. She had to have a wash.

Bhaiga continued to suck his lozenge, 'Once the lozenges drew everyone to that motor car, the other two left the place, blowing their horns loudly. There'll be great fun when they return in the evening.'

'Oh, Narayan!' Dase entered uttering. He carried a large brass plate covered with a banana leaf. Bhog from the temple. He placed it in a corner of the veranda and said, 'Bring me a jug of water, Bhaiga. I want to wash my feet.' Bhaiga brought a jug of water and put it on the upper veranda. After a wash, Dase settled himself. A lozenge in his mouth, and two sticky lozenges held tightly in his palm, Tukua fixed his eyes on his father.

'What is it that you are holding so tight? Show me.'

Tukua had put all the four lozenges into his mouth to find out how they tasted. He now opened his fist and showed the lozenges. His mother came in, four lozenges in her hand.

'Where have Jayi and Bata gone? I don't see them here. I am sure they are with the canvassers, listening to songs from the gramophone. Oh, now that the election has come, these rogues will have a great day. I saw the campaigners on my way home. Brunda Nahak had joined them.'

'Why should it bother you? Would you like to have green chillies with fried badis, or you want me to roast a few dry chillies?' Tuku's mother asked, seated near the fireplace.

'Give me a roasted chilli. I admit it is none of my business. But see what a calculating fellow Brunda Nahak is. Listen to this. Those who came in the motor car got down, and were busy doing whatever they came to do. This Nahak sat inside the car, sweating, and looked at everyone out of the car window, and talked to them about the election. When he caught sight of me, he said, 'Dase, these people have again come to you.' He mentioned the name of one baboo—I forget who— and said that he was a candidate this time. He went on, 'This gentleman invited me home, was very hospitable, took me into his confidence and told me that no one in the village should have any cause for complaint. If any one had any problem, he would certainly sort it out. It would not matter in the least if you did not vote for him; all he wanted you to do was to give him a chance to serve your village. He would change this village beyond recognition. The villagers would see for themselves, there was no need for him to elaborate. . .' He went on and on like this. I thought he would come out of that suffocating cage and talk, but he wanted to sit in the car and lecture. Of course, how could he let go of a chance to find himself inside a car? The fool thought he had got the opportunity to fly in an aeroplane. I have paid this month's tax. So I wasn't scared of him. I said, 'All right, Nahake. I must go now. I am late.' He said, very politely, 'Yes, yes. Please go.' Normally, he would never utter a word like 'Please.' But today he was the picture of politeness. Shameless rogue.'

'Bhaiga was saying that this time two or three parties will fight this election.'

'What fight? It will be a grand farce. Brunda Nahak will run like mad from one motor car to another. There will be a lot of noise like there was the last time. In the end, as soon as this voting business is over, Brunda Nahak will finish the construction of his house which has lain half-built for the last two years. This is all there is to the whole thing. All the rest is of no account.'

'Get up now. You always talk like this. All your life you have maligned others. How does it matter to you if someone built a house, or how he went about building it?'

'Oh, you misunderstand everything I say. Whenever I tell the truth, it seems to you as if I am speaking ill of someone. I should never tell you anything.'

Dase came and sat down on the veranda. A cool breeze blew, fanning his face. He spread his towel on the veranda and lay down. Plastered with a paste of burnt straw and fresh cowdung, the veranda felt very clean.

On second thought, how does it matter to me what someone else does? Why should I bother if Brunda Nahak constructs a house? There is no point in lowering oneself in the eyes of others by speaking ill of someone. Anyway. One may keep quiet about it, but it is difficult not to notice what Brunda Nahak did that year. Like a leech with two mouths he sucked both the parties fighting the election. The candidates never turned up. Perhaps they had been asked not to, for some reason. They sent others to plead with people to vote for them. Those who came here were their servants, and worked for whoever paid them for their services. These people can work miracles. Like betalas they fly from one place to another. Like a ghost calling from a shami tree, they scream from some instrument and make the earth quake. They have mastered the arts of enchantment. They'll burst into laughter one moment and sing and dance the next.

They charm everyone, using all manner of tricks. They are great experts and know how to talk. With the power of their words they can sweep people off their feet. Never underestimate these fellows. The moment they set foot in the village, Brunda Nahak will unfailingly join them. Government officers will come, a room for people to cast their votes in will be found, an awning made of coconut branches will be set up in front of it. And it will be Brunda Nahak who will organize all this. The officer, like a fool, will hand him the money. Last time, their truck got stuck in the sand of the river bed. Nahak got the young men of the village to lop off branches and lay them on the sand. The truck was driven over these with great difficulty. Later we were told that Nahak asked for and got money for all this, which he quietly pocketed. Where would the officer stay during the polling time? Brunda Nahak found a place for him to stay. What would he eat? No problem. . . The fishermen cast their nets into the village pond and caught fish. Nahak brought the fish and organized a kitchen. Two fish were sent to Nahak's house; the other two were sold to the sahibs at five rupees. The officer wanted eggs. Nahak got a few eggs from Palei's house. To the officer he said, 'We are poor people. Who among us can afford eggs? Give us whatever price the government has fixed for these. Palei wants only eight annas.' When the officer looked askance at him, Nahak understood and hastened to add, 'All right, huzoor, six annas will do. That's final. I'll tell Palei. Things like this don't happen every day. We must be very lucky to get an opportunity to set eyes on great people like you.'

He arranged a boy from somewhere, and organized a tea-stall at the polling station. The boy took his meals at Nahak's place. When the sahib was busy working, Nahak would bustle in, breathless, stop and ask. 'Huzoor, should I bring some tea?' That day the young officer could not have drunk fewer than forty cups of tea. It was as if Brunda Nahak kept pouring tea into the officer's mouth, and the officer kept gulping it. When it was time for the polling party to pack up and leave, Brunda Nahak got the villagers to leave the place, and approached the sahib. But Palei managed to stay behind and listened to all that passed between Nahak and the officer. After all, wasn't Palei the grandson of that wicked old woman, who could not help eavesdropping on people before she entered their house? Nor did she forget to linger on the veranda for a minute trying to eavesdrop while leaving. She was notorious for quarrelmongering. . . Like seed, like sapling. Palei went round the back, and listened to everything.

'It's government money, after all. If huzoor wants, any amount can be spent. Just a fistful flung with your left hand could end these people's misery and help them survive. I am not pleading for myself, huzoor. This poor boy opened a tea shop; he had also supplied provisions for huzoor's polling party. He would not dare come before huzoor and ask for payment. It is on his behalf that I humbly beg for only sixty rupees. He says he had spent fifty-seven rupees, and his wages come to rupees five. I'll tell him to forget about two rupees. Huzoor, please give him sixty rupees.' The sahib took out the money and handed it to Nahak, who put it into his bag. Palei saw everything and told everyone in the village about it the very next day. The villagers made Nahak's life miserable. They couldn't stop talking about his misdeed. At last, fearing loss of face, he donated ten rupees to Lord Lakshminarayan's temple fund. Otherwise a seasoned thief like Brunda Nahak, given half a chance, would think nothing of gobbling up property belonging to gods or brahmins.

Even such an unpleasant experience did not cure him of his bad old habits. See how he is back again at the election business this year. How can he stay away, having tasted blood once? The same things will take place again. People will go from house to house distributing pieces of paper. Brunda Nahak will be with them. But he will never approach them openly; he will whisper into my ears, 'Listen Dase, you and I are but one soul. We are of the same age. You are as bald as I am. Isn't that a marvel? It is amazing how both of us have a bald patch in the same spot. You and I are of one mind. Nothing separates you from me. Anyway, since you know all this, I need not elaborate. Never say yes or no to anyone before consulting me. I'll come when it's time and tell you which box you should put your ballot paper into. You will do as I tell you. Will you hesitate to trust me after we have been together for so long? There is another thing I want to tell you, which I haven't told anyone else.' He'll go on like this. No matter how sensible you are you can't help falling under the spell of his words. Later, you'll find out what a clever show it all was; he would have said the same thing to everyone. People like Brunda Nahak are extremely dangerous; for them nothing matters except their self-interest. It is best to keep a safe distance from them. They belong to a race of predators. They will pamper you as long as they have work with you. After it is over, you cease to exist for them.

But come to think of it. All this farce took place only because people had to put a piece of paper into that ballot box. What was the use of so many rules, so much care? Everything is fixed well in advance. How did it matter, where you cast your ballot paper, who got elected, what happened if he got elected—no one had the time to bother about such matters. Vote where the people of your village tell you to. Can one go against the wishes of one's fellow-villagers? How could one look them in the face when one met them the next day? After all, who got elected made not the slightest difference to us. Our food or clothes were not going to get any cheaper. Things were becoming so expensive these days it seemed impossible to get on. Who cared who got the votes. The best thing was to give one's vote to whomever one chanced upon first and live in peace for a few years afterwards.

'Hey, what were the two of you doing there for so long?'

Bata and Jayi came in, hand in hand.

'That gramophone played so many songs. We were listening to them.'

'All right. Go now. That funny instrument made a strange noise like some animal, and these two fools wasted two hours listening to it. Go and tell your mother we will all eat now.'

A Prayer

Om apohistha mayobhuba stana urje dadhatana, maherayana chakshase.

Dusk was approaching. Seated on the veranda, Dase was preparing to say his evening prayers. Bhaiga had gone to the temple to offer worship. A feeling of unhappiness had been oppressing Dase all day long. How could one feel happy with two patients in the house? This woman never fell ill, but she spent so much time nursing Jayi, she too would certainly catch the fever. Someone in every house in the village was down with it. How could we escape? Comforting himself in this way, Dase offered his prayers.

Someone in a shabby shawl walked past his house. Dase could not figure out who it was.

Who was it? Oh how deserted the village felt. All doors were bolted so early. Not even a bird twittered now.

Suddenly a cursed dog in the distance lifted its head and set up a howl which sounded like a human cry. Dase felt disturbed. However, he collected himself and resumed chanting his prayer—*Om asana mantrasya meruprustha rushih, sutali chhaadah, Sri kurmo devata, asana suddhaye biniogah.*

That day the weather too was terrible. If only they had a heavy rain, this feeling of discomfort would give way to one of relief. But it did not rain, and the clouds did not disperse. A few drops of rain fell, then the wind dropped. One did not feel like stepping into the house. One felt suffocated. It was drizzling outside. How could one go out in such weather to get medicines or do anything for that matter? Oh, a really sensible man should do everything to avoid worldly life. Once you enter it, there was no end to your misery. No matter how wonderful a human being you were, you ended up being utterly worthless, once enmeshed in the web of earthly attachments. No, I am not going to that Baikunthia. Who would spend two days waiting in front of his house like a supplicant? This fever epidemic has been a godsend for Baikunthia. You have to pay to see him, you have to pay to talk to him. Put the money before him and then move your lips. He would prescribe a couple of nostrums, but these have to be taken with a thousand other things. To hell with him. I'm not going to him at all. *Om pruthitvaya dhruta lokah debituam Vishnuna dhruta. Tuancha dharya mam debi pabitramasanam kuru.*

Forget it. These enemies will rest only after they destroy me. First there was one patient in the house; now there is another. They will be my undoing. I had hoped that the son who has made his way in the world would help me out in times of crises. But he chooses to live away with his wife and children. Here everyone is crushed with misery. When everyone in the family was in good health, we needed little more than a poor man's diet, to get on somehow. With patients at home to care for, now, it seems as if everything is over for me. Where is the money for medicines? In the end I'll have to do what Tuku's mother asked me to do: I'll take that brass pitcher to old Patra, pawn it and collect whatever he chooses to give me. What else can I do?

The dog howled again. The sky seemed to lower itself. It kept drizzling. Dase opened his eyes. He could hear Bata and Tukua chatting in a room in the inner wing of the house. And yet the house seemed eerily empty. Just at this time, someone carrying a hurricane lamp approached from the other side of the village. Half walking and half running, the man approached Dase's house. He was going in the direction of the river. Dase now recognized him.

'Isn't it Gandhia? Where are you going so late in the night?'

'Who? Oh, Dase! Pundit's wife has taken ill. Today he got to know that Baikunthia Kabiraj is here since morning. Isn't Pakua Mishra his father-in-law? The Kabiraj has come from Patapur, and he is going to stay here for a few days. I should say our village is lucky to have him here. He has already been informed. I'm going to fetch him now.'

'Is Pundit Nilakantha at home? He must be. All right, I'll also go to his house. On the way back, I'll request the Kabiraj to step into my house. I'll ask Pundit Nilakantha to put in a word for me. I could tell him myself, but. . .'

'You are right, sir. The Kabiraj can never say no to Pundit. Let me proceed, sir.'

Feeling restless, Dase finished saying his prayers and rose to his feet.

'Oh, Hari Narayan—*Sarbe bhabantu sukhinah sarbe santu niramaya, sarbe bhadrani pashyantu ma kashchit dukha bhag bhabet*. Bata, my dear, bring the oil lamp to this room. Is your mother sleeping?'

'No, Nana. This Tukua insists he must sleep beside mother and he wants Jayi to move aside.'

'Oh, should you not keep that boy under control? Where is Tukua? Has he gone and lain beside his mother?'

Dase came to the inner wing of the house.

A small oil lamp hung from a nail driven into the wall. Its feeble light fell on two string cots placed side by side. The beds covered by two dirty quilts sagged and hung low like cloth bags. Darkness lay thick under the beds and spread itself under the lamp. The air in the room was heavy with the sickening smell of ghee, sunthi and garlic which blended with the smell of warm perspiration. Dase felt even more depressed than before. Just before he entered the room he stopped dead, startled by his own shadow on the wall. He felt a sudden pain in his chest. Just at this moment, the sickly black cat jumped over the threshold and darted away. His heart sank within his breast. To reassure himself, he said 'Teh-tch get lost, you inauspicious cat.'

Tukua lay in his mother's lap, pretending to be asleep. Jayi, too, was asleep. But he moaned. Dase bent down a little, gently felt his wife's forehead with his hand, and then removed his hand.

'Oh, she still runs a high temperature. What shall I do? The fever shows no signs of remission.'

'Let me see how this boy is doing'—he felt Jayi's forehead, and quickly removed his hand.

'He is running a high fever, and see how the idiot has thrown the blanket off his back.'

Dase covered Jayi with the blanket.

'Lift your legs a bit, Jayi. Pull this over yourself. You will begin to perspire soon. That's good. Now, go to sleep.'

'Tukua, come, my son, let us sleep in the other room. Hush hush. Don't make a noise. Don't you see mother is ill?'

He persuaded Tukua to go with him to the room in the upper wing of the house. Here he laid Tukua on a reed-mat with a sheet spread over it, his head on a pillow. Then Dase threw a shawl over his shoulders, picked up his walking stick, and went out. The road lay buried in darkness; and he had to grope his way along.

Before leaving he said, 'Bata. I'll be back soon. When Bhaiga comes, tell him I have gone to bring the Kabiraj from the pundit's house.'

The Kabiraj went to the pundit's house because he would get paid for his services. Why should people like us matter to him? Even if we pay him as much as he receives from the pundit, I wonder if he'll give us good medicine. Oh, what an excellent man Narayan Kabiraj was! You only had to utter his name to be cured. How sweetly he talked! His voice used to fill the hearts of his patients with hope. Alas, this man, who was like a loving father to all, is now no more. He had the magic touch; he would simply touch you and hand you a few leaves of duba grass and your illness would vanish. This bastard Baikunthia's hand is poisonous—a single touch and a year of your life was reduced to a day. He was also disgustingly tight-lipped when he talked; words seeming to issue from deep crevices. He had a foul, waspish temper. He chewed ten paans in an hour, and chewed them throughout the day like a goat. Nevertheless, people treated him with respect.

Why did someone in Pundit Nilakantha's family fall ill? Everyone there took good care of their health. . . Nonsense! What's the point of being careful? Isn't man's body a storehouse of diseases? How many ailments can you guard it against? The pundit's wife was a good woman, who observed vows and fasts without number. And the poor woman had gone down with fever! Why worry about people like us?

Dase smiled inspite of himself.

See, how the thought of others' suffering brings us comfort! The sight of someone else's misery makes us happy rather than saddening us! We feel reassured because we are not alone in our suffering; the disease has not spared a single family in the village. There is a patient even in a rich man's house. It seems one's grief grows less oppressive if one suffers in the company of others. How strange human nature is!

A light burned inside the pundit's house. How big his newly built house looked against the darkness. The fellow had spent a lot of money constructing it.

'Gandhia. Ei Gandhia!'

'Who is it?' A hurricane lamp in hand, Pundit Nilakantha came out on to the veranda. He raised the hurricane lamp and looked at Dase.

'Dase, what brings you to this part of the village at this hour?'

'I'll tell you later. First, tell me if Baikunthia Kabiraj has arrived.'

'Why do you ask? He hasn't arrived yet. I have sent someone to call him over. What happened? Is anyone ill in your family?'

'Not one, but two. My wife and that boy Jayi have been down with fever for ten days now. I thought the Kabiraj should take a look at them. But the problem is I don't know him that well. It'll help if you could put in a word for me.'

'That can be done. But the fact is he is a very busy man; everyone wants him to pay a visit to their families. All the same, there should be no problem. All you need to do is to pay the Kabiraj his fees. I'll tell him.'

'Tell me, your wife is down with the same fever, isn't she?'

'Oh, how many times I've told her that observing so many rituals and fasts will not take her to heaven. You can earn merit only if you stay alive. I have no objection to her doing these things within a limit. But all kinds of excesses should always be avoided. She has grown so thin, and she still runs a temperature. I think the Kabiraj has arrived.'

Dase saw the Kabiraj, a stout crooked stick in hand, walking behind Gandhia, who held a hurricane lamp.

Pundit Nilakantha received him with every mark of respect and ushered him in.

Baikunthia Kabiraj recognized Dase and enquired, 'How are you, Dase? Is everything going well?' But he did not wait for a reply, and Dase saw his crocodile-shaped gold earrings dance as he entered the house.

Dase thought that it mattered to the Kabiraj not in the least whether everything went well with him or not. He felt his own earrings dance. Never had he taken these off no matter how big a crisis had faced him. But times were so bad, he might have to sell them off one day. 'Well, let's wait and see. Things have not come to such a pass yet.'

Since Dase was sitting on the veranda, Gandhia had left the hurricane lamp burning there before he went inside. In its light Dase could see drops of rain falling through the air. Except the forecourt of the pundit's house, it was pitch dark all around. And the air was absolutely still. Dase stared unblinkingly into the dark void. He felt nervous and restless. After quite a while, he heard voices coming from the inner wing of the pundit's house. . . He felt a little relieved.

'I have given her a dose of medicine now. Give her another at midnight. The third dose she should take before sunrise. We'll decide the next course of action after seeing the patient in the morning. Send your man with me. I'll send some homemade honey through him. Dissolve two tablets in this honey and give it to the patient.'

The pundit, the Kabiraj and Gandhia now came to the outer veranda. Dase rose to his feet. The pundit said, 'Sir, there are two patients in Dase's house. Dase came here to ask you to visit his house on your way back.'

The Kabiraj looked up at Dase, while tying his shoe laces. The pundit added, 'Of course, he'll pay you your fees.'

'So, who in your family has taken ill?' asked the Kabiraj putting a paan into his mouth.

'My younger son Jayi and his mother have been lying ill and feverish for over ten days.'

'All right. Is your house on the way back?'

'Yes, sir.'

'Let me take leave of you, pundit. Don't worry at all. It is common these days to suffer from this fever, which is caused by an excess of bile. You have no reason to fear.'

'We have faith in your healing touch, sir.'

'Come with me. What's your name?'

'Gandhia sir,' he replied moving two steps ahead of the others, hurricane lamp in hand.

Not a word was exchanged while everyone walked down the village road.

When Dase arrived at the doorstep of his house, he said, 'Here, sir.'

'It seems we have passed this way earlier!'

'Yes, we have, sir. We could have taken another route which lies through the Bauri locality but that was circuitous.'

When Dase stepped into the house, he found it filled with smoke. He could not see anything.

'Hey Bata, has your elder brother come? Why is there so much smoke?' said Dase.

Bhaiga came to the upper veranda, rubbing his eyes hard and said, 'Mother felt thirsty. So I lit the fireplace to boil some barley water left over from the morning. I have already spent an hour blowing into the fireplace, but the firewood is not catching fire, it is only smouldering.'

Just at this time, the fire suddenly leapt up. Encircled by the smoke, the flames looked pale and sickly. Dase heard a voice saying from behind, 'Where are the patients, Dase? I can't see anything in this smoke.'

Dase started.

'Oh, they are in that room in the inner wing. Please come in.' He said this and stepped into the room. Baikunthia Kabiraj followed him, reluctantly. Dase set out a wooden stool—Raghu had brought this soon after getting a job—for the Kabiraj to sit on. The Kabiraj gently felt Tuku's mother's pulse for a while. Then he took a deep breath and sighed. He got up, saying, 'Let's now have a look at your son.'

How thin and stick-like Jayi's hand had grown in these few days! Oh God!

The Kabiraj examined his patient. He motioned to Bhaiga that he wanted to wash his hands. Bhaiga poured water from a tumbler.

Without uttering a word, the Kabiraj made his way straight to the outer veranda and stood there.

Dase felt his heart sink.

'What did you see, sir?'

'Both are down with the same fever. And this fever is difficult to cure. Not that there is no hope; but it'll take time.'

'Oh God, what shall I do?' Dase's voice broke, and he felt shaky and nervous.

'Let's get through the night somehow. Come to me tomorrow morning. I'll give you the medicine. And. . .all right. We'll talk about that tomorrow morning.'

The Kabiraj stepped out on the road. Gandhia led the way.

Not a word passed Dase's lips. After some time, when he heard the shuffling of Bhaiga and Bata's feet, he sighed deeply and quietly went inside. He felt as if his legs were giving way under him.

'Do you hear me?' A feeble voice called him from the inner wing of the house.

Dase instantly regained his strength and, in two strides, reached Tuku's mother. The two boys stood close beside him.

'What are you saying? How do you feel?'

'Why do you take the trouble of calling these Kabirajs and Vaidyas? They are thieves after all. Why pay them? In any case, where is the money? Oh. . . Bata, my son. One of my toes is getting cramped. Please straighten it out!' Bhaiga and Bata straightened the toe in no time. Bhaiga gently massaged his mother's legs. Bata stood by.

'May you live for a hundred years, my darling!'

'You wanted to drink barley water. The boys have boiled it. Let me bring you some.'

'Give it to Jayi. He said he felt thirsty.'

Dase brought barley water in a dish and woke Jayi.

'Get up, my son. Drink this and go back to sleep.'

High fever had parched Jayi's throat. He gulped down the barley water and threw himself on the cot. Breathing more easily now, he said. 'I want to lie down beside mother.'

'Mother is beside you sleeping on the other cot. There is no room on this cot for two. Stay where you are.'

Tuku's mother turned on her side painfully, faced Jayi and said, laying her hand on him, 'I'm here, my child. Go to sleep.'

Jayi went to sleep, resting against one of the sides of the cot, as if it was his mother.

'This boy had to leave my side when he was very small. So he always longs to be with me. He is a big boy now. But how he loves to sleep in his mother's lap! But this Tukua won't let him come anywhere near me.'

'That's right. Here, drink a little of this.'

'I don't feel thirsty now. Leave it under the cot. I'll drink it whenever I feel like it. You said you would do the cooking.'

'Yes, we'll do something. What is the hurry? It's not dark yet. Bhaiga, go and boil some water. Once the rice is cooked, roast three brinjals in the fireplace.'

'No, don't do any such thing,' enjoined Tuku's mother. 'Today is a Thursday. Instead cut the brinjals into two halves each, and boil them with the rice.'

The two sons and their father left the sick room. Bhaiga and Bata set about cooking. Dase sat quietly on the upper veranda.

Everything seemed like a dream to him. The next morning, the Kabiraj wouldn't give him medicine unless he handed over the money. By the time old Patra opened his shop, it would be late morning. Who knows how much he'll pay if the brass pitcher was pawned to him.

'The bastard said that this fever would not be cured easily. Why? Have we killed a cow or what? This is only a trick to make me pay up.'

'How much water should I add?'

'Take that large glass, and put two tumblerfuls into it.'

'No. No. One will do.' Tuku's mother protested. 'You need two tumblerfuls of water to cook rice for eight persons. Oh, the son is as useless as the father. These are utterly hopeless. And I am down with this fever.' Her voice came from the sick room quite disturbed.

'All right. Do whatever your mother says. Would you like to have a little barley water?'

'You all first eat. I'll drink it later.'

'All right. Bata get me some to drink.'

He felt much better after he drank it.

What's ordained will happen. What good will come out of worrying about it? But the poor child has suffered unspeakable tortures. It seems as if all vitality has drained out of his body, leaving only a little bit on the tip of his nose. Even so, this godforsaken fever refuses to relent, and boils the poor boy in a cauldron of pain.

It was quite late by the time the rice cooked. The water left in the rice was so little, it wouldn't drain. So to make it evaporate, they placed the pot on the fireplace again. Now the rice became extremely soft and soggy. Bata, Bhaiga and Tukua ate this rice somehow and went to sleep in a room in the upper wing of the house. Dase rolled out a reed mat on the veranda of the inner wing. Before lying down on it, he went into the sick room.

'Listen. Have you fallen asleep? Drink this barley water.'

Tuku's mother writhed in pain.

Her whole body seemed to be burning.

'Lie where you are. I'll pour it into your mouth, spoonful by spoonful. Now, open your mouth. That's good. Only two spoonfuls more. Fine. Now you go to sleep. Do you want to be covered with a blanket? You don't? All right, as you wish.'

Her eyes closed, Tuku's mother said, 'You too go and sleep. Oh— your body can't take the strain—it's too sensitive. . .no, no. Don't sleep by my side. Oh. Go now.'

'All right. I'm going. Don't be so restless. You'll get a headache. Try to sleep.'

Dase came out and stood in the courtyard. The sky remained overcast, but not a drop of rain fell. There were two patients in this wing of the house and in the other, the children slept. He felt deeply disturbed. All manner of worries crowded his mind. He also felt helpless. A strange shadowy fear seemed to creep over him.

'Oh Lord, Your will be done. If the Lord protects me, who can kill me, and if the Lord wants me destroyed, who can save me? Whatever is fated will come to pass. There is nothing that man can do.'

The reed mat lay on the veranda. Dase sat on it leaning against the wall for quite a while. At long last, his eyelids felt heavy and he dropped off into a deep sleep.

Later, Dase screamed in his sleep. He woke up, startled. He had broken into a cold sweat. He rushed into the sick-room, his heart pounding, oppressed by the fear of a calamity. He ran his hand over the mother and the child, and standing motionless, felt their breath. Oh. I feel life coming back to me—what a strange game you are playing, Oh Hari! Lakshmi Nrusingha, Lakshmi Nrusingha—saying this, Dase came back to the veranda and flopped down on the reed mat.

'Oh, what a terrible nightmare! How scary the grey eyes of the buffalo were! And that man, whose complexion was pitch black, filled the doorway, his head touching the ceiling. He was streaming with perspiration. On his head was a huge turban, and he carried a staff as big as that pole. Lord, O Hari, who saves us from all calamities, spare us this once. O Lord Janardan, save us from the jaws of death!' He then rose to his feet and emptied a whole jug of water into his mouth. He could sleep no more. Every so often the image of the nightmare recurred to him, and he repeated Lakshmi Nrusingha, Lakshmi Nrusingha.

The Dead Shall Never Rise

'Father. I can't bear to see you like this,' said Raghu as he knelt beside Dase, weeping.

It seemed as if Dase, who sat leaning against the wall, had become deaf and mute. His eyes, which had sunk into their sockets, stared unblinkingly. The world around him was full of such noise and wailing. But he appeared utterly deaf to it all.

Raghu had come home with his family two days ago. Baikunthia Kabiraj too, kept an all-night vigil. But when he could no longer feel the patient's pulse, he quietly informed Raghu and left. Incoherent with grief, adults and children alike now broke down and wailed like frightened animals. As for Dase, he sank slowly to the ground. But his eyes remained absolutely dry.

Raghu, to whom it fell to console everyone, broke down and wept. When he finally came to his father, he found him dumb struck. He shook him, called out to him—but Dase did not move. After a long time his eyes seemed to regain their sight. He saw people encircling the cot and wailing in an agony of despair. Everything seemed uncannily strange to him. Only Tukua, who had just woken up, stood quietly by the cot. From under the blanket, one could see his mother's hand. Tukua kneaded her index finger, tears drying on his cheeks.

Dase experienced a dam-burst of grief, which wrenched his guts and rose in waves. He suddenly lifted himself, gathered Tukua into his arms, and sank down again. Every tear that fell from his eyes seemed to silently shatter a bone inside. Tears flowed ceaselessly, like the rain-fed streams in the month of Shravan. The lips trembled, and the nostrils were dilated. He sat, eyes closed. It seemed as though his entire being, melted by grief, was flowing away.

Once the tide of wailing began to ebb a little, a certain alertness asserted itself. Raghunath and his wife took the children away from the sickroom into the upper wing of the house. Bhaiga too, calmed down a little. Wiping his tears, he carried Tukua into the upper wing. Dase, however, continued to sit, his head wedged between his knees. The ribs on his back rising and falling. Raghu balked at the thought of calling him. How would he console him?

What had happened was simply incredible. No one would believe it if you described it. The mother and the son both died the same day, as if one wanted to accompany the other. The sight melted every heart with pity. That boy, Jayi, would not stop crying because he wanted to die. He insisted 'I want to go to mother.' 'I want to sleep beside mother.' It was the cry of his soul. Everyone had warned against laying him by his mother's side, for that would fulfill his heart's last desire and snap the thread that tied him to life. In the end that was exactly what was done. The moment he was placed close to his mother, he slipped an arm and a leg over her, as if he was going to fall asleep comfortably. At this time, his mother's body was slowly beginning to turn cold. For a moment everyone was overcome with drowsiness. Then they all woke up with a start, but found that everything was over. It seemed unbelievable, but it appeared as if mother and son decided to undertake that final journey together.

It was some time before daybreak. Raghunath's two children fell asleep again. Tukua, resting in his sister-in-law's lap, dozed. He was very tired; perhaps he would fall asleep in a little while. Bata sat quietly on the upper veranda, staring intently into the void, as if stunned. Bhaiga came in from the outer veranda, and said, 'Brother, the uncles from Patapur have arrived.'

There were five or six of them. They came straight into the courtyard, where Raghu found them pattering about quietly. He understood everything. Unable to contain himself, he burst into tears. They surrounded him, comforted him, patting him on the back. An elderly person among them said, 'Raghu, this is not the time to lose heart. There should be no delay. Let's set to work immediately, or else the corpses will start to deteriorate.'

Dase felt as if someone had thrust a burning torch into him. He suddenly got up. But his head reeled. He would have come crashing down like a felled tree had he not steadied himself against the wall.

'Hold him, Raghu. Hold his other arm,' saying this, someone led him into the courtyard and seated him on a wooden stool and sprinkled his face and head with water. After a drink of water, Dase closed his eyes and rested for a while. Then he said slowly, in a broken voice, 'I knew she would give me the slip and she cheated me in the end. . .well!'

He heaved a deep sigh and remained silent for a long time. Then he said, 'Go, Raghu, my son. Make the preparations. This will be the end of everything for her.' Tears kept streaking down his cheeks.

Everyone busied themselves. Turmeric had to be ground into a paste. New clothes, new earthen pots, pitchers, lac dye, and vermillion had to be arranged. The drummer had to be sent for. Someone had to get some khai. Someone else had to look into the making of the litter.

In the middle of all this bustle a problem had to be sorted out: should they make one litter or two? At last it was decided that one large litter for the two bodies would do.

Dase sat inert and indifferent in the midst of all this hectic activity and noise. The past rose vividly before him like a tableau, and memories of bygone days, happy as well as sad, returned. Tears welled in his eyes. He remembered the day he had brought a matha saree for Tuku's mother.

'You should not spend so much money on a saree. Should you not have brought my children things to eat with this fifteen rupees?'

'Oh, put it on. Let's see how you look in it.'

Tuku's mother smiled.

He remembered that smile.

Is this all an illusion, then? Was she alive?

Dase blinked and stared again, his eyes wide open.

The smile of Tuku's mother faded away. All he could see was a lot of bare legs running around in the gathering.

No. Everything was over for Tuku's mother. And whatever he saw was nothing but a dream. Death was truer than life.

Dase could not remain seated any more. It had already become light. Someone had ground a plateful of turmeric. He got up and went into the sickroom, carrying the plate of turmeric paste.

He pushed the shroud aside and rubbed turmeric paste all over her body. Tears slid off the tip of his nose.

What crossed his mind no one could say, but he also rubbed turmeric paste all over Jayi's body. No one said anything. What could anyone say after all?

There was no turmeric paste left on the plate. But he sat scraping the plate and running his hand over Jayi's cold chest.

Someone said, 'That'll do. Now it is time to put lac dye on her feet.'

Without saying a word, Dase took the cup containing lac dye from his hand and bathed the feet of Tuku's mother with it pouring whatever was left over them.

He put a large quantity of vermillion powder on her forehead. The red dust rolled down as far as her eyebrows.

The litter was laid out in the courtyard in a north-south position.

'Here. Take her,' said Dase, withdrawing his hand smeared with turmeric paste and vermillion powder. Then he stood staring vacantly.

The pallbearers lifted the bodies of the mother and son and laid them on the litter.

Everything was done as if by a machine. The earthen pot was positioned. The puffed rice was carried in. The drummer arrived. Now it was time for the litter to be borne to the cremation ground. Despair rose in Dase. When the litter was lifted from the ground, he rushed in and gripped one side of it. But the litter did not stop for him. Only his trembling hand groped around for something. A nameless grief gnawed at his vitals.

'Go on your way, my goddess Lakshmi. The house will be empty after you are gone. Go, go. On your way.'

'Let me take leave of you, my Lord. We're never going to meet again in this life'—Sita Devi's last words to Lord Rama before she disappeared into the earth. Dase muttered those lines tearfully in a low voice. No one heard him.

Raghu's eldest son had woken up. He had been made to hold a bunch of burning wicks. Living in a town had made the boy knowing and clever. He walked cheerfully at the head of the funeral procession. Raghu scattered puffed rice and cowries on the ground as he went. Holding Tukua's hand, Bhaiga made his way slowly. Bata walked a little ahead of him.

The pallbearers proceeded in silence.

The drummer led everyone else, and Dase followed the procession. The cool morning breeze had made Raghu's son feel fresh and energetic. To him it all seemed like a festive occasion. So he was full of fun and laughter. The sight of ghee-soaked wicks burning away amused him no end and made him laugh.

The women of the village watched, peering around their doors. They talked to each other, making inquiries, expressing grief and pity. Now and then their words reached Dase.

'She was like Goddess Lakshmi. See how she makes people laugh and feel happy as she goes on her final journey.'

Dase's eyes were drying up. He moved on, like a machine.

That boy Jayi, left me, his heart full of grievances. How often had he pleaded, 'Father, please get me a cloth bag like the one other boys take to school. I'll carry my books in it.' And I cheated him saying, I'd bring it the next day, or the day after. In the end, he went away, never to come back. Oh, what a son he was. He was like Bhagirath to my family, who would have saved us all. What a broad forehead! Now he was gone. Why should he have lived such a wretched life in this poor house?

How your mother scrimped and saved to buy rice and molasses for your sacred thread ceremony, which would have been held in Baisakh this year! Oh my son. If only you had remained alive, you would have raised libation to me. Why did I live to see this day?

A pair of small feet, which looked like a rabbit's ears, stuck out from under the shroud.

Tears burst his bones and gushed forth. The litter disappeared from view. Dase walked on.

Raghu turned round and said to Bhaiga, 'You take the children and go back from here.' Bhaiga took Tukua by the hand. Bata held his nephew's hand. These tear-stained dim faces receded past Dase.

What passed through Tukua's mind, one couldn't say, but he kept looking back. It seemed his tearful eyes carried all the grief that weighed on his soul. After taking four or five steps, he stopped and wailed 'Ma-a. . .' The bitter cry of the last-born little boy, who had lost his mother.

'Ma-a. . .'

Oh!

The cry tore the sky to shreds, and the earth smouldered and gave way under his feet.

Dase felt as if a large boulder had pushed its way up from within his bowels and blocked his throat. He thought he could not bear it any longer, that he would explode, and sink. But he stood like a rock.

Resting his head on Bhaiga's shoulder, Tukua shivered like a puppy and kept wailing. Bhaiga moved on. Dase melted into tears. He felt as if his life-breath would escape him and leave him dead. If one had cared to listen to the words uttered by Dase's quivering tear-soaked lips, he would have heard him say, 'Try as hard as you may, you'll never find her. From today, whenever you call your mother, no one will answer.'

The litter was carried further on.

A pyre had been set up on the sands of the river bed. The dry sand mixed with ash had been trampled upon by human beings and jackals.

On this lay scattered a half-burnt string cot, a couple of broken earthen pots, a torn winnowing fan, and a few charred faggots.

An old gnarled mango tree stood on the ridge. Pradhan's brick kiln had been reduced to a pile of broken bricks, anthills, ash and wild undergrowth.

The cremation rites were performed one after the other. Dase went through the motions in a dream-like state. His body looked dark and emaciated. How miserable he looked! His face was covered with a beard, and his eyes were sunken. One could bear to look at him only because he was tall and big built. But grief had withered him.

Dase did not utter a word. If someone asked a question, he only looked up with vacant, unfocussed eyes, nothing made sense to him. Only occasionally could he be roused from his reverie.

'Wait. Let's lay the boy by his mother's side.'

For a moment Dase would regain consciousness. He would fully understand what was going on. Then he would be back in a world of dreams once more.

'Hey take the sudasha thread off her arm. Or else it'll be burnt.' Dase was again all attention. A moment later, his unseeing eyes would fix themselves on the void.

The pyre blazed up. In the broad light of day, the fire looked ugly, trivial and ominous. Everyone was sweating heavily. Raghu was thoroughly exhausted. He was a boy after all. Not equal to the task before him.

One of the pall-bearers said to Raghu, 'Take your father home. We'll stay here. We'll join you after finishing the job and taking a ritual bath. He is heart-broken. Can't you see how he is sitting over there, speechless. Take him home, and give him something bitter-tasting to eat. Bring him round. Go.'

'Father. Let's go home now.' He had expected Dase would only gaze vacantly at him, as he had done before.

But, raising his eyes from the pyre, Dase replied, in a clear voice, 'You go home. I'll sit here for a while. I'll wait until everything is over. I'll follow you. Where is my box of chewing tobacco?' He searched the fold at his waist, but did not find it there.

Puria was Dase's cousin. He was listening to him in surprise. He came forward and handed him his own box of chewing tobacco.

Dase tipped some chewing tobacco onto his palm. Puria said, 'We have to endure what is fated to pass. None of us will be spared. The

Lord had given, the Lord has taken away. What will we gain by grieving? She was extremely fortunate, for she died before her husband. And, as for that poor boy, he was not fated to enter worldly life to enjoy its pleasures. The time allotted to him was up, and he took his departure.'

Dase said nothing. But a little smile seemed to play across his face. He put the chewing tobacco into his mouth, and nodded as if he agreed with Puria.

After being ravaged by a terrible storm, the earth lies buried under a heap of broken branches and wet leaves on which the sun glints. A squirrel scurries over it, a sparrow takes off only to come down again. Dase's face looked like this storm-ravaged earth, empty, deserted, filled with wreckage, and utterly exhausted.

'Father, do I go back home then?'

'Yes, go. Why wait? Both of you go together. I'll stay here only a little longer.'

The fire was dying. Dase sat, watching it intently. Two mortal frames were being slowly reduced to ashes. Lost in thought, Dase looked on.

'Bhaina, it's getting late. Let's go. We'll come back later, cool the ashes and collect the bones. Don't brood like this. You are a wise man after all. Get up, let's go.'

Dase rose to his feet, heaving a sigh.

On the way back, everyone went on talking. But Dase said nothing. At last they reached home.

An earthen pot had been posted in front of the house. Raghu stood on the veranda. He looked wretched and miserable. One could not bear to look at his unshaven face.

But to Dase, few things made any sense now. The shadow of the funeral pyre had rendered every aspect of life obscure, opaque and grey. Now, nothing that happened could affect Dase. The pyre that reduced Tuku's mother and Jayi to ashes had destroyed much that was meaningful in Dase's world. For those who had passed away, he grieved no more, nor did he feel that anything bound him to those who were alive.

Raghu handed out new sacred threads and oil to the pallbearers returning from the cremation ground. They would go out to take a purifying bath. Scraps of conversation reached Dase. Raghu said, 'No, why should we stay here? I have found Bhaiga a job there. We'll all go to Madanpur.'

'And this house?'

'We'll do something about it.'

Dase heard what was being said. But to him it seemed it was all taking place in some far off place. He sat down on the veranda, leaning against the wall and said, 'You Bata, give me my box of chewing-tobacco.'

'Bata is sleeping, father.' Saying this Bhaiga handed him a box.

'Brother came and searched for your box of chewing-tobacco everywhere but couldn't find it. He found mother's gundi box—will it do?'

A wave of grief rose as far as his throat. Dase controlled himself with difficulty. He lowered his tearful eyes and silently stretched out his hand.

Maya, the Mover

It was already a month since they had moved to Madanpur. Raghu
felt glad when he saw Dase going out of the house. He asked,
'Are you going to the temple, father?'

Although the house where Raghu lived was a small one, it had a
fenced backyard. Dase had his bath there every morning, and spent
all his time indoors doing puja. Never a talkative man, these days he
had become even quieter. It seemed he had nothing to say, no opinion
to offer.

Occasionally Raghu suggested he go to the market, in order to
cheer him up. But he had found that such trips left him depressed.
Not that Dase ever broke down, he only looked sad and forlorn. One
had to repeat a thing thrice before he paid any attention to it. Nor
was his heart in anything he said. He felt detached from everything. If
you asked him something, he would take quite a while to answer, as if
he was speaking from a far-off world. It did not matter to him if he got
something to eat or not. He would not bother if his clothes were washed
or not. He seemed completely indifferent to everything around him.
Now and then he watched intently and long when Tukua played before
him. Tukua had many friends among the children of the colony now.
He had grown fond of his brother and his sister-in-law. He would run
away to be with his playmates, and, while doing so, glance timidly at
Dase. But Dase did not notice him and merely stared at the place
where he had been playing before. Then he would look around, as if
startled, and leave the place sighing.

That day, after bathing in the morning and dressed in a freshly laundered dhoti, Dase set out for the Dhabaleswar temple, carrying a dudura flower in a plate. Raghu came in and asked, 'Are you going to the temple, father?' Dase looked at his son, smiled and said, 'Yes.'

Even though it was a wan smile, it pleased Raghu. He said, 'It may get very hot by the time you return home. Take my umbrella.'

Raghu had not had his bath yet. He brought the umbrella and propped it against the wall.

Dase left the house silently, the umbrella tucked under his arm, carrying the puja plate in one hand and the walking stick in the other. Raghu and his wife, Bata, Bhaiga and the children came silently to the door and followed him with their eyes.

The figure of Dase receded. The rim of the brass plate caught the morning sun and glittered like gold. Dase walked on.

Raghu turned round and found everyone in the family standing behind him. He understood everything but said, to show that he was the head of the family, 'What are you all doing here? Get inside.'

But why had he himself come to the front door, a twig in his mouth?

Dase slowly made his way. Perhaps he thought to himself, 'I'll ask Satpathy Mahasaya when I meet him, the meaning of all this. She is no more. It seems I am past grieving for her. Then why does life seem so utterly empty?. . . This must be happening to many. And they get on somehow, living with those who are alive. How do they bring themselves to re-enter worldly life? But they know life has to be linked. True, Bhaiga has got a job. But the other two boys have to be settled in life. One may not do anything for them; at least one could give these two motherless children a little warmth, a little affection. They are my offspring after all.'

But why does my heart remain totally detached, uninvolved? It's not that I don't feel sad when I set my eyes on that poor Tukua. But I no longer feel the urge to gather him into my arms. As for him, he too does not want to come to me, he has grown to like his sister-in-law. Now I have no one I can really call my own; there is no longer a purpose in my life. I am restless. I feel my time is running out. When life loses all its meaning and value and grows utterly empty, it becomes difficult to go on living. I had never expected that grief would suddenly darken my life. How could You be so cruel, O Lord? How could You shower blows on someone like me who did not get even two square meals a day and had been crushed by suffering, defeated by life? I had never dreamt that You could be capable of such deception, such double-dealing!

The temple came into view. There were only two or three persons on the premises. Dase saw the gardener limping towards the pond. Memories crowded his mind. The place was familiar, so was this man. A current of chill dew-soaked breeze. Memories revived him.

Has the gardener gone blind? He couldn't recognize Dase at all! Or was he trying to recall him?

The gardener struck his own cheek and said, 'Is it you sir? Oh! How strangely altered you are! Only a fraction of your earlier self. Oh, what a well-built man you used to be. Now one has difficulty in recognizing you.'

Dase stopped smiling.

He would have liked to say, 'How does it matter? Why bother to look after the body? How much time am I left with? I'm like a water bubble. Here now, gone the next moment.'

'I know everything, sir. It must have been a terrible blow. How could fate do this to a man like you? Day before yesterday, maybe the day before that, I heard the bad news in the market. I was telling someone about it here when Satpathy Mahasaya came out of the temple. Perhaps my words reached him, he stopped and turned around. I told him everything. The mention of your name made him pause and ponder a little. Then he walked away, saying nothing. Are you on your way to the temple? Go there. Of course, Lord Dhabaleswar understands the state of your mind. Open your heart to Him, and you'll feel relieved.'

Dase made his way towards the temple. Inside, the temple was extremely quiet. Only the stream of water falling on the head of Lord Mahadev glittered like a silver wire.

Dase tiptoed into the temple.

He found Satpathy Mahasaya deep in meditation, seated in the lotus posture in his usual place. His body glowed like a copper wire, inspiring in Dase feelings of fear, reverence and hope. He gently laid down the umbrella, the walking stick and the plate on the floor, and prostrated himself behind the stone bull. The temple was so quiet, one could even hear the sound of one's breathing. Dase feared that his presence would disturb Satpathy Mahasaya. Then he rose quietly and threw himself at his feet. When he felt a hand on his head, he raised himself and sat silently before Satpathy Mahasaya.

Satpathy Mahasaya smiled. The smile expressed not only affection, but pity and love as well. Dase had nothing to say to him. For his part, he knew everything. In silence, one understood what was passing through the mind of the other. After a while, Satpathy beckoned Dase into the sanctum.

Dase offered the dudura flowers to the linga and, following Satpathy's directions, raised the little tumbler, filled with water.

'A-u-um! Namah Shivaya.'

The stone walls of the temple echoed this mantra and carried it into the innermost recesses of Dase's heart. Without being conscious of it, Dase's voice united with Satpathy's.

For a long time this mantra comforted Dase's tormented heart.

Someone rang the temple bell, pulling it hard. Suddenly, there was a bustle. Large brass plates clanged as they were placed on stone. Dase turned around and saw that the Marwari family had arrived. The gardener stood behind them. There were three fat Marwari women carrying a basketful of ripe bananas and two buckets full of milk. Behind them loomed the figure of a pot-bellied Marwari sporting big whiskers. The sight was most irritating.

But the expression on old Satpathy's face seemed to say, 'Wonderful. These people have got up early in the morning to come to the temple. Great.'

Dase looked a little put off, as a child is, when roused from light sleep.

Old Satpathy returned to his seat. Dase sat beside him in silence. The Marwari made a lot of noise. The bell never stopped clanging, the brass plates were dragged noisily across the floor and the milk buckets thumped down on it.

After a time Dase thought it would be nice if someone comforted him, with a few kind words. Strange! He had never felt like this before.

'You suffered a lot, didn't you?' Satpathy's smile seemed to ask him. Dase looked away. The touch of Satpathy's hand patting his back seemed to say, 'These things are bound to happen. The value of life will be diminished if these things don't happen. Its meaning will change.'

Dase turned to look at him. His innocent eyes seemed to query, 'Why should this happen to me, of all people?'

Satpathy Mahasaya pointed a finger at the sky, as if he understood the question. He seemed to say, 'You must be terribly unhappy with God, must be beginning to lose faith in Him.'

Dase only stared.

That's right. Why should I not feel aggrieved? Someone in whom

I had placed so much faith, has let me down so badly! I have never harmed anybody!

Satpathy opened his mouth. 'We suffer on account of our own faults. Ignorance clouds our judgement. We form so many ties for ourselves. When these snap, we suffer unbearable pain. Attachment is a creeper we tend lovingly. If someone harms it, our hearts bleed. One achieves detachment only by loosening the bonds of affection. In doing so, one ceases to suffer.'

Whatever little Dase understood convinced him. He said, 'But we are no yogis who have conquered desire. We do get drawn into the web of worldly attachments. These matter if you recognize them; they don't if you refuse to recognize them. My mind is at the end of its tether. Life holds no interest for me at all. I'm also losing faith.'

'You haven't lost faith at all; why did you come here, then? That you don't find any joy in anything is also not true. What is happening is that the bonds that have kept you tied to the world are loosening. But that is an auspicious sign. True liberation consists in the struggle to escape bondage. The soul finds its strength in the fierceness of this struggle. The river will surely flow down to the sea.'

'Then why have so many obstacles been put in its way?'

'It should be given an opportunity to test its strength. Likewise, adversity determines the true worth of a human being. Do you agree?'

'I do, but these are profound things. There is something that bothers me and I want you to explain it to me. You are a learned man. I am asking you because I have faith in you. My wife went her way. How do the others who were left behind matter to me? I have been trying to comfort my youngest child, but I have a feeling that he doesn't need me at all. I get the impression that he's completely cut off from me. I'm also not in the least bothered about him. This is something that comes straight from my heart, but it seems perverse. I look upon you as my guru. Tell me what I should do.'

'I understand. The wound in the heart hasn't healed yet. Some people form new attachments even while the wound is still raw. Others take longer. But if the wound heals on its own, the heart will reach a wonderful state steering clear of all attachments. Nothing will be able to enslave it. But it will be so soft it can feel even a breath of wind. It'll drip with love and pity.'

Satpathy smiled and took Dase by the hand. Although much of what was said passed over his head, Dase felt the emotion that animated his words.

Satpathy pondered for a while and said, with great severity, 'Have you thought about making a tour of the four great centres of pilgrimage?'

Oh, so this was what he had been driving at all along. Dase smiled and said, 'Such things are beyond unfortunate people like me. We can never come anywhere near people like you. It's difficult for us to arrange two square meals a day.'

'Oh, you misunderstand me Dase. Did I say something wrong? The thing is I have decided to go on a pilgrimage for a year, two days before the full-moon night in the month of Aswin. I had planned to go alone. Let's go together. The money I planned to spend on myself will easily cover your expenses too. There are only eight days to go. Think it over, be decisive. Follow the example of great men. I can see clearly that your wife's soul will be pleased if you do this.'

Dase was overwhelmed. What marvels were taking place? It seemed like yesterday: he could not go to Puri to see the Gobinda Dwadasi festival. And now he was being taken to visit the four holy places of the country!

Just as light floods into the sanctum when its door is thrown open, his inner being was suddenly lit up. He lifted his tearful eyes and gazed into the void. In the meantime Satpathy had gone back into the sanctum.

'Well, You played all these games only in order to pull me to Yourself! But should You show Your generosity only after violently cutting me off from the world! So be it. This is Your practice. Tell me, was Tukua's mother in Your way? Oh, poor woman. She was desperate to set her eyes on You. How excited she would have felt had she accompanied me! She has gone her way. What can be done? As long as we were fated to live together we travelled the road of life as companions. At the crossroads she parted company and went her way, as if she was dragged away. As for me, I stayed enmeshed in the web of earthly cares. Oh, how hard it is to burst through these ties and break free. Oh Lord, if You are pulling me towards You with a silken rope, pull hard and make this my final journey. The soil around the tree of my life has been washed away. I have abandoned all hope, I repose my faith only in You, O Lord.'

Dase was seated, leaning against the wall. His tears had washed away the sandal paste on his chest. He hurriedly wiped his face and looked around. Had Satpathy Mahasaya gone away? The temple premises were deserted. The Marwaris had long since left the place. He rose to his feet and peered into the sanctum. Inside, Satpathy was deep in meditation.

Dase sauntered out of the temple premises. A pleasant breeze blew. The pond had bloomed with many water lilies. Dase suddenly felt a lightening of heart and spirit. It seemed to him as if many things inside him were changing, being turned upside down. A mysterious nameless grief curled up from the deepest recesses like a line of smoke. But the heart fluttered happily like a kite in the bright, turbulent air. Just one tug, and it would soar away.

Dase's eyes were wet with tears and he looked mournful.

He absent-mindedly ran his hand gently over the bare sharp-edged rock of the hill.

A Cripple Scales a Mountain

The train sped along.

The compartment was packed with nearly a hundred and fifty passengers, and it seemed as though they spoke three hundred different languages. Every bundle seemed to be announcing haughtily, 'Hey you. We too have been paid for. How dare you push us aside. Do you think the train belongs to your father?' The compartment was suffocating. The smells of smoke, of bidi, sweat, the toilet and soiled clothes blended and filled the compartment. The train rushed forward, dragging along a few such compartments.

But nothing seemed to affect Dase. He sat absolutely still in the corner which he occupied after boarding the train with Satpathy. Satpathy was seated directly opposite him, but Dase took no notice of him at all. He seemed lost in thought. Satpathy watched him silently, like Sanjaya in the Mahabharata. A fierce and bloody battle raged inside Dase.

Lord Hari was helping the Pandavas cross the wide and dangerous river of the war, like an expert helmsman. Satpathy Mahasaya understood what was going on and what was going to come about. He was simply looking on as a silent but curious spectator.

It was two o'clock at night. They had steamed by many stations. Many people got down, many others boarded the train. Everyone in the compartment dozed, leaning against each other. They looked innocent and vulnerable like children. They all had the same destination. Among boxes, trunks and luggage dozed a mother and her child.

Dase awoke slowly.

But he could not utter a word, as if he was terribly exhausted. Satpathy felt Dase was trying to make sense of his situation. After looking about him vaguely, his eyes fell on Satpathy. He cleared his throat, peering into the outer darkness enquiringly, Satpathy Mahasaya said, 'The compartment is very crowded. This is usual. There'll be an even larger crowd when we change trains in Calcutta.' But finding that his words brought no response, he fell silent.

Dase said, hesitatingly, 'Raghu came to the station. Did his wife come with him? I think she did.'

'I don't remember having seen her. Aren't you talking about Chittarajan's wife? She is my eldest daughter-in-law. She was insisting that we travel in a higher, more expensive class. She'll grow more sensible in time. I don't think anyone else came. Now I understand what happened. Raghu handed me a paper packet of paan. It was your daughter-in-law who sent those, isn't it?'

'That's right. I somehow got the impression that my daughter-in-law had come to the station.' He took a paan out of his pocket and chewed it. As for Satpathy Mahasaya, he didn't take paan, wouldn't even touch chewing tobacco. How inconvenient! Would the heavens fall if one ate these? But this man has mastered all desire. You could never persuade him to touch a paan.

'Day will break soon. We'll reach Calcutta early in the morning. We'll have plenty of time before the other train arrives. It'll be a good idea to visit Dakhineswar. Let's see. We'll decide after we get there.'

Dase looked up at him. Then he said, 'Tell me what I should do, sir. The thought of Tukua keeps tormenting me. Why did he shy away from me?'

Satpathy realized that all this time Dase had not been listening to him at all. He smiled to himself. Dase went on, 'Yesterday he gazed at me all day long but never left his sister-in-law's side. I have detached myself from everybody. And yet I get the feeling that I'll never see my boys again.'

'What nonsense! We will spend a year travelling to many holy places. Of course, you will return to your family. But you'll have achieved true understanding, and you will have broken free of all worldly bonds. The world will seem a wonderful, pure place. The Lord will wash your heart clean and restore you to the world.'

'I have nothing to say. As it has been said. "I have lost all hope and surrendered myself to Lord Hari." Let the Lord do whatever He wants with me. If He feels like it, He will take me everywhere and finally drown me in the sea. Let Him do so. I'm helpless. . . He does everything. Or else how could someone like me go on a pilgrimage to the four holy places. Why should you have taken pity on me?'

'The truth is, Dase, not even a leaf moves without His will.'

The train came to a stop at a station. There was a lot of bustle and activity on the platform outside. Some ten to fifteen passengers entered the compartment at this station. There was no space inside for even a mustard seed. But they crowded into the compartment, paying no heed to protests and objections. Someone pushed a passenger aside to make room for himself. Another settled himself on his box. The one who was to get off at the next station seemed to be in no hurry. He climbed up to an upper berth and went to sleep.

'How strange!' Dase thought to himself as he watched them. People from so many different places found themselves in the compartment. They had no choice but to jostle each other. Each one of them had work to do, each one must have fixed a day on which he had to get back home.

He watched all this as if he were looking at a picture unfolding itself before him.

That man with a gold ring on his finger, smoking a bidi. The bare-bodied boy sitting next to him. How frightening that old man looks! Maybe, all old men look so horribly ugly when they are asleep. Mouth open and not a single tooth in it.

What a lot of people there were in this compartment!

He turned away and looked out. The stars were clearly visible. Three of the stars in the Great Bear shone brightly.

Satpathy too watched his fellow passengers. He too curiously noted the countless desires which animated the hearts of all these people. But the enormity of the task filled him with amazement and made him feel diffident. Enmeshed in the web of earthly attachments, how eagerly yet how helplessly they clambered up their chosen paths! Each one was weighed down by all kinds of baggage, all kinds of responsibilities. If only they would care to see beneath the surface, they would realize the futility of it all. But they would never have the time. They were being pushed from behind, and pulled from the front. The Master uses them merely as a means to His own end. He alone knows what amazing things He does by assuming countless forms in this great journey of the living and non-living universe. I salute you—the One with thousands of heads, thousands of eyes and thousands of feet.

Satpathy Mahasaya folded his hands, and closed his eyes.

Hours passed.

Suddenly someone inside the compartment sang loudly.

O, Lord, listen to the prayer of a poor man.

O Lotus-faced one, save this defenceless creature.

'Hey you, stop it.' Someone shouted sleepily. 'Why do you howl at the dead of night?'

'It's already morning sir. Take the name of the Lord and wake up. Take pity on this poor blind man. You will earn merit. The Almighty will grant all your wishes.'

Why did the ocean of pity dry up for me?

I know my fate is sealed and irredeemable.

O Lord, listen to a poor man's supplication.

Dase took out a few coins from the waist-fold and dropped them into the blind man's hand. 'May God bless you sir!' Following the example of Dase other passengers too placed some money on his palm. He prayed to God for their well-being and moved on. Satpathy Mahasaya gave him an eight anna coin. He guessed its worth from the sound it made and profusely expressed his gratitude.

Others in the compartment looked at Satpathy Mahasaya in surprise. But he seemed utterly indifferent, uninterested. Not being in a position to understand anything, Dase too sat quietly.

The train moved on.

After a while, Dase thrust his head through the window and looked out. Yet another dawn in his life!

Oh, how deserted these places look! And how old the stars!

Dew-soaked shadows reeled past in the thin darkness. In the distance, a misty darkness lay drowsily on the rice fields. To Dase it suddenly appeared as if the sound of the moving train was receding. And that star in the sky seemed to stand absolutely still. The sky too seemed utterly motionless. Why does it all seem so quiet? Why didn't the train move? Why do I feel so light, so weightless?

Actually the train had stopped between two stations, in the middle of nowhere. No one got off, nor did anyone board the train. There was silence all around, inside the train and outside.

Dase kept gazing out of the window. Some profound emotion charged his whole being and he trembled all over. Satpathy Mahasaya noticed it, but he said nothing and meditated, his eyes closed.

A little later, he opened his eyes when a piercing cry reached his ears. Dase was slowly turning his head.

His eyes were wide open, staring. Cold sweat beaded his forehead.

He desperately clutched at Satpathy's hand for support. His own hands shivered. Satpathy guessed that a shatteringly painful thought had crossed Dase's mind. The train started moving, spouting smoke. There were movements inside the compartment. Sleepy voices began talking. Dase stammered, 'I felt very uncomfortable. My head reeled. It seemed to me as if I was dropping into an abyss. My spine trembled and I screamed in fear. . . I get the feeling that one of these days I'll die at the hour of dawn.'

Satpathy Mahasaya understood the state of Dase's mind and why he was so upset. Everyone in the compartment dozed in the quiet hours before daybreak. Only the train rushed on, rattling loudly. Any sensitive mind would become unhinged in a situation like this. The wound in Dase's heart was still raw; it bled whenever fresh breeze blew over it.

He said, changing the topic, 'Well, let's go to Dakhineswar and do our morning ablutions there.'

'I'll do whatever you say. But tell me why do I feel like this? Did I not set out on this pilgrimage because I thought the world held no interest for me? It seems to me that Raghunath, his children, Tukua, Bhaiga and Bata are calling me, and that I am running away from them, not turning to look back. I was being pulled in two directions and my heart was being wrung. However, I feel a little better now. I realized that I'll never turn back. If one trips up and a nail comes off one's toe, can the nail dripping with blood be made to grow back into the foot? It has to be pulled off and flung away, no matter how much it hurts. Raghunath's elder son was not well. He is very fond of this boy.'

'Don't think about it anymore. What does it hold any more for you?'

Dase ran his hand over his head. He said, as if talking to himself absent-mindedly, 'Distance dilutes affection, doesn't it?'

Satpathy sensed the battle raging inside Dase's heart, but said nothing. He somehow got the impression that the conflict was coming to an end. Now shall Yudhishtira ascend the throne and the clan of the Kurus be wiped out.

A change came over Dase.

Oh, poor old Dhrutarastra. His hundred sons had amounted to nothing in the end. Five Pandavas could finish them off. This has been going on for ages. The Lord controls everything. Unarmed himself, He acts as a mere charioteer; yet at the same time He uses everyone, from Brahma to an insect, as a means to His own end. Of course, the victory will be Arjuna's, no one else can win. But even being used as a means in the great battle is no small matter.

He opened his eyes and saw that it was light. The sun was rising. Satpathy Mahasaya calmed himself and started chanting a mantra— *ajjagrato duramudaiti daivam tadusuptasya tatheibeti—*

durangamam jyotisham jyotirekam tanme manah shiva sankalpamastu.

Dase had dozed off. He opened his eyes wide and wondered if it was Pundit Nilakantha reciting slokas from the Vedas. Dase used to think the pundit made himself ridiculous whenever he recited the Vedas in this manner.

He found Satpathy Mahasaya completely absorbed in the act of chanting the mantra. He took in the compartment at a glance. Everyone was awake now. It was a bright day. He greeted the morning by swiftly chanting the Prabhati, as he always did.

Brahma Murai Stripurantakari, Bhanu,
Sashibhumisutobudhascha.
Guruscha Sukram Sani Raghu Ketu Kurbantu sarve mamasuprabhatam.

Eyes half closed, Satpathy Mahasaya gazed out of the window. It seemed as if he had been transported to another world. Words issued from some deep recesses of his being—*tasya prasasane Gargi.*

Dase was filled with reverence. He saluted Satpathy Mahasaya mentally and waited. The darkness inside him was slowly dissolving. The doubts that assailed him had also faded. As the day grew brighter, light came filtering into his heart, penetrating its various layers.

Some of the shabby-looking passengers had in the meantime disembarked. The rest were busy arranging their luggage, and taking care of their children, who had just woken up. Some smartly dressed passengers boarded the train. They sat apart, making sure no one brushed against them. All of them would get down in Calcutta.

Dase got up and stretched his limbs. His joints had become stiff. Satpathy Mahasaya remained seated as before. Dase wondered how he came to be associated with such a great soul. Worldly attachments seemed to mean nothing to this man. 'Oh Lord. It's all thy will.'

Two educated young men stood guarding the door and laughed, watching Satpathy Mahasaya. Why was this old man staring so funnily, and why was he chanting so many slokas!

After quite a while Satpathy Mahasaya opened his eyes, which dwelt compassionately on everything around him. It seemed as if he was blessing everyone. On either side of the compartment, railway tracks stretched away, like long snakes. How many trains must be running along these rails? The sight of Dase watching with wide-eyed childlike wonder amused him. The train rattled on, slowly. Some passengers gathered at the door, and leaned over one another to watch something. Dase thought the train would come to a stop, but it moved on.

The train stopped after a long time.

The two young men were the first to get down. They paid their respects to someone and stood aside. The man whom they saluted was about forty-five years old. He was very fat. He came straight into the compartment, threw himself at Satpathy Mahasaya's feet and saluted him several times before getting up.

Satpathy blessed him, placing his hand on his head.

'Well, Bimal. What brought you here?'

'Ramu informed me that you were coming to Calcutta. He wrote to say that you were travelling third class this time. Was your journey a comfortable one, sir?' he asked in Bengali.

The two young men standing outside stared, wonder struck. It took them some time to recover.

Seeing Dase, the gentleman said, hesitating, 'Is he your. . . I mean . . .'

'Yes, he is travelling with me. We are on this pilgrimage together.'

On hearing this, the gentleman bent low to touch Dase's feet. He got coolies to carry Satpathy's box and took Dase's shoulder bag himself and stepped down.

Satpathy Mahasaya explained to Dase that this gentleman was one of his old students. He was a professor now. A worthy man.

When he got off the train, Dase found himself in the midst of a milling crowd. Electric lights, bright like the moon, burned overhead. A coolie walked past him, like an elephant balancing six boxes on his head, holding a piece of luggage in one hand, and a pitcher of water in the other. 'Oh what a load he is carrying! I shudder to think what will happen if he trips over and falls!' Oh, how fair-skinned everyone here is! This man must be above forty, but he looks young for his age. A plump woman walks behind him. Her skin glows so brightly, you would see the reflection of your fingers if you shook them before her face. A tall young girl whose shiny plait of hair reaches down to her ankles, followed her. She handed something she was carrying to the young boy, who looked like a sahib—he must be her younger brother—and walked towards Dase and his companions. She paid her respects to Bimal babu, and stood, her head lowered. He asked her. 'Where were you?'

The parents of the girl also came up and paid him their respects. But Bimal was busy lifting Satpathy's box onto the coolies' heads. He said to them, 'I hope you won't mind. I am very busy right now.'

They looked at Satpathy Mahasaya in surprise. They also looked Dase all over, and then walked away, talking to each other in low voices.

The area outside the station was crowded. There were many motor cars and horse-drawn carriages. Dase felt overwhelmed. What a big place Calcutta is! How many people live here! Here, a human being is no more than a fly. The huge Howrah bridge loomed on his left. Many came all the way just to look at it. Everyone in this new city was a stranger to Dase. Many looked like the coolies he had just seen; many others resembled the tall young girl and her parents. There were others who looked dirty, shabby and dark-skinned, and did not seem to belong to this crowd. He knew no one here, and not even one person in this vast crowd knew him. Amazing!

Bimal babu's shiny motor car was waiting for them. First Satpathy Mahasaya got into it, Dase followed him. Bimal babu got in after them. The seats felt very soft and were covered with silk. Dase was a little nervous at first and would not rest his full weight on the seat, but soon he settled himself comfortably.

The road down which they drove was lined with houses. There were houses as far as their eyes could reach. The road was filled with people. Countless cars and buses passed. Oh, did human beings actually live in these houses which seemed to belong to some fairyland?

Satpathy Mahasaya said, 'Bimal wants us to spend a day at his place as his guests! His wife was also my student. She insists that we go to her house. She would have come to receive us, but there was some problem. What do you say?'

Dase smiled. He said nothing. To Satpathy the smile seemed to say, 'What's the point in asking me?'

No one contradicted Satpathy Mahasaya. He always seemed to say the right thing.

They were quiet on the way.

Bimal babu lived in a very big house. Many flowering plants grew in front of the house. His wife was a beautiful woman with chiselled features. They had two handsome boys. It was a happy, contented family. They all came and touched first Satpathy's and then Dase's feet. Dase blessed them silently. 'May your husband live long and may your children live to a ripe age.' Arre, this young boy reminds me of Tukua. If Tukua had good food and nice clothes, he would look exactly like him.

Satpathy Mahasaya had asked him to get ready quickly. Dase suppressed the thoughts crossing his mind, and set about finishing his ablutions. But he kept looking at the little boy, who showed him where the bathroom was, brought out his tumbler from his cloth bag and handed it to him.

Dase patted his head and asked, 'What's your name, my son?'

He replied shyly, 'Name? My name is Santosh.'

What a charming little boy! Dase's heart warmed to him. He stretched out his arms but quickly withdrew them, after merely touching the child's shoulder. The boy looked him in the face and said, 'Mother has told me to attend to you. Whenever you need anything, call. . . Santosh. I'll come running. And I have been told I must salute you, for you are an elderly man.'

The lisp with which he spoke and his plump cheeks made Dase very fond of him. He blessed him in his heart, 'Lord Jagannath, may this boy live long.' Then saying 'Hou,' indicating satisfaction, he made his way towards the bathroom.

'What does that word "hou" mean?' Thinking he had done something wrong, the boy bowed penitently, and said holding his ears. 'I am sorry. I should not have done that. Mother has asked me not to bother you. I'll go and ask her what it means.' He ran off.

Dase stood a while, looking in the direction in which he ran. He sighed in amusement, 'Naughty boy.'

It was late in the morning by the time they finally got ready and set off for Dakhineswar. Bimal babu drove the car. Satpathy and Dase occupied the back seat.

In no time the buildings of Calcutta receded from view. Small houses with fluted tile roofs, and little hutments surrounded by ditches and drains stood on the low-lying land below the highway. Stray dogs wandered all over the place. This was another face of Calcutta. Thousands on their way to Dakshineswar must have seen all this. But had anyone ever stopped his car to take a good look at people living there? Even someone like Bimal babu kept his eyes focussed on the road ahead of him as he drove on. Dase let out a deep sigh and turned to look at Satpathy, who calmly stared into the distance.

The car turned left and came to a stop. The three of them got out of the car. Wherever Dase looked, he saw women with their hair let loose. Some were buying flowers, others were buying prasad. Dase wondered if the land was full of women. Satpathy Mahasaya had by now completely withdrawn into himself. He would not utter a word. He only expressed himself through gestures to Bimal babu when they got closer to the temple. Turning to look at Dase, he only smiled. Then he entered the temple alone, without looking back.

Smiling, Bimal babu said humbly, 'He has asked me to look after you. Please come with me.'

There were many smaller temples inside the precincts. Dase came across many saffron-clad, tonsured sanyasis. One of these came up to Bimal babu and embraced him. From what transpired between them, and from the way they mentioned Satpathy Mahasaya and saluted him, Dase gathered that he was no ordinary man. Outside the temple wall, Dase and that sanyasi fell to talking under a branching tree. The sanyasi talked to him, in all humility, about Ramakrishna and Swami Vivekananda. Dase felt that these two were great soul-like figures in the holy scriptures.

Bengali, when simplified, is easy to understand. Dase listened, fascinated. It was getting late. At last, Bimal babu called them. The three of them went into the temple of the goddess. A feeling of ecstasy came over Dase, and he lay prostrate on the ground for some time. When he rose to his feet, he found Satpathy Mahasaya seated in the lotus posture in a corner. He could not take his eyes off him, did not want to call him or disturb him. It seemed to Dase that Bimal babu very politely beckoned to him to step out. Dase quietly left the place with his new-found friend, the sanyasi.

The bhog in the temple was delicious. Dase had some of this, and rested on the cool veranda. Many thoughts floated through his mind. Soon it grew dark. A religious meeting was organized. Many sanyasis, young and old, arrived and sat on the floor. Bimal babu came there with Satpathy Mahasaya. Someone got up and respectfully requested Satpathy Mahasaya to say a few words. He sat down on a raised platform, his legs folded, and his back as straight as a ramrod. Only a few of the things he said were intelligible to Dase. Satpathy spoke in pure Sanskrit on profound subjects, and everyone listened to him with bowed heads. Dase's heart was filled with wonder.

Oh God. How insignificant I am compared to him! I don't deserve to stand beside him. Lord Jagannath is playing his pranks. Or else, how could someone like me, utterly ignorant and worthless, find himself among these learned men?

Dase's eyes grew moist. In a state of ecstasy, his mind dwelt on the divine sport of Lord Krishna in the *Bhagavata*. He felt he was lost.

The meeting came to an end. Everyone silently walked up to Bimal babu's car. Dase now hesitated to sit next to Satpathy Mahasaya but he took Dase by the hand and made him sit beside him in the car. He warmly responded to everyone saluting him while he took leave of them. They paid their respects to Dase too, but Dase did not dare to raise his hands and bless them.

Dase felt that being with Satpathy Mahasaya had brought him this honour. He was on the verge of tears. He wanted to surrender himself completely—he would not mind if someone were to rush him to the top of a hill; he would not complain if someone flung him into the sea.

The car began to move.

Far away, someone was blowing a conch.

Manikarnika Ghat

Ever since his dip at the sacred confluence of three rivers at Triveni, Dase seemed to sink into a state of abstraction. If he sat somewhere, he would remain seated for a long time, staring for long hours into the void. He would talk but rarely. It appeared as if his consciousness had melted into the air. He gazed vacantly for some time before breaking into a sad smile, as if he was accepting life in its totality. It was difficult even for someone who knew him, to recognize him now, for he had shaven his head. One would wonder if he was indeed Sanatan Dase.

Satpathy Mahasaya watched everything closely. But there was nothing for him to say or do, since things were taking their own course. The Kumbha Mela ground near the ghat at the conference stretched in every direction the eye could see. When he got there, Dase looked around like a child, wide-eyed with wonder. Satpathy asked him, 'How do you feel?' Speechless, Dase gave him a vacant look. It was as if at that moment a feeling of vastness had suddenly swept into his heart.

This happened ten days ago. Finding Dase so indrawn, Satpathy Mahasaya took it upon himself to do everything. At times, Dase suddenly became conscious of his duties, as if waking from sleep. Feeling ashamed of himself, he would set about doing the chores. But coming under a spell, the next moment he would sink into abstraction. His thoughts floated far away like tufts of silk cotton. His glassy eyes saw nothing.

Satpathy Mahasaya realized that the holy war raging in Dase's heart, which he watched like Sanjay, had at last come to a close. But there was an eerie lull after the din of battle. A deep silence had descended on the vast battlefield. Only the faint sound of the Panchajanya conch reverberated far away on the horizon. The whole of Kurukshetra quaked at the sound. As for Dase, he did not know what that sound signified, which direction it came from, and who produced it. This might be the reason why he seemed so lost in wonder. But Satpathy said nothing to him.

That night they reached Kashi from Prayag. Their plan was to visit the temple of Lord Viswanath after taking a bath at the Manikarnika ghat. Early in the morning Dase's unseeing eyes were fixed on the void. Suddenly he opened his eyes. He saw that Satpathy had folded his blanket and laid it aside. Maybe he had got up early and had gone out to perform his ablutions. Dase felt embarrassed. What a shame! I sit here like a ghost, and he got up, finished his chores in my presence and I noticed nothing. I should be ashamed of myself.

He sprang to his feet. He rolled the blanket and came out onto the veranda. It was the beginning of the month of Kartik, and the dharamsala seemed empty and deserted. It was a three-storied building constructed around a circular space, like a well with stone rings. In fact, in the middle of this space was a deep well. Dase remembered, 'Oh! today we are to go to the temple of Lord Viswanath after a bath at the Manikarnika ghat.' He hurriedly went out and drew a bucket of water from the well. He suddenly noticed that Satpathy Mahasaya was standing behind him. He respectfully placed the bucket of water before him and stepped aside. In that misty darkness it seemed to him that Satpathy left after having a wash, a smile flitting across his face. Dase's eyes kept following him. He would have remained like this, but with a start, he came to himself, drew another bucket of water from the well and set about finishing his ablutions.

After some time, the two made their way along a deserted narrow street towards the banks of the Ganga.

The path was paved with bricks. It was flanked on either side by five-storied buildings almost jostling against each other. The small doors fitted with metal knobs seemed to guard the passage to the underworld. Darkness seemed to lie heaped at the turnings.

It was quite chilly. Dase's step quickened with the slope. Satpathy Mahasaya followed him.

Just at this moment the faint sound of someone reciting the Vedas reached their ears. They slowed down at the same time. The sounds became more distinct: a chorus of voices chanted the Mahima stotra of the Vedas. A shiver ran through Dase. Satpathy placed a hand on his chest, stopped for a moment, and then proceeded. As they came closer the sounds reverberated. Dase told himself. 'I have been saved. I am redeemed.' Their path now met a wide road, and they stood on this for a while. The ghat lay on their right. A high wind, cold and moist with the water of the Ganga, blew. 'Ah, let me breathe this to my heart's content.' The words of the Sama Veda resounded in his ears. Dase walked down the sloping road, taking long strides. He had left Satpathy far behind, and it seemed as if he was running away.

There were no houses around. The luminous space ahead of them was perhaps the river Ganga, which washed one clean of all sins.

Dase's heart was stirred. His walk was almost a bound. In the misty darkness, someone in wet clothes hurried past him. Who was it? It must be someone returning after a dip in the river.

Inspite of himself Dase stood, as if dazed. There was an immense crowd before him.

Oh, so many thousands were bathing in the river! Dase only stood and stared. How could he make his way through that crowd? Thousands of sanyasis were on their way back, carrying tumblers filled with water from the river. They went their way, taking no notice of Dase. They brushed past Dase. What a lot of matted hair lay coiled on their heads! Their bare bodies gave off a peculiar smell. Swept up by a roaring wind, thousands emerged from that lustrous water.

Suddenly Dase felt that someone was calling him from far away. Then the voice came closer and he felt someone shaking him gently.

He was startled. He saw Satpathy Mahasaya standing beside him.

'Why are you standing in the middle of the road, Dase? Let's go.'

'Sir, I found it impossible to go any further. So many people were returning, having bathed! Did you see them?'

'No. I saw no one.'

'What? Where have they all gone?'

'Who?'

'How can I describe it to you? Thousands of sanyasis, with long matted hair passed along this road. I could not make my way in that crowd. Oh, there were so many of them!'

'Your mind is still disturbed. That's why you could see the souls of the dead wandering in this sacred place. This is a very auspicious sign. Let's go and bathe. It's getting late!'

'Wandering souls?'

'That's right. This is a great cremation ground. There is nothing to be surprised by all this.'

Dase felt as if the ground beneath his feet was slipping away. He collected himself with difficulty and followed Satpathy Mahasaya.

It was still a little dark. Although the Manikarnika ghat was not very crowded, some people were bathing there. Satpathy descended the steps one at a time, without turning to look back. Dase stood, fascinated by the wonderful, white river. His feet slipped from the edge of the step, but he steadied himself and sat down on the step.

People chanted all kinds of stotras while bathing. Many people now stepped into the river. The darkness made it difficult for Dase to see far ahead, but the wind blowing off the river made his inner being open up and expand. People seemed to float past his eyes.

A strange scene again unfolded before Dase's eyes: swirling crowds, the press of people, millions of bathers appearing from nowhere and stepping into the river to have their bath and millions stepping out of the ghat. More people. . . More and more and more. Countless human beings, like clouds in the sky!!

Dase felt breathless. His head reeled. Unable to bear it any more, he closed his eyes and remained seated. Even so, he could not wrench free from that ocean of humanity.

Waves rose and crashed in that strange ocean. He pressed his temples to calm down. His ears buzzed; his throat felt parched. His whole body was bathed in cold sweat. Wherever he looked, he only saw millions of faces.

A shudder ran down his spine. He felt he was expanding, becoming larger—he was spreading over the Manikarnika ghat like a gigantic shadow. His head rose high. Millions of human beings issued out of him like winged termites when rain water enter their mounds, and they disappeared into him again. And becoming weightless, he was melting into the air.

He became insensible to everything after this and lay crumpled on the step. Satpathy Mahasaya climbed the steps carrying a tumbler filled with water from the Ganga. His eyes were still. The world now claimed only a tiny fraction of his consciousness, which was enough to make him reach the temple of Lord Viswanath. The rest of his consciousness had been detached from the world outside and lay concentrated deep within him. When his eyes fell on Dase, he had difficulty in recognizing him. Then he threw a handful of water on his face and walked off.

Dase's eyelids trembled and opened. His head was still heavy. He propped himself up on his arms and rose. It was already light. The sight of the river in the early morning light revived him a little.

On their side of the ghat, a few persons sat under umbrellas to apply tilak to people's foreheads. There were also people to keep a watch on the clothes of the pilgrims.

Brahmins, young and old, wearing freshly laundered clothes and rudraksha chains wandered about, waiting for gullible pilgrims, whom they would purify in the river, chanting mantras.

Dase felt as if he lacked something, and was looking for someone. Oh, where was Satpathy Mahayasa? Perhaps he had gone off. He must have gone to the temple. I can meet him there. But, why do I have these fainting fits from time to time? Very strange.

At this moment a young boy, about twelve years old with a rudraksha rosary and sandal-paste marks on his forehead came up to him. Dase looked him in the face. He smiled and said in Hindi, 'Come with me. I'll help you with your purificatory bath. The water of the holy Ganga will wash away the sins of all your lives. After your bath, I'll take you to Lord Viswanath. There are other temples such as the Annapurna temple. I'll take you to those. Where are you staying? You are like our guest. If you like, I could render you all kinds of services.'

Dase understood what was being said. But he could say nothing. He simply stared at the boy. His face was fresh, bright and beautiful and his features finely moulded. Dase's heart prompted, 'What a handsome boy! How sweetly he talked! How can I turn him away?'

But, chaos reigned within him. His heart, his mind and his deeds were no longer in harmony with each other. The boy seemed a little put off. Before Dase could say anything, he went off in search of other pilgrims.

After a long while, a smile full of pity and love played on Dase's lips. There was no one around who could have seen it. Dase, too, was not aware that he was smiling, because his mind wasn't behind his smile.

Something must have happened.

Dase came back to himself with a start, harmony and faculties restored once more. He kept gazing in a single direction. Was that Tuku's mother? How could she be here? And that boy with her was Jayi. Unbelievable! The same gait, the same way of covering her head with the end of her saree. What is this that I see? Should I believe my eyes?

He scratched the back of his head whenever he got agitated or confused. His hands touched the bristles growing there. He was quite conscious, after all.

His heart fluttered. He fixed his gaze on the mother and her son. After a long while, they turned to look back. Dase's face glowed. I will be able to see them now. It seemed as if the woman smiled at him. He was taken aback. It was exactly the same smile. . . In every respect she resembled her, but she was not fair. And, as for the boy, he looked like Jayi when viewed from behind. He smiled like Jayi too and resembled him closely, but, all the same, he was not Jayi. Face to face, he looked so different. No, these were strangers.

But Dase could not get over the shock easily. At last the woman went away, talking with her husband. Dase followed them with his eyes, as before.

What had they felt when they saw him acting strange? But what else could Dase have done? He got up, proceeded to take a bath at the river's edge and sprinkled water on his head. Then he gently stepped into the water. All around him, people immersed themselves, stopping their noses and ears with their hands. An old man stood waist-deep in water, offering handfuls of water to the sun. White stubble, like the stamen of a kadamba flower, covered his chin. Standing up to his neck in water, Dase observed everything.

A boat floated down the river. It had an awning drawn over it. A sahib and his wife were seated under it. They looked at the river-banks through a telescope. The two fine lines left in the wake of the boat soon vanished. There was water as far as the eye could see. The currents were so strong they could easily sweep the divine elephant Airabata away.

Dase looked on, all kinds of thoughts crossing his mind. The water felt warmer than the air. After a time he quite forgot that he was still in the water. People who came much later than him had left after their baths. But he continued to sit in the same spot unable to exercise any control over his mind. Thoughts floated into his mind, and then drifted away. Dase simply did not know what to do and kept gazing at the flowing water. Then he looked up at the pilgrims, wide-eyed. Nothing seemed to make sense to him. Human beings seemed like shadows to him. The river, the bathing ghat looked like pictures. But what about the current of water? It caused in him a feeling of deep unease. To which destination did such an immense quantity of water flow on? Where did it originate? Where would its journey end? These questions kept coming back to him repeatedly, but he had no answers.

What was the matter? It was already late in the morning. The sun had started beating down on him. Dase was utterly confused. To an outsider observing him Dase behaved as if he was drugged, or a bit unbalanced.

The crowd at the ghat was thinning. Two or three brahmins at the ghat pointed at Dase and talked to each other. From their gestures, one gathered that they took Dase for a madman. It was but natural that they should think so.

At this moment, chattering endlessly, a large number of men and women arrived from Chhattisgarh. Regular pilgrims. They even travelled as far as Puri. People everywhere laughed at them, and swindled them, taking them for fools.

There was no knowing what thoughts passed through Dase's mind. He took three or four dips and came back to the steps of the ghat. He squeezed out his wet clothes, collected some water in his tumbler and made his way, taking care not to brush against anyone. His eyes were as dazed as before. But he had become aware of the world around.

As he climbed the steps, two or three people approached him and asked him to mark their foreheads with tilak. Dase only glanced at them. He would have said something if he had understood what they said. By the time he made sense of what anyone said to him, and was able to translate his understanding into some form of action, that person would have lost patience and gone away, perhaps smiling in amusement at this strange man.

Someone said something when Dase reached the uppermost step. Dase must have heard it, but it took time to register in his consciousness. He walked a little distance and wondered, 'Why did that man say, "This fellow is not a mad man, he is an ullu." Do some people here take me for a madman? Maybe, they do. Do I really look and talk like a lunatic?' He smiled to himself. What have I done to deserve being called a mad man? He felt amused. Then he wondered why they called him an 'ullu'. A funny language, indeed. Must mean something abusive.

Dase stood by the road and laughed to himself. Beggars sat on either side of the road. Although he looked like someone who had nothing to give, the beggars stretched out their arms to him. Dase walked on, saying nothing. No one seemed real to him any more; it seemed to him as if he had come across them all in a dream. They were all shadows. He felt that he himself was borne aloft by a current of wind.

Two persons who had bathed in the river, walked in front of him. They carried their wet clothes in a bag, making their way slowly, wearing dry dhotis and covering themselves with warm shawls. But Dase's body was bare and the clothes he wore were wet. A wet towel thrown over his shoulder, he followed them.

A cramped lane branched off the main road to his right. It was dark and cold. If one stretched one's arm across the lane one could touch the houses on the other side. It was as narrow as a split in a length of bamboo. Dase noticed the shapes lining the lane. He then walked on, avoiding contact with anything.

After he walked a short distance, he came upon a brown bull, blocking his path. Two large shiny horns stuck out of its huge head.

Dase felt scared. Consciousness of the world outside returned with a rush.

How would he get past the bull?

He glowered at it for a time. It stood like a hill, like Shiva's bull, Nandi. It was chewing cud, sleepy-eyed. This was a dangerous beast. It could knock down a big tree with one push. Face to face with its grave countenance, Dase was unable to decide what to do. He wondered, 'How did the two walking ahead of me get past it? They must have squeezed themselves against this wall and got through.'

Nerving himself Dase moved forward.

The bull did not give way at all. While getting past it, Dase poked his elbow into its hind part and said, 'Hey, move off. Why are you standing like this, blocking the way?'

Oh, what a strange animal! It would not budge an inch!

There were many shops selling flowers, bel leaves, and bhog. But for the wet dhoti he was wearing and the wet towel thrown over his shoulder, Dase's body was bare. The shopkeepers on either side of the lane did not call out to him. They knew a man like him had no money, and so could not buy anything from them.

As for Dase, he walked on, his head lowered. 'Can't I have flowers worth two paise? Anyway. How does it matter if I can't buy some flowers? Won't the Lord accept a little water if I offer it to him with deep devotion?'

An old shopkeeper, a vermillion mark on his forehead, called out to Dase. After he called him two or three times, Dase raised his head and looked in his direction. He had never expected someone to call him in such a place. The old man humbly saluted Dase. Confused, Dase forgot to give him his blessings. The old man respectfully handed him a leaf carrying flowers, bel leaves and some bhog. Utterly confounded, Dase only smiled awkwardly at him.

The old man said, 'Sir, offer these to Lord Viswanath. Don't worry about money. I'll be blessed if the Lord receives this offering from a good soul like you.'

Dase thought he had nothing to say in reply to this, and moved on. After he had gone only ten paces or so, another shopkeeper handed him a leaf with flowers, bel leaves and offerings. Dase could not make out what he said.

Dase held the tumbler in one hand. It was inconvenient to carry so many things in the other. He spread his towel, and put all these things in a corner, tied it up and walked on.

He found it difficult to make his way. More and more shopkeepers filled his towel with flowers, bel leaves and bhog. At last, he found himself in front of a shopkeeper, towel spread before him. What? He had ended up begging for alms. Many thoughts passed through his mind. He stood in the middle of the lane. The Lord himself is an old beggar, having given everything away. He wandered from door to door. Why go into His presence as a man of means. One ought to go to Him, a begging bowl in hand.

He thought it was great fun. He stood motionless. Shopkeepers before and behind him came up and loaded him with gifts. At last, someone placed a bamboo basket before him. People now put their gifts in this, after reverentially touching his towel. More and more people surrounded him. Dase stood transfixed, as if dazed. A crowd gathered around him. Some got busy trying to protect him from the press of people. In the middle of all this bustle, Dase realized that people were falling at his feet and offering flowers to him. How extraordinary! Had all these people gone out of their minds? Dase made an effort to get ahead. His feet lay buried under something a foot deep. How could he move? Hefty young men parted the crowd and made way for him. Fixing his eyes on the void, Dase headed for the temple, step by step.

He saw the wonderful forms of Lord Viswanath in his mind's eye. He regarded every devotee with fresh interest. Hundreds of them dissolved into a smoky haze and became one. People excitedly crowded round someone possessed by a deity, and in the hubbub it would be difficult to tell who the possessed one was.

Dase was now encircled by a similarly agitated crowd. But he walked on, saying nothing, looking ahead of him. At another time Dase would have panicked, screamed in fear and fled from the place. But now he was guided by a force stronger than himself. Something magical had pervaded his being. He walked, as in a dream.

He did not have to find his way to the temple of Lord Viswanath. Like a current, the crowd swept him towards it. He entered the precincts though the silver gateway on the left. The crown of the small temple was plated with gold. A huge crowd milled about.

So, this then was the temple of Lord Viswanath. Deep in thought,

Dase found himself behind the statue of Nandi. Suddenly back in his senses, Dase saw a shiny black linga rise before him from the holy vessel, a stream of milk poured continuously on it, like the waters of the river Ganga.

Someone must have taken the puja things from Dase's towel, without his knowledge. There was a fixed stare in his eyes. He trembled and collapsed on the stone bull.

After a long time the crowd inside the temple thinned out. Satpathy Mahasaya came out of the temple of Panchmukha Mahadeva, which was opposite the temple of Viswanath. Lost in meditation, he had not yet opened his eyes fully. He looked about him, as if roused from a reverie. He saw Dase lying unconscious before him. It took him a while to comprehend what might have happened. He was amazed when he found out by talking to people there that they now regarded Dase as a saint. He waited until Dase came to his senses. Someone had draped a silk dhoti on Dase. He lay on the ground, looking utterly helpless. Satpathy Mahasaya sat beside him for a while, his hand on Dase's body. It was some time before Dase opened his eyes. 'I have gone through a terrible time, sir. You went to the temple and I followed you later. I was miserable all along the way. My head is so muddled I can't see things properly. Tell me, sir, have people here gone mad?'

For Dase, Kashi was a completely unfamiliar place. But Satpathy Mahasaya knew what a marvelous place this abode of Lord Shiva was, and how casually people took life and death here. The book of life lay open here; a thin thread crept through its leaves from the beginning to the end.

Nothing was impossible in Kashi.

Here there was nothing uncommon about a new saint coming into being every day. It also took very little time to turn someone into a saint. People here were a peculiar lot. Inhabitants of Kashi were easily swayed. They were, after all, devotees of Lord Mahadev. Dase's simple dress, his unassuming demeanour made them take him for a saint. There was nothing surprising about it. Things happened here with unexpected swiftness, like leaves drifting down the currents of the Ganga. In no time all these devotees of Dase would never be seen again. Such thoughts crossing his mind, Satpathy took Dase with him and stretched his hands out for the 'paduka'.

The priest poured a little paduka with bel leaves into Dase's cupped hand. Sheer habit made Dase chant a sloka, '*Akalamrtyharanam sarbabyadhinibaram.*'

A narrow path lay behind the temple. It finally led to a wide road.

Satpathy and Dase walked a short distance and looked around. From nowhere a horse cab appeared, and they climbed into it.

Satpathy's face wore a solemn expression until he had a wash at the dharamsala. Dase felt a little nervous. How much trouble he had given this good man! On his way back from Prayag, Dase had brought a few guavas and bananas. Now he took them out and put them by. From the shop in front of the rest house he bought some milk mixed with sugar crystals in mud pots and a few sweets.

He went out and had a wash.

As he wiped his mouth, the length of silk fell off his shoulder. Dase felt terribly awkward, took it off and put it on the rolled-up blanket.

Satpathy burst into laughter.

'Well, Dase. You have got a very nice silk dhoti. I brought your dhoti and towel from where they were lying. Tell me how all these extraordinary things came to pass. Wait. It's getting late. Let's first sit down and eat. I am starving. Great. I see that by the grace of Lord Viswanath our day has been a wonderful one. Where did you get these fine jalebis from, my saint?'

'I haven't paid the shopkeeper for this yet. I told him through gestures that we were staying here, and that he'd be paid. I don't know if that stupid fellow understood me or not; he only smiled, his whiskers dancing. He also nodded his head, and I brought the stuff.'

'Don't worry about the payment. First let me know how you became a saint?'

'All this happened when I was totally oblivious of the world outside. Something came over me this morning and since then I have been dazed by terrifying things that presented themselves and appeared to be real. And what happened on the way to the temple would seem like illusions to a sane man, not to speak of someone like me. I must tell you, sir, people here have great capacity for devotion. Or else, how could they behave like they did?'

Satpathy Mahasaya found this talk of dreams and illusions impenetrable. He looked only in one direction unblinkingly. Dase went on eating, his head lowered.

After a while, Satpathy said, 'Let me tell you Dase. You have been blessed with the boundless mercy of the Lord. Let's now wait and see where the currents take you. How do you feel now?'

'I feel as if the breezes of the dawn have invigorated me on being roused from sleep. I feel elated, for no particular reason.'

'After all, you have got a silk dhoti for free. It's natural that you should feel happy.' Satpathy gently mocked him.

Dase smiled.

It had been a long time since Dase had felt truly happy. The rusted iron doors in his heart creaked as they were flung open. They would never be closed again. To shut them again, a host of ghosts, with eyes like burning cinders, would have to labour hard on a drizzly night. Satpathy was now convinced that day had dawned in Dase's inner space. There was no cause for fear.

Dase said, smiling, 'Tell me sir. Who put this on for me? See, how he has tucked the end of the left side. Really, I was not aware of this until now. I really had a hard time.'

He hurriedly finished eating, got up to tuck the end of the silk dhoti the right way. Satpathy and he doubled up, laughing heartily.

Dase went out to the veranda where he rinsed his mouth and draped the towel.

Satpathy looked at him for a while. He realized that the dark night of the soul had ended and the great battle within had drawn to a close. Lord Krishna was now returning, turning his back on the ravaged battlefield. He looked a little fatigued. That was all. He was perspiring profusely. He thought it was time to go back to Dwaraka. A lazy smile played softly across his face.

Satpathy Mahasaya called out, 'Dase, Let's go to Vrindavan next.'

He smiled with amusement, saying this as he sipped his milk.

The Renunciation

'**D**ase, you are happy, aren't you?'
'Oh, it's such a wonderful place, Sir. From the moment the train moved I haven't been able to take my eyes off this land—it's as flat as the surface of a becalmed sea. Nowhere does the land slope or rise. Everything about this place—the land, the water, the air—seems pure. Or else, why should all the holy places belong only to the northern part. One must be blessed to be born in this land.'

Dase's heart was swelling like a tidal wave. Whatever he came across he lovingly embraced, accepted. To him, everything now seemed beautiful. The trembling light of the setting sun filtered into his heart like grains of powdered musk. The living warmth of the earth permeated his whole being, and dashes of colour pervaded it. The high wind blended with his life breath. Feeling a profound intimacy with the world outside, he was overwhelmed with ecstasy. His heart overflowed with bliss, the foam-crested waves crashed in his eyes.

Satpathy Mahasaya, too, felt happy. He soaked in the marvellous beauty of the evening.

The compartment was not very crowded. Dase's eyes dwelt on the faces of the few passengers seated around. Their faces looked tearful, like those of children about to be kissed. His eyes caressed them. How simple-hearted, uncomplicated these people were! That man sitting across would be about forty-five. A long moustache sprouted on his broad, fair face. He looked quiet and peaceful. His shirt was buttoned up to his neck. How nice he looked! And there, that boy!

His tuft hung out of his cap like the tail of a mouse. He had put on a shabby dhoti anyhow. But it looked good on him. And that young man resembled a young sal tree. Dase's affectionate glance moved from one face to another. Satpathy Mahasaya for his part, fondly watched Dase.

He thought Dase seemed to have risen above ordinary emotions. All divisions, all differences had dissolved in a spontaneous flood of love. To him, everything seemed blessed with loveliness. How the grace of God had led him towards a state of bliss! To be able to transcend the body and reach the world beyond the senses requires such austere self-denial. But Dase needed to climb only one more step. After that he'd come face to face with the transcendent being.

Satpathy Mahasaya looked at Dase again and again. A feeling of wonder and delight made him shiver. He thought, 'The Lord's boundless grace has rained upon a pure soul.'

This thought absorbed him and filled him with bliss. Dase's eyes gave him an enlarged view of existence. His face seemed heavy with tears and smiles, ready to burst any moment. The more Satpathy Mahasaya gazed at him, the more ecstatic and restless he felt. His reverence for Dase grew. Dase suddenly rose to his feet, and shook himself free of thousands of invisible gossamer threads. He stamped the ground twice and running his fingers through his hair, he said 'Seems very strange, sir. I think I am going out of my mind. Why do I feel like this from time to time? My limbs seem to have become numb and lifeless. Someone is sucking me, as it were, into an abyss. Slowly the world outside is becoming a blank, and I feel as if I am being hollowed out. A bottomless chasm is opening up inside me. I can't explain things properly to you. Just as one can't see or hear anything when one's mind wanders. . . I'm exactly in that state. I think I am lost.'

Smiling as before, he continued shyly, 'I fear I'll burst. I'm feeling breathless. Sir, it's difficult to make someone believe what I say. . .but, actually, I get the impression I don't have many days left.'

Dase felt embarrassed when he saw Satpathy Mahasaya watching him silently and smiling. He scratched his head with one hand, and took out the betel pouch with the other. His daughter-in-law had put a quantity of ground khaira in it. There was not much of it left now.

Every time he kneaded a mixture of khaira and quicklime, his thoughts would often return to the days gone by. But today there was no pull of memories. When he placed chopped arecanut on the betel leaves, memories of Tukua's mother blew into his mind like a strong current of wind. It stirred up dust and old dry leaves from the ground, but soon everything became quiet once more. Dase folded a betel leaf and tucked it into his mouth. The other two paans he put into his pouch.

'Let me tell you, sir. . .' He discovered that Satpathy was not there any more. It was getting dark. So, maybe, he had gone to the toilet.

Dase stood up. He paced up and down the compartment, which was more or less empty. He spat out the betel juice, and returned to his seat.

He gazed out of the window. The air was growing chilly. How tender and beautiful the evenings were in this part of the country! This, then, is the hour for cows to come home. Cowherd boys in Gopa would be driving their cows home. One of them would be softly playing his flute. The honey-coloured light of the dusk lying on the parrot-green fields slowly faded as Dase looked on, without batting an eyelid. Inspite of himself, he burst out singing:

Eager to set his eyes on Krishna,
Safala's son yoked horses to his chariot
And took to the familiar road.
'Go' he commanded.
In a flash he crossed the border of Mathura.
The sight of Him riding His chariot would thrill whose heart.
The lord of the gods would sit in his chariot.
Kansa's messenger thinks
'Blessed am I today. Blessed are my
father and mother, for I'll set my eyes
on the king of the gods.
Blessed are my eyes for they will
have a glimpse of the cloud-dark
figure and be washed of all sins.
Kahnu will be sitting on Nanda's lap
among cowherd boys.'

Dase was unable to go on. He only went on endlessly repeating the last two lines. '*Blessed are my eyes*'. . . His voice grew fainter just as the crying of a baby gets feebler when sleep overcomes it. His lips kept mumbling but soon they too became still.

When Satpathy Mahasaya came back he found Dase fast asleep. Drops of tears were suspended in the corners of his eyes. A little betel juice trickled from that side of his mouth where Dase had lost four or five teeth.

Satpathy Mahasaya watched him fondly. Dase lay still before him for a while. Then he looked away and sat cross-legged. The compartment was empty. All the passengers had disembarked on the way. The compartment seemed deserted in spite of the two of them sitting in it.

The train tore through the dusk, roaring. The tracks lay motionless underneath. The iron wheels pounded them. The carriage rocked as they raced. Dase's limbs shook. But Satpathy sat absolutely still. Night fell, but the two of them remained frozen in the same posture.

After a long time, the train halted at a station. Here, some twenty or thirty passengers burst into the compartment. The sound of people excitedly calling out each other, shouting, and dragging their boxes across the floor disturbed Satpathy. He felt uncomfortable. He could not concentrate any more. He moved off to one corner, took a deep breath and closed his eyes.

As for Dase, he remained where he was seated. No one awakened him or disturbed him. They all stood at some distance. After a time, one or two of them humbly sat at his feet. The train left the station. The hubbub subsided a little.

Satpathy Mahasaya gradually became sensible of his surroundings and looked about him, with disinterested eyes. He smiled to himself. He found a man aged forty or forty-five standing beside him. He immediately made room for him and requested him to sit down. Grateful and pleased, the man fell into talk with Satpathy Mahasaya as if he had known him intimately. From him Satpathy Mahasaya gathered that the train would reach Mathura around nine at night. There were two hours to go at most, before they got there.

Dase lay on the berth opposite, as if unconscious. His head was shaven, his body bare. On his chest glittered a thick white sacred thread. The sandal-paste marks that had been placed on his forehead and chest in the morning were still there. Tear drops stood in the corners of his eyes. In the middle of all that bustle, Dase lay fast asleep. Satpathy Mahasaya looked at him closely. It seemed as if Dase's heart overflowed with bliss and wonder. The expression on his face seemed to say that he had come to purify his mind. Or how else could the impurities get washed away so fast?

Elated, he watched Dase. He felt that Dase had embarked on his great journey.

The word 'Mathura' repeated in the course of the conversation fell on Dase's ears. They must have penetrated beyond the layers of his consciousness, for he stirred, opened his eyes and stared. He hurriedly rose to his feet and looked about him, confused. Dreams seemed to cling to his dim eyes. Seeing that he was not himself any more, Satpathy took him by the hand and gently made him sit down.

'Wash your face. You went to sleep at the wrong time of the day.'

The voice of Satpathy Mahasaya made Dase rub his eyes and look in his direction. He was able to see properly only after a little while. He said, 'Do you have water in your tumbler, sir? I am feeling thirsty.' Satpathy handed the tumbler to him.

Dase put his head out of the window, cupped his hand and threw water onto his face. He drank the water in the tumbler at one go and relaxed, leaning against the wall.

Satpathy Mahasaya told him, 'The next station is Mathura.'

Dase only gazed at him. He hurriedly put another paan into his mouth and said, smiling, 'Sleep overcame me at this evening hour. When you went into the toilet, I occupied myself with singing lines from *Mathura Mangala*. I don't know when I drifted into sleep. I saw a very strange dream.'

'All your dreams are bound to be out of the ordinary.' Satpathy Mahasaya smiled sweetly.

'No. This was really unbelievable. I had the rare good fortune of setting my eyes on the Lord. I saw in my dream that I stood behind Garuda and beheld Lord Jagannath. It seemed as if the Lord looked at me out of the corner of his eyes, from inside the sanctum. I had a feeling that you, too, were there. You and I rolled down the twenty-two holy steps. And the two of us were convulsed with uncontrollable sobs. A south Indian woman danced in ecstatic abandon crying, "Animesh, Animesh." The dream seemed real, sir. My heart longs for more.'

'Beholding the Lord in a dream is an auspicious sign. And the name the woman called out was the name Chaitanya gave Lord Jagannath. Wonderful. You have been truly blessed. Tell me, Dase, have you been initiated by a guru?'

Dase started, as he was not prepared for this question. He was also put out. Not looking at Satpathy's face, he asked, shyly, 'Does such good fortune come one's way easily?'

Satpathy Mahasaya said, 'That's right. Unless one is lucky, one can never find a true guru. If we have really earned merit, we'll find a guru in this holy place, who'll initiate us.'

Dase looked at him in surprise.

He thought to himself, 'You too have not found a guru yet? I wanted to make you my guru. Now we'll both look for a guru.' But he kept quiet.

They arrived at Mathura station.

The passengers rose to their feet, and got ready to disembark, carrying their luggage. Dase, too, stood, holding his cloth bag, enjoying the scene outside. There were so many lights! There were rows upon rows of them.

Everybody got off when the train came to a stop.

Satpathy Mahasaya knew Mathura like the back of his hand. He looked around like a man familiar with the place.The moment he stepped out, Dase longed to have a glimpse of Akrura, the charioteer, Kubuja, the hunch-backed woman and Udhaba, the great devotee, in the dazzlingly bright light. But what met his eyes were countless motor cars, horse cabs, and a milling crowd. And yet he found everything lovely and enjoyable. What sacred land, what a holy place it was! He longed to pick a little dust and rub it on his forehead.

They loaded their things onto a horse cab and got into it. What Satpathy said to the driver Dase could not follow. But the driver understood him, and cracked his whip without once looking back. When the horse leapt forward, raising its front legs, Dase and Satpathy clutched each other and rolled about in the cab. They found it funny. Soon they steadied themselves.

From the time they talked of seeking a guru together, their affection for each other had grown stronger.

Dase asked, like a child, 'Tell me, was the chariot Akrura rode drawn by horses like this one? He must have had set out from Mathura. Have you looked at this driver closely? Do you see how gorgeously dressed he is. Is he Akrura?'

Satpathy Mahasaya, too, got carried away under Dase's influences. He said nothing, and only smiled.

A little later, Dase broke into full-throated singing.

> *Kansa's messenger thinks he is blessed.*
> *Blessed are my parents for I shall set*
> *My eyes on the king of the gods.*

The horse-cab driver looked back at him and smiled. He turned and lashed the horse.

They drove through the crowded marketplace, and Dase went on singing lines from *Mathura Mangal* soulfully, his eyes closed.

At last the horse-cab stopped in front of a resthouse for pilgrims. Dase no longer sang in a loud voice, he only hummed the lines. He hopped down holding his cloth bag, feeling as restless as a young man brimming with vitality. From a distance, a stranger would have mistaken him for a twenty-three or twenty-four year old. An unspeakable elation made his heart leap, he felt as if he had returned to his father-in-law's house eight days after his wedding. In the way he now carried himself, one could notice the bliss, a sensuous bashfulness associated with the first experience of love.

They were allotted a small room on the second floor of the rest-house. When they opened its window a cold wind lashed its way in. Dase looked out, clutching the bars of the window. The darkness had blotted everything out. Peering hard, he spotted a river in the distance.

Dase turned and said, 'Is that the river Yamuna, sir?'

'Yes, she is the beautiful sister of Yama, the god of death.'

The answer amused Dase greatly, and he laughed out loud. What animated this laughter was difficult to tell. Satpathy Mahasaya, too, was feeling happy for several reasons.

Dase said, 'She looks shabby and ugly all right, but she should never be dismissed lightly. She deserved this punishment for having tormented her elder brother. This river Yamuna is a shameless woman.'

Arguing with Dase upto a point, Satpathy Mahasaya said, 'You are right, but the story has a deeper meaning. Anyway. One drops all his masks when one takes a dip in this river. One should discard the shells concealing one's soul. Once one succeeds in offering up his naked soul to God, there will no longer be any need for a mask.'

Although Satpathy Mahasaya did not say this seriously, what he said bore a profound meaning. Dase went on laughing like a young man. It was as if he was saying—'All this is fine, but the story does not end here.' But Dase did not say this openly, nor did Satpathy Mahasaya suspect what was going on in Dase's mind. After some time, Dase couldn't restrain himself any further and said, 'Aren't all the Gopis stupid? They knew that there was a prankster full of mischief in their village. Why did the shameless ones take their clothes off and get into the river? If you give him a chance, will he spare you? Has he ever spared any one? It has served those barefaced milkmaids right. In fact, they must have enjoyed it thoroughly. Deep down, they wanted this to happen to them. Their shock was only a pretence.' Saying this, Dase again burst out laughing. He was behaving as if he was very close to the gopis, and on joking terms with them.

Satpathy Mahasaya now detected traces of abnormality in Dase. It seemed as if Dase had turned into someone else. He seemed to be possessed.

He thought that Dase had left the shore behind and begun his onward voyage. He had now been summoned by the divine flute. The Lord would not spare him now. No one could snap the cord that pulled him away. He gazed vacantly at Dase for a while. Then he opened his bag and set about arranging his things. Dase followed his example. The towel and the tumbler had to be taken out of the bag. Things like these had to be attended to. Work like this might appear trivial and people who have opted out of worldly life may find this a great burden.

At this moment someone entered their room.

'We're meeting after a very long time, sir!'

He had the looks of an elephant who had assumed human form. For the first time Dase set eyes on a man of this size. When Satpathy Mahasaya made some remarks he raised his arms, as big as pillars, and saluted Dase. Nonplussed, Dase gave him his blessings. The man then began to talk with Satpathy in a tone of great intimacy. Dase merely looked on in surprise. Dase observed how the wooden bed creaked and the whole room from the floor to the ceiling quaked every time the man burst out laughing.

Oh God! This man must have been a descendant of the demon Kansa. Satpathy Mahasaya looked like a child before him. Their talk went on for a long time. At last the elephantine man gingerly squeezed himself through the door.

Seeing the questioning look in Dase's eyes, Satpathy Mahasaya said, 'He is Mathuraprasad Chaube. A very old friend of mine.' He realized that this information was not enough. Dase felt curious not so much about the name as about the superhuman size of the man's body.

'These Chaubes are in fact Chaturvedis. They are brahmin by caste. But he abandoned all the four Vedas and is now concentrating on Ayurveda, the science of the body. He leaves his bed two hours before sunrise. Dressed in only a brief loin-cloth he goes to the gymnasium. There he does push-ups till dawn. While doing this he must have by his side a heap of chick peas soaked in water, raisins and chopped raw carrots mixed with dry molasses. He takes a handful of this after every hundred push-ups. This goes on for a long time. You will not believe this unless you see it personally. He would sweat profusely even in the dead of winter. Four or five persons like him breathlessly doing countless push-ups is quite a sight. At the end of it all he would be massaged with a large quantity of mustard oil. After a bath he helps himself to a ball of crushed almonds mixed with boiled milk and butter.

In addition to these, he also has fruits and cakes. He settles down after such a breakfast. This should help you guess how much he eats throughout the day. Eating gave Mathuraprasad the greatest of all pleasures and his figure was his chief concern.'

Both laughed heartily. Satpathy Mahasaya went into the bathroom to have a wash, laughing all the way. Wonder and amusement slowly drained out of Dase's eyes. His curiosity also abated. He put the thought out of his head. Towel in hand, he waited for Satpathy to come back. He would then go out for a wash.

Humming, Dase paced the veranda. He stopped abruptly. He looked up and saw the Kruttika star glowing like a burning cinder in the sky. As he stared at it for a while, memories buried deep in the heart stirred. The past came alive and brought memories of Tuku's mother nestling against him and brushing past him. The memories had an extraordinary vividness about them. Dase felt as if the past had knocked him down. Nonplussed, he stood paralysed. The crust on the old wound cracked open and blood oozed. Dase hurriedly turned around and looked at the light burning inside the room. Scratching his tonsured head, he collected himself. The steamy clouds parted to reveal a patch of blue sky. Dase now wandered about, not choosing to stand still in one spot. But it did not help. He felt weak and dispirited. How strange! Since leaving home, his thoughts had returned to his worldly attachments only after he reached Vrindavan and they kept oppressing him. He was confident he had left Tuku's mother far behind. He had burnt her, and her ashes had mingled with the sand on the river-bed. But it seemed she had risen from her ashes and come here. Dase saw her now; she was coming from the lower wing of the house to the veranda of the upper, she was tying her hair into a bun, standing on the veranda, smiling, amused at everything that was said to her.

Dase stood gazing into the void.

Satpathy Mahasaya came out of the bathroom and saw Dase, standing motionless. He shook him. Dase was roused from of his reverie. He felt embarrassed in Satpathy's presence. He smiled and proceeded towards the bathroom.

Satpathy Mahasaya looked into his eyes and said, 'Get ready quickly.'

Dase came out after a little while. He hung the wet towel on the window to dry and asked Satpathy, as if murmuring to himself. 'Tell me, why did the thought of Tuku's mother enter my head? For the last one hour, memories of her kept recurring. I feel very disturbed.' He turned round, came closer to Satpathy and said, 'A long time ago when Raghu was a little boy, she once said, "What kind of places are Mathura and Vrindavan? It would be nice if we could go there. A woman from the Santra family has made a trip to these places." I made fun of her at the time. It is possible that her soul never forgot this incident. She has followed me all the way to this place. Entering me, she would set her eyes on Vrindavan. I was an utterly worthless person. Not even once was I able to take her anywhere.'

Sighing deeply, Dase's eyes focussed on Satpathy's face.

Satpathy Mahasaya said, smilingly, 'Put these things out of your head, Dase. We travelled this far in order to be able to forget her. Why think of her now? Why pursue a shadow?'

'No, sir. If you enter a zone of light, you have to drag your shadow along.'

Satpathy suddenly became alert. He was delighted and amazed at the dawning of wisdom in Dase's heart. He also noticed that Dase looked detached. His eyes expressed an inner calm. Satpathy said, to test him, 'If you stand facing the source of light, your shadow will fall behind you. Why worry about it?'

'But does that mean the shadow will fall away? It will always cling to you. Man has to trample upon it in his journey towards light. The closer the source of illumination, the longer the shadow. Once you lose yourself in the light the shadow too will merge in it.'

Satpathy could not conceal his interest and amazement any more. He took Dase by the hand and seated him on the wooden bed. Suddenly a cloud filled Dase's mind. He was soon lost in ecstasy. He bit his tongue and said smiling, 'I must certainly have gone crazy. Or else, how would I dare join you in a dialogue on the scriptures. Just look at my audacity.'

Satpathy Mahasaya wondered, what was this? His state of mind was very complicated. This complexity had nothing to do with his conscious mind; it originated in the depth of his being. There was no doubt that a new awareness was dawning on him. Otherwise he could never have managed to sum up effortlessly the Panguandha principle.

'I am sorry, Sir. Please forgive me. I am no longer in control of what I say or do.'

Satpathy smiled and said, 'No, no. You haven't committed any mistake. I know of none. I asked a question and you gave an answer. That was all.'

At this moment, a boy of about seventeen or eighteen entered the room, carrying a few things on a plate. His coarse brownish hair had been tied into a tuft at the back of his head. His dhoti, draped high around his waist, did not cover his legs. His cotton shirt had been buttoned up to the neck. His skin was covered by a layer of dirt. It was clear he worked in Chaube's hotel, which was on the other side of the resthouse.

'Chaubeji has sent me.'

Satpathy pointed to the plank-bed and said to him, 'Put it there.' He left the plate on the bed, wiped his nose with the back of his hand, and went off. On the plate lay two glasses of steaming milk, two apples, and eight large bananas.

Dase was very happy when his eyes fell on the plate. He said, 'Excellent bananas. Have you seen them? What are these?'

'These are apples. Very good fruits these. People here are very fond of them.'

'Shall we eat and go to sleep?'

'All right.'

Dase did not want to drink the milk after his meal. 'My stomach will churn if I have this hot milk.'

'Nothing will happen to you. Drink it. Everyone here has milk after their meals.'

Dase drank it with great reluctance and tucked two paans into his mouth afterwards. It was quite late in the night by the time they put out the lights and went to sleep. Like a child Satpathy Mahasaya fell into a deep sleep as soon as he lay down. But Dase did not feel sleepy. He merely lay on the bed, eyes closed. All kinds of thoughts crowded his mind. He thought about how the Lord had driven him from place to place till he had reached here. He was like a coconut shell, swept towards the shore by mighty ocean waves of the sea. The sea swelled, and wave crashed upon wave. It never quietened down. It remained restless, disturbed and tumultuous. But to Dase it seemed as if out of the depths of the churning, bottomless sea, someone had stretched out an arm and lifted him up, and dropped him on the beach. The salt water had seeped into his veins. All along, tossed by an ever restless swing, he had seen life only in terms of loss and gain. Would he be able to survive when suddenly deposited on the fine sand of the seashore?

Dase felt as if someone really held him in the palm of his hand. Or else, how could he, a non-entity, find himself in Vrindavan on the banks of the river Yamuna? How could he, who never had the means to make a trip anywhere, have arrived here? A tide of feeling swelled in him. Warm tears flowed from the corner of his eyes and he shivered from time to time. The words kept echoing in Dase's heart.

My eyes you are blessed, for you have fallen on the cloud-dark figure.
Kanhu sits on Nanda's lap, surrounded by cowherd boys.

His breathing was heavy. Tears streamed out of his eyes. His lips quivered and his whole body trembled.

A horse-cab rattled past the rest house. At the sound of the horse hooves piercing the stillness of the night, Dase felt as if he had been transported in time to the Dwapar era and was seeing Akrura's chariot.

The two horses were white like agasti flowers. They would fly away before one could blink. Dase was Akrura riding the chariot, his head adorned with a silk turban. But why was he crying? Of course he must, or else his heart would burst. Hot tears rolled down his cheeks and flooded his ears. He wanted to wipe them with the silk turban, but he could not. He gently prodded the horses, who ran like the wind and reached the bank of the river in a flash. Then the chariot and the horses melted into thin air. The fragrance of kadamba flowers permeated his whole being, and he turned into a tree, putting out branches and leaves. He was now laden with a million kadamba flowers. And beneath his feet lay the dust of the land of Braja, soft like drifts of petals of nameless flowers. Did the aroma of sandalpaste and camphor radiate from this? As far as the eye could see, there were bowers, some of which sagged under a profusion of flowers, and some others were weighed down by jasmine creepers. Flowers of all the seasons bloomed here. But why did all these bowers seem so deserted? Had they hidden themselves at my approach?

Oh, how inky the waters of the Kalindi river are! Is it deep, or is it that no waves wrinkle the surface of the water here? Do you see, Tuku's mother, how marvelous these places are! How sacred? What about having a bath in the river? The water here will wash all our sins away. You women have no patience at all. Take a good look. Let the mind take all this in. There'll be plenty of time to take a dip in the river. Oh, why do you pull a long face? Let's go. We haven't grown old yet. Let Raghu get a little older. Then we'll make a trip. Come, come near me.

Dase turned over on the plank bed, talking incoherently in his sleep. A voice calling to someone far away broke the silence of the night. Ho. . .i. . .la. . .la.

Dase woke up, as if he was still dreaming.

'Wake up. Let's go.'

Dase got out of bed, picked up his towel and tumbler in the darkness. Something about him gave the impression that he had become a different person altogether.

Satpathy Mahasaya woke up, with a start. Still lying in bed, he watched Dase. 'Arre Dase! Walking in your sleep?'

Dase bent down and took out his cloth bag from under the plank bed. He paid no attention to Satpathy.

When his eyes suddenly fell on Satpathy Mahasaya he hurriedly went to the other side of the bed, and said, overcome by shame and embarrassment, 'Why did you bring me here, can't you see that Satpathy Mahasaya is sleeping here? You are utterly useless. When did I say that he was not a saintly person? But so what? Come, let's go. Your tumbler? I am holding it. Come.'

Satpathy watched him, amazed.

Dase hurriedly opened the door. Satpathy followed him quietly.

He had no doubt that Dase had fallen into some sort of a trance. But wasn't it unusual that while his faculties were in perfect order, his mind should fall into such a reverie.

Dase tiptoed down the steps and went outside. The place was deserted at that hour. From there the Akrura ghat of the river Yamuna was only a short distance away. If one turned right, one came to the path leading to the ghat.

The Mathura junction lay on the left. Dase did not hesitate for a moment. He took the path that led down to the ghat as someone who knew his way and had been treading that path for a very long time now and was very familiar with it.

Satpathy followed Dase, keeping a distance of about forty cubits from him.

The outer layer of Dase's consciousness was dominated by memories of his late wife, but deep inside he was experiencing the bliss of reunion with her. It seemed as if he was conversing with an invisible person, as if Tuku's mother was engaged in a normal conversation with him. In the exchange Dase's questions and answers remained unuttered.

Akrura ghat lay very close to Vrindavan . This was where most of the pilgrims bathed. So it was very clean. At night the river Yamuna looked as if it carried millions of molten stars in its womb. One could not bear to look into the fathomless depths of its waters.

Dase came to the water's edge and said, 'Oh, why are you behaving like this? Why are you making a racket like a child? What would someone who hears you say?'

Satpathy Mahasaya heard everything.

Dase was quiet for a few moments and then continued, 'Why should I not shout? Will this wonderful opportunity ever come again in life?'

Saying this, he broke into a dance. Because he was entranced, his movements were a little sluggish, but otherwise he was in a state of frenzy.

'O Radhamathav, the lifter of the mountain, the one adored by the gopis.' He repeated this line as he danced with abandon.

Satpathy felt that Dase had soared to a higher level, leaving Tuku's mother behind. But Dase stopped dead, flung his arms wide and called, 'Come, let's step into the river, come. What if the gopis are there. Who are the gopis? Don't I look like one to you? Come, come with me.'

Satpathy felt a flush of excitement. From Dase's gestures it seemed that he was stepping into the river with his wife.

Satpathy waited anxiously. He wondered if Dase would return to the conscious state now. But nothing of the sort happened. Dase stood neck-deep in water, in silence.

'No, I must take him away from here. He is no longer himself.' But Satpathy Mahasaya thought the better of it for some reason. Taking a deep breath, he looked around him.

Until this time he had not noticed the wan moon of the dark fortnight in the sky. Akrura ghat lay empty and quiet. The misty light of the moon rained down dreams. He slowly came under its spell.

'Oh, how peaceful! Why not sit down here for a while?'

Satpathy sat down where he was standing and let his eyes dwell lovingly on everything around him. Then entirely unaware, he drifted into a trance.

Dase continued to stand in the water, completely oblivious of the world outside, immobilized, as it were, by the gossamer threads of a beautiful dream. And the play of moonlight across a cloudless sky had led Satpathy into a rapturous contemplation of the relationship between Purusha and Prakriti as he sat on the river bank.

It seemed as if one of them would melt into the water of the river Yamuna and flow away, and the other would turn into stone.

After a long while, one heard the anklets of the night tinkle. Perhaps sixteen thousand girdles jingled. It could well be the faint sound of a flute playing on the other side of the river, wafting in.

It was as if a breath of wind had charged the moonbeams with a strange longing. The earth throbbed with passion. Satpathy Mahasaya felt this restlessness in the air he breathed and opened his eyes. Something unusual was happening without his knowledge, and he fretted about it. He rose to his feet.

Far away a feeble voice called.

'Ho. . .i. . .la. . .la. . .a. . .'

Immediately after this, came a sound from the river. Dase got up and fell again into the water. Satpathy hurriedly dragged him to the shore.

Dase's body seemed lifeless. Only the upper portion of his body shuddered like a deer pieced with an arrow. There was a blank look in his staring eyes. He could hear nothing nor could he open his mouth to utter a word.

Satpathy felt very guilty, but he had no time to think. At the same time, it was impossible for him to lift Dase up and carry him to the resthouse. He looked about him, but there was no one who could come to his rescue. He was at his wit's end. He ran towards the road.

Just when he was running left along the main road, he glimpsed in the street light someone preparing to go to sleep on a veranda. The man cast a glance at Satpathy. Satpathy went up to him and pleaded. 'Will you do me a favour, brother?'

Something about Satpathy's voice and personality impressed the man. He looked at Satpathy, taking the torn blanket off his face. Satpathy noticed that the man was a little less than forty and quite well-built. His face was covered with a velvety black beard, and his eyes were bright but soft.

The man said, 'Tell me how I can help you?'

'Not far from here, a friend of mine is lying unconscious. We have to take him from there to the resthouse. I can't carry him by myself.'

The man got up immediately and said, 'Let's go.'

They came where Dase lay. Before Satpathy could say anything, the man wiped Dase with his torn blanket, covered him with it, and lifted him up all by himself.

'Tell me where I should take him. He is in very bad shape.'

Satpathy, carrying Dase's cloth bag, walked ahead of the man as fast as he could. Worries filled his mind.

The watchmen of the resthouse were absent. It was the early hour of dawn. Satpathy led the man into his room and pointed to Dase's plank bed. He covered Dase with his blanket.

The man left the place, without saying anything. After a little while, he returned, carrying a bundle of faggots. He asked Satpathy to make a fire as it would warm Dase. Before taking his leave, he said, 'Not to worry. I will come with the Sadhu Maharaj immediately. Everything will be all right once he comes.'

The worldly side of Satpathy's nature told him that what Dase needed urgently was a doctor. But somehow he felt he should rely on this man.

Outside, people were already up and about. A couple of motor vehicles passed, Satpathy Mahasaya was hard at work trying to warm Dase's ice-cold body.

Two men silently entered the room. One of them was Satpathy's young friend and the other was a sadhu.

Satpathy Mahasaya rose to his feet and humbly paid his respects to the latter. The sadhu smiled and blessed him, raising his hand. He then stood gazing at Dase for a while. Suddenly his eyes moistened. He turned around and asked Satpathy, 'Tell me, my son, where have you come from?'

A thrill ran through Satpathy's body when the question was put to him. He replied, 'We have come from Orissa.'

'Wonderful. Lord Jagannath has sent you here.' Every word he uttered exuded boundless joy.

As if he could read Satpathy's thoughts he said, 'Don't worry about him at all. He will be all right. We should nurse him the whole day today.'

Dase was cared for throughout the day. Towards evening warmth crept into his limbs; his pulse could be felt, and he began to run a high fever.

The others left Dase's side at night but Satpathy and the sadhu stayed on and continued to discuss profound matters.

In the end, Satpathy threw himself at the sadhu's feet. At long last, the river of his knowledge flowed into the sea. Beaming, the sadhu laid his hand lovingly on his head.

Dase appeared to be staring at this rite of initiation, but his unseeing eyes took nothing in.

Puri

Satpathy Mahasaya looked after Dase. Dase did recover, but lost his power of speech, staring at people with leaden, uncomprehending eyes. If for some reason he felt pleased, he would break into a smile. His eyes would light up with love, but there was always a faraway look in his face. It seemed as if he floated through the mists of a Margasira morning. For most of the day he would sit leaning against the wall and not notice if anyone entered his room and talked to someone else.

When Satpathy Mahasaya brought Dase into the ashram of the sadhu, he learned that the name of the sadhu's friend was Jugal Kishore. He was a young ascetic. He was fond of looking after sadhus. Most of the time he took care of Dase. Only occasionally, Satpathy, too, had to help.

Satpathy Mahasaya observed Dase. It often seemed to him that not only was Dase unable to speak; but that he had gone deaf and lost his sight as well. But he was proved wrong sometimes. Dase had drawn himself in, like a tortoise into its shell; he had lost contact with the world outside. Once, he fell asleep and woke up only after two days.

The sadhu came to see Dase every alternate day. On seeing him, Dase would join his palms and motion to him to sit down. It was clear that he was very pleased and excited, but he could speak only with his eyes. On occasion, the eyes seemed to look from some faraway place out of such unfathomable depths that Satpathy wondered if Dase knew him at all. And it was expected that Dase would not recognize him. But the look in those eyes was soft and caressing like the morning sunlight on tree-tops, descending in waves from the great void above,

and folding everyone into its warm embrace. At other times, the eyes
would grow leaden and lifeless, filled with emptiness. They would lie
still, like wooden puppets, when the hand moving them is suddenly
withdrawn. Then suddenly, consciousness would flow back into them
and the face would grow lively again.

Dase did his chores out of habit. But there were days when he would
forget everything. On such occasions, he had to be looked after.

Tears often streamed from Dase's eyes. But Satpathy Mahasaya
knew these tears had nothing to do with either joy or grief. He would
wipe them carefully, reverently. As for Dase, he noticed nothing. By
and by, he got over this trance-like state. He cheerfully set about doing
his daily chores.

One day, he stopped dead and stood staring at Satpathy Mahasaya,
who noticed that he was trying to tell him something after many days.
He was unable to speak, but his eloquent eyes made it clear that he
wanted to say something. Satpathy waited eagerly. Dase put the tumbler
down, and wrote on his left palm with a finger: 'Puri'.

Satpathy looked at Dase, whose smile was benign and open-hearted.
To Satpathy it seemed Dase's heart, now washed of all impurities,
glittered like gold in that smile, white like a new lily. There was no trace
of hesitation, doubt or uncertainty in it.

Dase, then, we won't stay at Vrindavan any longer? Why should he
leave Vrindavan and go to Puri? Should he ask Dase and find out?
What was the point of questioning him?

Satpathy told the sadhu what Dase wanted. The sadhu sat still for
a while, then said, as if talking to himself. 'He is being taken to Puri.'
Satpathy understood that Dase's journey to Puri was not a matter to
be decided by mere humans.

The two of them got up and headed for Dase's room. Dase silently
fixed his gaze on the sadhu's face for a very long time. To Satpathy
it appeared as if the two were engaged in a pleasant and intimate
conversation.

It was decided that Dase would set out for Puri the very same day.
Jugal Kishore would accompany him. No preparation was necessary.
Dase picked up his cloth bag. Satpathy took it from his hands and put
in it his soggy towel, tumbler and grinding stone (for making sandal
paste). Dase waited, rubbing his palms, and smiled. After an hour and
a half they would board a Calcutta-bound train. Satpathy went to the
railway station to see them off.

Dase was gone.

He left behind a Vrindavan overflowing with bliss and encircled by the river Yamuna that was dear to the gopis and cowherds.

As for Dase, he seemed thoroughly detached, unmoved. He seemed at peace with himself. He did not notice that Satpathy too had fallen behind after their long journey together. He now missed no one, longed for nobody. No one was near or far away from him.

Satpathy Mahasaya stood by Dase's compartment and gazed at him. But Dase sat uninvolved, unmoved. Now and then his eyes would grow lively and focus on Satpathy. And a smile would play on his face. Then suddenly everything would go still. Dase would withdraw from the world and move into the depths of consciousness, where awareness, now focussed, achieved unusual intensity.

The train moved.

Dase stared, oblivious of everything around him.

Satpathy Mahasaya stood on the platform, gazing into a vacuum. The shadow of the moving train flitted across his motionless eyes, from left to right.

Consciousness flowed back into Dase, and he found that the station had vanished, and so had Satpathy Mahasaya. Satpathy's nose, straight like a flame, rose before him and then dissolved into the air.

Dase turned to look into the compartment. He caught sight of that young man. What was his name? Oh, it had completely escaped my mind. Dase's gaze remained focussed on him. Suddenly he felt like bursting into laughter.

Why has Satpathy Mahasaya grown a beard? A very whimsical man! And he looks quite plump and well-fed doesn't he?

Dase's eyes lit up. They were dreamy and moist. Now and then they reflected a consciousness of the world outside. He looked at the young man whose name he had forgotten. Did he look like Satpathy? Or was he Satpathy himself? He felt confused.

The train had in the meantime crossed a few stations on the way. Dase's eyes closed. Jugal Kishore thought that Dase had fallen asleep and laid him down on the berth.

It is a very long way from a dark cave in a hill to the turbulent, cold and restless sea. The river winds, branches off, joins other rivers, eddies on its way before joining the sea. Why it does so, even the poor river can't say. As the estuary draws nearer, the sea calls across the sand banks, and the flowing river stands still. The roaring ocean gathers it into its arms. It loses itself ecstatically in foam-crested waves of salt water.

In a few minutes, Sanei—no, Sanatan Dase—no, Dase of an unknown village called Patapur, who used to wear only a cotton towel, would reach Puri and lose himself there. He wouldn't be able to retrace his steps. Can a river flowing down to the sea ever turn back? Pebbles, big and small, roll on the floor of the estuary, pulsating with memories. They have all been worn smooth, and look like seeds of jack-fruit—all their rough edges rubbed off. But who cares for these memories? They lie buried under deep, turbulent waters. And the river's currents are at rest. They had carried the pebbles this far. Now, all they could do was to wait for the tide, when the water would churn and leap upwards to the sky, making it difficult to tell the sea from the river. All their troubles would end if they could now tumble into the bottomless depths of the sea.

Dase looked solemn and calm when he disembarked at Puri, and walked across to the other side of the station. But if someone had looked more closely, he would have seen that all the hair on his body stood on end like the stamens of a kadamba flower. He kept his mouth sealed tightly, or his teeth would have chattered. His eyes looked bleary under grey eyelashes as if he were tipsy.

Despite all this, Dase was eager to press forward, pushing his way through the crowd. His heart had grown wings. It rushed ahead, not caring for obstacles in the way, but the body staggered. It seemed as if awareness had been sucked from every fibre of his being and concentrated in one place. Vitality seeped from his joints.

But he pressed on.

Jugal Kishore, Dase's cloth bag in hand, followed him. If Dase was his normal self, he would have liked to suggest that they take a rickshaw, but how could he? Dase's eyes saw nothing and his legs were unsteady. Still he walked on, his feet dragging.

Suddenly Dase turned off the main road on to an untrodden path. Seeing Dase heading into someone's house, Jugal Kishore understood that he was not able to see anything. He remembered what Satpathy had told him. 'Take care of him when he loses control.'

He took Dase by the hand and made him sit down in a rickshaw. They proceeded in the direction of the Lion Gate of the temple. Dase sat in the rickshaw, speechless. He was not even aware that he had been made to climb the twenty-two holy steps and now stood before Lord Jagannath.

Here he recovered his senses. He looked about him, wide-eyed. He felt as if a miracle had occurred that very moment. Did the blue hill of his heart melt and turn into stone again?

It seemed to him as if a vastness had opened inside him. Grief and joy crushed his ego, his body and his soul. He leaned against the temple wall and slumped to the floor. Like pollen, his consciousness scattered—on the stone, in the sky.

After regaining consciousness, he found that the dream-world had not vanished; it was still there, real and palpable. He sat surrounded by heaps of the rough stones of the blue hill into which he had breathed life. The wind blew through him, and the sky melted and poured over him. But everything about him seemed normal from the outside. It seemed to him as if, to gather a lotus from a pond he had waded from knee-deep water to where he could drown trying. Inside and outside him, water eddied and swirled and he was being sucked into its depths.

He propped himself up with trembling hands and rose to his feet. He took a step, trying to walk. It was as if his shadow had blotted out everything around him. Steering clear of others he moved forward, as if he were eager to jump onto the Garuda pillar, taking it for a pond, or to become the pillar itself. In the end, he clasped the pillar and became one with it for a moment. After a time his grip loosened, and his left side sagged. His eyes remained open. He could no longer close them. His limbs hung listless. The stone floor under him and the stone wall near him might or might not have melted, but he surely dissolved, and flowed over the barrier of his physical self. A vast emptiness was mirrored on his face and his body. He was now nothing more than a brittle, lifeless shell.

Dase lost all control over himself.

Jugal Kishore, for his part, stood near the inner sanctum, absorbed and deeply moved. A sudden commotion made him turn round and look. When he came to the Garuda pillar, wiping his tears, he saw some people fanning Dase and sprinkling water on his face. He was shocked. What a terrible thing to happen inside the temple! Without stopping to think, he lifted Dase up and stepped out of the temple, carrying him in his arms. A crowd followed him. His thoughts went back to the deserted bank of river Yamuna, that silent night, and Dase's wet, unconscious body.

Where would he go now? Let my feet carry me wherever they would, he thought.

It was beginning to get dark. Once their curiosity diminished, the crowd following Dase fell back. After a while, Jugal Kishore discovered that he had reached the seashore. He laid Dase out on the sand. It was quite dark by the time he made Dase finish his ablutions. He felt calm and undisturbed by worries. He had been instructed to wait and watch.

The sea also fascinated him. It looked as if the sky had melted and dripped into it. Drops of the molten sky kept falling on the blue boundary of the sea. When the waves rose, it seemed as if a hill had dissolved, crashed and turned into foam. A deep rumble issued from the bowels of the earth.

Night descended on the sea. Cottonwool clouds in the sky were chased by a cool breeze.

Dase lay motionless on the sand.

Jugal Kishore watched over him, feeling his heartbeat from time to time.

The night advanced.

The clouds dispersed.

Millions of stars appeared on the hot, steamy sky of the month of Baisakh.

A high wind blew noisily.

The sea swelled and roared in the darkness and churned.

The stars twinkled and glittered.

But the sky looked down severely. A boundless, trembling, clear blue sky.

And the earth underneath lay absolutely still.

The dense dark night hung over it. It was receding silently. A heavy shadow encircling the earth was closing in from all sides.

After a time, the darkness quivered. The sea grew quiet. The enchanted night wind dropped. The stars looked pale.

Dase's body shuddered like a coconut frond in the wind. His perspiration dampened the sand.

Dawn was breaking.

Dase's eyes opened and the tears flowed. He recovered himself. When a little water was poured into his mouth, it trickled out from one corner.

He tossed his head from side to side, as if he was deeply worried about something. But the rest of his body lay motionless. Then his whole body, from head to toe, became taut like a bow-string. His thin arms were flung wide. A breath forced its way through his mouth. It made no sound. It was his life's last gasp.

Jugal Kishore thought he heard in that soundless gasp, the last prayer offered up by Dase—Ja-ga-nnath!

He sat beside the corpse.

The cremation would be at dawn.

The End

One day, around dusk, Pundit Nilakantha, while walking down the village path, ran into Brunda Nahak in front of Kanchi's house. Nahak bowed before him.

These days the pundit went for a stroll along the village track every day. His son Indramani had bought him a pair of carpet slippers to make it easy for him to walk. He had also given him a walking stick made of horn, fitted with an ivory handle, believing that regular walks would help his father's flatulence.

'Namaskar, sir.'

'May you prosper, may the evil forces acting against you be pacified. Where are you off to, Nahak?' Pundit's betel stained teeth gleamed through his beard.

Brunda Nahak stopped. So did Pundit.

'How are you? Since you gave up your job as tax collector, one rarely sees you these days.'

'I'm your servant, after all. I would definitely have called on you. But for the last six months, this pain in my chest has been bothering me. I fear I won't last long.'

Nahak looked away when he saw pundit staring somewhere absent-mindedly. He understood and said. 'Alas. Fate meted out a harsh treatment to Dase and wrecked his world. Shouldn't that boy Raghu do something about this house? Kanchi, the oilman's wife, was saying it would be convenient to her if Raghu would let her buy Dase's house.'

Pundit, still looking in that direction said, 'I'm told Dase went on a pilgrimage from Madanpur. Hasn't he returned yet?'

'It's strange that you haven't got the news yet. I was under the impression you knew everything. Dase passed away.'

'Oh!'

'That's right. I too learnt of it only today. Raghu had sent some money owed to old Pradhan along with a letter, which said that Dase had breathed his last in Puri. The news came from the gentleman from Vrindavan, with whom Dase had gone on the pilgrimage.'

'Oh, the man was really blessed. He was simple-hearted. His heart was absolutely pure. Or else, would he have had the good fortune to die in Puri?'

'But when he died, there was no one by his side to pour a little water into his mouth. If only his son had been informed in advance. Anyway. Whatever fate has decided will come to pass. What can his son do?'

Brunda Nahak paid his respects to the pundit and walked away, shoulders drooping.

But Pundit Nilakantha stood there, his thoughts going back to the old days. The past flashed before him vividly. 'Go to that conference of pundits. Your being there will bring us glory.' Dase had said this with an untainted heart. The other day, he had been so apologetic and awkward while asking Baikunthia Kabiraj to go to his house on his way back. Just because he had no money at that hour of crisis, he had had to humble himself and plead like that. Now that man was no more. If luck had favoured him, he would have gone to Kashi and trained himself as a pundit. But the man was really unfortunate. Hope you will not hold this against me, my brother. I am as helpless before fate as you are. It chose to raise me higher, and it did. But do these things matter? Is anyone as blessed as you?

Pundit Nilakantha was a man with a heart. His eyes moistened when he looked at Dase's shabby, abandoned plot of land. He took a couple of steps. Then he suddenly turned back. He would go no further that day.

Glossary

Akrura	:	The messenger whom King Kansa, Lord Sri Krishna's cruel uncle, sent to Gopapur to invite Sri Krishna and his brother to Mathura to take part in a festival.
Astika	:	the saviour of snakes.
badi	:	a fine paste of black gram pressed through moulds and dried in the sun. They can then be deep fried like wafers.
Badi Pala	:	Pala is a folk form of semi-religious dance, traced to the Mughal period.
betalas	:	spirits, beings of the occult world.
Bhagirath	:	a figure in Hindu mythology. A sage who brought the river Ganges from heaven to sanctify the ashes of his ancestors.
bhekta	:	large fish.
Bhisma	:	the great legendary hero of the Mahabharatha.
Bhrukuti	:	an attendant of Lord Shiva.
Birachana	:	to write, to build, to create.
bratas	:	vows, religious observances.
Dasia Bauri	:	a devotee of the untouchable class had sent a coconut through a pilgrim. Legend goes that it was picked up by Lord Jagannath.
Dwapar	:	the era preceding Kali Yug. Association with Sri Krishna.
ekoisia	:	the twenty-first day of a child when after a ceremony the child can be held by the father and others.

Ganga-jal	:	water from the Ganges, the sacred river of India is stored in most homes to be administered to the dying.
Garuda	:	the emperor of birds and scourge of snakes.
golden mangala	:	who brought down goddess Ganga from heaven to earth.
gundi	:	a preparation of tobacco and other ingredients normally taken with paan.
gunia	:	exorcist.
handi mangula	:	the consecration of cooking vessels for the wedding feast: the first stage of the ceremony.
Jaksha	:	a supernatural being that guards wealth.
kada	:	a bunch of 80 leaves.
Kali Yuga	:	according to Hindu Puranic calculations the fourth (and present) age in world history, often called the dark age; marked by strife, unnatural hatreds and treachery, when righteousness appears to be losing the eternal battle with the unlawful forces.
khai	:	puffed rice.
khainga	:	a variety of high quality fish found in Chilka lake.
khaira	:	the extract from a tree; bitter in taste, is an ingredient of paan.
kosa	:	approximately a mile.
kusa grass	:	a kind of reed-like grass used for auspicious rituals by brahmins.
kusapatra	:	oval-shaped, copper shallow bowl pointed at one end with dried kusa grass in it, used for offering oblation to ancestors.
Lakshmi-narayanan	:	Sri Mahavishnu when he appears with his consort.
Lingaraja	:	literally the king of Lingas. The deity worshipped at Bhubhaneshwar.
mahimna stotra	:	sacred ceremonical verses that glorify a particular text (in this case the Vedas) or concept.
Margasira	:	a month in the lunar calendar roughly coinciding with November.
matha	:	coarse silk.
maya	:	the invisible mover of the complex of creation/illusion.
Mohini	:	the form Vishnu took as the divine enchantress, first to charm the demons and cheat them out of their share of the nectar of immortality and on a second occasion to seduce Shiva the great ascetic and interrupt his concentration.

nabata	:	crystallized molasses.
nakshatra enduri	:	star-like small and delicious idlis.
Nandi	:	the sacred bull of Lord Shiva.
natamandir	:	the dance-yard in a temple; a part of temple architecture.
Nrusingha	:	Lord Narasimha, the fourth avatar of Lord Vishnu. A terrifying manifestation, the very thought of whom is supposed to give the devotee courage.
one bisha	:	about two and a half kilograms.
oshas and brathas	:	rituals and fasts.
paan	:	betel leaf smeared with lime, and stuffed with sugar, spices, arecanut. Chewed as a digestive.
patri	:	copper spoon used in puja/rites to offer water.
phirika	:	dragonfly.
Prakriti	:	In the Samkhya school of Indian philosophy, material nature in its germinal state, eternal and beyond perception. Prakriti when it comes into contact with the soul (purush) starts on a process of evolution that leads through several stages to the creation of the existing material world.
Purush	:	In Indian philosophy the soul or self. In the dualistic philosophies of Samkhya and Yoga, purush is opposed to Prakriti as the two ontological realities.
Raghunatha	:	another name for Sri Ramachandra, Lord Ram.
saag and dal	:	a poor man's diet.
sage Suka	:	the son of Vyasa—wisdom incarnate.
Sakshigopal	:	a temple some twenty kilometres from Puri where Lord Krishna is worshipped as Sakshi or witness according to a legend.
Sanatan Dase	:	Dase is to be pronounced as Dasay.
Sankirtans	:	group singing by devotees.
Sankranti	:	the day the sun passes from one zodiac sign to the next.
Shumbha and Nishumbha	:	Demon brothers whom Goddess Durga slew before slaying Mahishasur.
sika	:	a rope-hanger.
Sudhasha	:	Sudasha is good fortune. If the tenth day of the bright moon falls on a Thursday, there is a ceremony in which goddess Lakshmi is worshipped. A ten-strand thread with

		ten knots is worn on the right arm by housewives, and ensures family well-being.
sunthi	:	dried ginger.
the book of Chitragupta	:	Chitragupta is the record book of Yama, the God of Death.
tol	:	a school where Sanskrit is taught to students.
Treta Yuga	:	according to Hindu cosmology, the second age in the world's Puranic history. A less happy age than the first in which virtue drops by a quarter.
ullu	:	stupid, fool.
vaidyas	:	practicer of traditional medicine.